AA308
THOUGHT AND EXPERIENCE: THEMES IN THE PHILOSOPHY OF MIND

Language and Thought

ALEX BARBER

This publication forms part of an Open University course AA308 *Thought and Experience: Themes in the Philosophy of Mind*. Details of this and other Open University courses can be obtained from the Student Registration and Enquiry Service, The Open University, PO Box 197, Milton Keynes MK7 6BJ, United Kingdom: tel. +44 (0)845 300 60 90, email general-enquiries@open.ac.uk

Alternatively, you may visit the Open University website at http://www.open.ac.uk where you can learn more about the wide range of courses and packs offered at all levels by The Open University.

To purchase a selection of Open University course materials visit http://www.ouw.co.uk, or contact Open University Worldwide, Walton Hall, Milton Keynes MK7 6AA, United Kingdom for a brochure. tel. +44 (0)1908 858793; fax +44 (0)1908 858787; email ouw-customer-services@open.ac.uk

The Open University
Walton Hall, Milton Keynes
MK7 6AA

First published 2005. Second edition 2010

Edited, designed and typeset by The Open University.

Printed in the United Kingdom by TJ International Ltd, Padstow.

ISBN 978 0 7492 1734 1

2.1

The paper used in this publication contains pulp sourced from forests independently certified to the Forest Stewardship Council (FSC) principles and criteria. Chain of custody certification allows the pulp from these forests to be tracked to the end use (see www.fsc-uk.org)

Contents

READINGS

Preface

This book has been written as a component of the Open University course, AA308 *Thought and Experience: Themes in the Philosophy of Mind*, and is best read in that context. It has benefited enormously from the combined wisdom of Mike Beaney, Sean Crawford, Keith Frankish and Carolyn Price, the authors of its four companions. Carolyn Price deserves special mention for her assistance with Chapter 5, of which she could reasonably claim to be joint author. Peter Wright and Nancy Marten (course editors) were merciless in pointing out obscurities, especially when editing my penultimate draft. Tim Crane (UCL), David Papineau (UCL) and Barry Smith (Birkbeck College) kindly agreed to be interviewed for a complementary CD. Audrey Linkman (visual resources manager) advised on and tracked down the illustrations. I thank them all, along with Jan Cant and Gerry Bolton (course managers), Tim Crane (external academic assessor) and Ian Chowcat (tutor assessor), for the improvements their interventions have forced me to make.

There are seven chapters. Grouping chapters 1 and 2 as a pair and chapter 6 and 7 as a pair gives five units of roughly equal workload.

CHAPTER 1

Introducing representation

One of the most impressive but puzzling capacities we have is the ability to represent the world around us, both in talking about it among ourselves and in thinking about it as individuals. When someone utters the sentence, 'The German economy is bouncing back', for example, they are able to convey to their audience something about the German economy. Their utterance may be correct or it may be incorrect, but either way it is making a claim about how things are, and in this loose but intuitive sense they are using language to represent the world to someone else. Another example – this time of mental rather than verbal representation – is of someone believing that cinema tickets are half-price on Tuesdays. This is a belief about how things are. Things may be that way or they may not be that way; in either case, the believer is representing them as being that way to herself or to himself – once again in an intuitive sense of 'represent'.

This short introductory chapter will outline some of the questions philosophers have asked, especially over the last hundred or so years, about our ability to represent, both in language and in thought. These questions are taken up in the six main chapters to follow. The book is divided into two unequal parts. Part One is about linguistic representation (chapters 2 and 3) and Part Two is about mental representation (chapters 4 to 7), though there are themes and interdependencies that reach across this division.

Representation and language

Consider some of the many different things we can do with language: express ourselves in metaphor, issue commands, ask questions, fill in crosswords, write shopping lists and diary entries, repeat nursery rhymes by rote, solve logical or arithmetical problems, make promises, tell stories, sign our names, etc. Impressive though it is, this variety in the uses of language is a potential distraction from our main interest, which is in the use of language to represent. It will therefore help if we abstract away from this diversity by focusing on a paradigmatic use of language: the use of words, spoken or written, *to transfer knowledge*. An utterance of 'The German economy is bouncing back' would ordinarily have this purpose.

One reason for focusing in this way is that a significant proportion of what we know comes to us via language. Sharing our thoughts about the world by talking and writing to one another allows us to pool our cognitive resources. Our task in Part One of the book will be to come to understand how this pooling process takes place. That is, we will attempt to answer, at least in broad outline, a question posed by the English philosopher John Locke (1632–1704):

Locke's question

How is it that 'the thoughts of men's minds [can] be conveyed from one to another' (Locke [1706] 1997, III.1.2)?

Locke's description of linguistic communication makes it sound like a kind of telepathy, and perhaps that is a useful comparison. By using language we are able to 'read each other's minds' quite effortlessly. Effortless it may be, but linguistic communication is a magnificent human accomplishment, every bit as peculiar as telepathy but more interesting because it actually occurs. What is it about producing a particular sound or pattern of ink that allows one person, the speaker or writer, to share information about the world with another, the hearer or reader?

An intuitive way of describing what happens when 'the thoughts of men's minds' are 'conveyed from one to another' is that the speaker invites his or her audience to accept that the world *is as it is represented to be* by the speaker's utterance, and the audience takes up this offer. This way of putting it can be elaborated into a simple theory intended to answer Locke's question:

The simple theory of communication

The successful communication of knowledge about the world is possible because speakers are able to produce utterances *with a specific meaning*, and recognition of that meaning by an audience enables them to appreciate what the speaker intends to communicate.

The key phrase is 'specific meaning' of an utterance. This is roughly equivalent to 'how the utterance represents the world as being', whatever that involves.

Saying what it involves is precisely what we must do if we wish to save this simple theory from the charge that it is hopelessly empty. For compare the simple theory with the theory parodied by the seventeenth-century French playwright Molière in *The Imaginary Invalid*. In this play, a doctor offers a spurious account of what gives opium its power to induce sleep in those who ingest it: it has this power, he says, because of its *virtus dormitiva*, i.e. its 'soporific virtues, the tendency of which is to lull the senses to sleep' (Molière [1673] 1879?, 73–4). The point of the parody is that the doctor has merely introduced a fancy-sounding name for the thing that needs to be explained, without having advanced us towards a genuine explanation. His putative explanation comes to this: opium induces sleep because it has the power to induce sleep. The simple theory of communication *as it stands* is little better than the doctor's theory. Like Molière, we can ask whether a term like 'meaning' as it figures in the simple theory (or 'represents' insofar as it plays the same role) is any more than a name for what we are trying to explain. Before we can sign up to the simple theory, we need to know how it differs from the following satirized version of it:

> **The empty theory of communication**
>
> The successful communication of knowledge about the world is possible because speakers are able to produce utterances with communicative powers, and audiences are induced by these powers to appreciate what the speaker intends to communicate.

Of course, if we supplement the simple theory with a substantial, plausible and independent theory of what meaning is – a theory that amounts to more than the claim that meaning is what makes communication possible – all will be well. That is our task in Part One, which considers attempts to develop a theory of the meaning of utterances, thereby rescuing the simple theory from the charge that it is empty as an explanation of how 'the thoughts of men's minds [can] be conveyed from one to another'.

Representation and thought

It would be surprising if the meaning of our utterances turned out not to derive, in part at least, from the thoughts and other mental states that these utterances express. Were that so, language would be failing in one of its main functions. Ordinarily, an utterance of the sentence, 'The German economy is bouncing back', is intended to express *the thought that the German economy is bouncing back*, typically so that the audience will come to adopt this same thought. It is hard to see how this could be so unless the meaning of the utterance did not derive, in part at least, from the representational properties – the 'content' as it is often put – of the thoughts and other mental states of the speaker. The discussion of mental representation in Part Two can therefore be thought of as a continuation of the project begun in Part One with the discussion of linguistic representation. Whereas Part One asks if and how the meaning of utterances derives from the content of the mental states of the utterer, Part Two asks questions about mental content *as such* rather than about how it finds expression in language. (This is a slight simplification of the relation between linguistic representation and mental representation. As we will see, some philosophers have argued that the content of our thoughts depends in part on what the words of our language mean, rather than entirely the other way round.)

Understanding the nature of mental content is taken by many to be equivalent to understanding how – presumably by virtue of possessing a brain, a complex physical organ – humans are able to think about the world around them. How can a state of the brain be *about* the world outside the skull of the person whose brain it is? This is the mental equivalent of Locke's question about language, and equally daunting.

Recent developments in theories of human cognition have added impetus to the search for an answer to this question. Many philosophers and cognitive scientists have been impressed by the explanatory benefits of claiming that mental activity in humans is akin to the operations of a computer. Crudely put, computers operate by transforming symbols within them in a blindingly fast but rule-governed manner. According to advocates of the computational theory of mind, the same is true of us. On most versions of the theory, for a human being to be in a particular mental state is for their brain to contain symbols of a kind of brain language, 'Mentalese' as it is usually called. The alleged attractions of thinking of the human brain as populated by symbols of a language will be considered in chapter 4, but they come to this: the computational theory of mind promises to explain how rationality is possible in a purely physical entity, as a living human body is assumed to be. Such an explanation has been a dream for many philosophers at least since Hobbes.

Not everyone accepts the analogy of human thinking with the operations of computers, but among those who do, the question arises of what gives the symbols of Mentalese their meaning. How can 'words' in a brain be about anything? How can they represent the world outside the skull? The meaning of the symbols of an actual computer – what makes it appropriate to call them 'symbols', in fact – derives from the interpretation imposed on them by computer designers and operators. The meaning of words in spoken or written language is also imposed, this time by the people using the language for the purpose of communication. But the source of the meaning of sentences hidden inside the human skull cannot be the interpretation imposed on them by an external interpreter, since there does not seem to be any such interpreter. So anyone who accepts the computational theory of mind is under an obligation to say what gives the symbols in the human brain their meaning. Many are sceptical of the computational theory of mind precisely because it is hard to see how this obligation could ever be discharged.

Discussion of mental representation, then, is often framed in terms of the meaning of inner symbols. But most of the difficulties that arise for those who accept the computational theory of mind also arise for *anyone* who (i) agrees that humans are capable of representing the world around them, but also (ii) wishes to claim that humans are in some sense essentially physical creatures subject to the laws of physics like other objects in the universe, and apt for study using scientific methods. Critics of the materialist world view are keen to stress how hard it is to show how both these assumptions could be true.

Three characteristic difficulties in discussions of representation

I have hinted that accounting for the nature of representation – whether it be the meaning of utterances or the content of our mental states – is not easy. There are several reasons for this, and it is as well to take note of some of them from the outset.

One is that there seem to be several different senses of 'meaning', 'represents' and related terms like 'stands for', 'being about', 'expresses' – differences that have been glossed over here but will need to be distinguished. Moreover, there are different *kinds* of thing that can ordinarily be said to represent or mean or stand for or express. Sometimes we talk of *people* meaning something, at other times we talk of their *words* meaning something, and often we talk of their *utterances* (i.e. the actions people produce *using* words) as meaning something. Different again is the meaning of a mental state, i.e. what is represented in thought rather than through spoken or written language.

Another source of difficulty is that meaning is not quantifiable in the way that, for example, temperature or humidity are. Generalizing from this point, ordinary scientific methods do not seem suited in any straightforward way to assist us in our efforts to understand either what representation is or how it is possible for human beings to represent. This is unfortunate because scientific methods have, without doubt, been extremely effective in other spheres of enquiry.

A further reason for thinking that science and the topic of representation are not well suited to one another has to do with the close connection between representation and the notion of *correctness*. Consider representation as it figures in belief. One way of distinguishing a belief *that cats have kittens* from a belief *that dogs have puppies* is that these two beliefs have different correctness conditions from one another. The first belief is correct if, and only if, cats have kittens. The second belief is correct if, and only if, dogs have puppies. But correctness and incorrectness – being right and being wrong – are normative or evaluative properties. As such, science seems ill-suited to describing them. Physicists and geologists, for example, do not include evaluative notions in their theories: a microscopic particle or a rock formation would never be described as 'correct'. It is true that geologists might evaluate a rock as a 'nice sample', but this is only an indication of its usefulness to the interests of the scientists, perhaps for illustrative purposes. Being 'nice', like being 'correct', is not part of any actual geological theory.

Finally, *represents* differs in strange ways from ordinary relations such as *bumps into* or *is late for*. To illustrate, consider our ability to think and talk about – to represent – things that do not exist. It is not possible to *bump into* things that do not exist. Similarly one can only swim in, read or kick things that actually exist. How is it possible that we can be related to a non-thing? Yet '*x* represents *y*' seems to be just such a relation. Were it not so, we would not be able to think about or talk about Santa Claus or God unless they both existed, and it seems plain that we can think about and talk about both without making any such assumption. For example, one can think about and discuss *whether* they exist. A phenomenon related to our capacity to think and talk about things that do not exist is our capactity to think and talk about one thing without thereby thinking or talking about a second thing, even though that 'second' thing is in fact identical with the first thing. Examples bring out the contrast with ordinary relations. With ordinary relations like *bumps into*, if *x* bears that relation to *y*, and *y* = *z*, then *x* also bears that relation to *z*. If by accident I bump into Mr Jones on the bus, and Mr Jones is identical with Plastic Freddy the performance artist, then it is also true that I have bumped into Plastic Freddy. *Representing*, or *thinking / talking about*, is different in this respect. When Oedipus thought longingly about Jocasta without realizing that Jocasta was his mother, there is a sense in which he was not thinking longingly about his mother. Representing someone as Jocasta is not the same as representing them as one's mother even when Jocasta *is* one's mother. (The example comes from the ancient Greek tragedy, *Oedipus Rex*. Oedipus unwittingly kills his father so as to marry Jocasta, taking out his own eyes on discovering his mistake.)

Some useful terminology and a convention

It will be useful to end this introduction by establishing a simple convention and introducing some terminology.

The convention has already been at work in this chapter, but has yet to be made explicit. It is a convention for marking the difference between *using* a word and *mentioning* it. Italy has a capital city, and the English language contains a word for that city, but the word and the city are distinct entities. When we are talking about the word rather than what the word is about, we are *mentioning* that word. When we want to talk about the city itself, we are very likely to *use* the word and not merely mention it. In oral language, this distinction between using a word and mentioning it is not explicitly marked. Spoken aloud, the first and third sentences below are indistinguishable, as are the second and fourth. In writing, however, there is a helpful convention of surrounding a word with inverted commas whenever it is being mentioned rather than used. Thus:

'Rome' has four letters. ✓
'Rome' is the capital city of Italy. ✗
Rome has four letters. ✗
Rome is the capital city of Italy. ✓

The convention of marking the distinction in this way will be adopted throughout this book, and it is used by the authors of the associated readings.

The terminology to be introduced concerns the use of 'subject', 'attitude' and 'content' in discussing mental states. The last of these has appeared already. What a mental state is about (its *content*) can be distinguished from both the person whose mental state it is (the *subject* or alternatively the *agent*) and the kind of mental state it is (the *attitude*). The distinctions are easily conveyed through examples of mental states:

Same subject; different attitude; different content

John believes that there are some biscuits in the biscuit tin.

John hopes that he can watch television undisturbed.

Different subject; same attitude; different content

John *believes* that there are some biscuits left in the biscuit tin.

Mary *believes* that she can watch television undisturbed.

Different subject; different attitude; same content

John believes that *there are some biscuits left in the biscuit tin.*

Mary hopes that *there are some biscuits left in the biscuit tin.*

This terminology assumes that every mental state involves three elements: a subject, an attitude and a content.

Contents are often expressed in the so-called 'that-clause' (underlined) of sentences used to attribute mental states: 'So-and-so thinks (or hopes, intends, imagines, expects, decides, etc.) that such-and-such.' This is true of the six examples above. When a content can be expressed in a that-clause, it is said to be a *propositional* content or, for short, a proposition. Propositional contents are capable of being true or false. But sometimes a content is not, on the surface at least, propositional. Being in love, for example, is a mental state, but one loves a thing, a person usually, rather than a propositional content. Someone can be correctly said to love *someone or something*, but it sounds peculiar to talk of loving *that* such-and-such, where the such-and-such is capable of being true or false. Contents of attitudes like 'love' are called *objectual*. Other mental attitudes relate a subject to a content of either kind. Someone can desire a person or a thing, but they can also desire that something be the case.

Differences between the attitudes will not be a large part of our discussion, but it is worth being aware that there are differences. The attitudes are traditionally classified as cognitive (e.g. believing or thinking), affective (e.g. being upset), or conative (e.g. intending, desiring or deciding). All three kinds involve representing, but in slightly different ways. The differences between them turn on the function of the attitude. Very crudely, we might say that the function of believing that p is to represent the world as it is, and the function of intending that p is to represent the world as it will become through one's own intervention. Part Two of the book will be about the representational properties of *all* mental states, not merely those involving cognitive attitudes such as thinking. But thinking will often be treated as a central case.

Finally, though I will often talk of 'speakers' and 'hearers', the philosophical point being made always generalizes to cover modes of linguistic communication other than oral. In particular, it applies to both sign language and written language.

Further reading

Detailed options for further reading can be found at the end of each chapter. For an advanced general introduction to the philosophy of language, see Blackburn 1984. Lycan 1996 is pitched at a more accessible level. Pinker 1994 is an informal but informative discussion of the hypothesis that much of our linguistic ability is innate, an important topic that has had to be left out of the present book. Crane 2003 and Sterelny 1990 both offer accessible introductions to issues covered in Part Two. Harder going but still introductory is Heil 1998.

PART ONE
REPRESENTING WITH LANGUAGE

CHAPTER 2

Is the speaker's mind the source of an utterance's meaning?

The distinction noted in chapter 1 between the representational properties of a linguistic utterance (its 'meaning') and the representational properties of a mental state (its 'content') gives rise, naturally enough, to the suspicion that one of these might be more fundamental than the other. In this chapter I will look at a theory, most closely associated with the British philosopher H.P. Grice (1913–88), to the effect that the source of an utterance's meaning is the speaker's mind, i.e. the content of their mental states. On this view, when someone produces an utterance, the meaning of this utterance can ultimately be traced back to the content of their intentions in producing it.

An alternative possible source of an utterance's meaning is the meaning of the words used, conceived of as dependent on the characteristics of the linguistic community the person belongs to and possibly other factors that are 'outside' the mind of the utterer. (We will examine the case for a particular version of this view, the one advocated by the American philosopher Hilary Putnam, in chapter 3.) Both views of the source of an utterance's meaning are appealing in their different ways. So a pair of questions that will stretch across both chapters is (i) whether the two views are genuinely in competition or merely apparently so, and (ii) if there is genuine competition, which of the views is more successful in locating the source of the meaning of utterances?

The source of an utterance's meaning: the words used or the speaker's mind?

How are we able to use language to communicate knowledge? Locke's question, introduced in chapter 1, was recast as the obligation to spell out what 'meaning' amounts to as it figures within a simple theory of communication, repeated here:

The simple theory of communication

The successful communication of knowledge about the world is possible because speakers are able to produce utterances *with a specific meaning*, and recognition of that meaning by an audience enables them to appreciate what the speaker intends to communicate.

This theory is, we saw, only genuinely explanatory if we can supplement it with a non-vacuous statement of what it is for an utterance to have the meaning it does. Our task in the next two chapters will be to explore ways of doing this.

There are two different and potentially incompatible approaches to carrying out this task, distinguished according to what they take as the source of an utterance's meaning. According to one view, the source is the meaning of the expressions uttered according to the language to which they belong. If a speaker utters the sentence, 'The German economy is bouncing back', what the utterance means is that the German economy is bouncing back. On this first view, it means this because *that is what these words mean in English*. If the speaker had unusual ideas about what the words 'German' and 'economy' mean – for example, that they mean what we ordinarily mean by 'folding' and 'bed' respectively – this would not (on this first view) change the meaning of the utterance. The speaker would still have said that the German economy is bouncing back, not that the folding bed is bouncing back.

Many find this thought intuitively appealing. To others, it seems unnecessarily prescriptive. Why, they ask, can we not use language in ways of our own choosing? If someone wants to use 'jealous of' to mean *envious of* rather than *possessive of* (its traditional or 'proper' meaning), then why shouldn't they? This second view treats the speaker's mental states as the source of the meaning of the utterances they produce. Supporters of the first view often respond to the liberal, speaker-centred perspective by pointing to the disastrous consequences of treating the actual speaker rather than the words the speaker uses as the arbiter of an utterance's meaning. They are fond of alluding to Humpty Dumpty (as he figures in Lewis Carroll's *Alice through the looking-glass* rather than as he figures in the nursery rhyme) to make their point. Below is a passage from the book in which Humpty proclaims his right to mean whatever he wishes by the words he uses.

> 'As I was saying [said Humpty Dumpty], that *seems* to be done right – though I haven't time to look it over thoroughly just now – and that shows that there are three hundred and sixty-four days when you might get un-birthday presents –'

Figure 1 Alice and Humpty from Lewis Carroll, 'Through the looking-glass and what Alice found there', illustrations by John Tenniel, first published by Macmillan & Co., London, 1872.

'Certainly,' said Alice.

'And only *one* for birthday presents, you know. There's glory for you!'

'I don't know what you mean by "glory",' Alice said.

Humpty Dumpty smiled contemptuously. 'Of course you don't – till I tell you. I meant "there's a nice knock-down argument for you!"'

'But "glory" doesn't mean "a nice knock-down argument",' Alice objected.

'When *I* use a word,' Humpty Dumpty said, in rather a scornful tone, 'it means just what I choose it to mean – neither more nor less.'

'The question is,' said Alice, 'whether you *can* make words mean so many different things.'

'The question is,' said Humpty Dumpty, 'which is to be master – that's all.'

Alice was too much puzzled to say anything; so after a minute Humpty Dumpty began again. 'They've a temper, some of them – particularly verbs: they're the proudest – adjectives you can do anything with, but not verbs – however, *I* can manage the whole lot of them! Impenetrability! That's what *I* say!'

'Would you tell me please,' said Alice, 'what that means?'

'Now you talk like a reasonable child,' said Humpty Dumpty, looking very much pleased. 'I meant by "impenetrability" that we've had enough of that subject, and it would be just as well if you'd mention what you mean to do next, as I suppose you don't mean to stop here all the rest of your life.'

'That's a great deal to make one word mean,' Alice said in a thoughtful tone.

'When I make a word do a lot of work like that,' said Humpty Dumpty, 'I always pay it extra.'

'Oh!' said Alice.

(Carroll 1893, 113–15)

We can distil from this dialogue a claim – call it *Humpty's thesis* – regarding the extent to which what we mean is under our own control rather than dependent on the meaning of the words used, where this latter is independent of our wishes:

Humpty's thesis

What we mean when we utter a word or sentence is under our own control; we can mean whatever we want and choose.

Though it is difficult to see exactly why, Humpty's thesis seems deeply misguided. Grice's theory, to which I now turn, sees the mental states of the speaker as the primary source of the meaning possessed by the utterances the speaker produces. He even claims that the relevant mental states are the speaker's *intentions*. This sounds as if he is just providing a 'Humpty-Dumpty' theory according to which what we mean is up to us. Whether this unflattering comparison can be made to stick is something to consider after seeing the details of his influential theory.

ACTIVITY

We will be examining a position according to which the meaning of utterances is inherited from the content of the speaker's mental states. Having just read Humpty's embarrassingly extreme statement of this view, you may be deeply unsympathetic to that idea. So, to counterbalance your sympathies, consider a reason to be suspicious of views at the opposite extreme, which treat the meaning of utterances as entirely independent of mental states. Suppose some rocks are found arranged in a pattern on the dusty surface of Mars, as below:

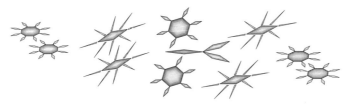

The rock pattern could be the equivalent in some alien language of a piece of clumsy but meaningful handwriting. Alternatively it could be a meaningless cluster of tiny fallen meteorites, any discernable pattern in it being a random accident. What would make you treat this pattern of rocks as a meaningful utterance – not a verbal utterance obviously, but an utterance in the same sense that a written letter is an utterance?

DISCUSSION   Arguably, in order to be meaningful the cluster would have to be judged as having been produced by some intelligence, perhaps with the intention of communicating with another intelligent being, or with us, or with God, or (as in a diary or a doodle or an arithmetical calculation) with itself. Considered merely as an unintended and accidental pattern in the dust on the Martian surface, it has no meaning whatsoever. If by outlandish chance a cluster of meteorites fell into a pattern that spelled out the English sentence 'Lo, Earthlings!', it would still not mean anything – though in that case we could be excused for incorrectly reading meaning into a meaningless event. This is a reason of sorts for suspecting that the meaning of utterances is dependent on the psychological states, perhaps even the intentions, of the producer of the utterance.

Grice on natural and non-natural meaning

Ironically, the word 'meaning' has many different meanings. There are four occurrences of 'mean' (or 'meaning' or 'meant', etc.), italicized, in the following paragraph:

> Roberto's instructor had been *mean* to put it so bluntly, but she was probably correct that his short legs *meant* he would never be a great dancer. He turned into the narrow alleyway, *meaning* to take a shortcut home. His life no longer seemed to have any *meaning*.

Here is the paragraph again, with each of the four occurrences of 'mean', 'meant' and 'meaning' replaced with an appropriate synonym.

> Roberto's instructor had been *cruel* to put it so bluntly, but she was probably correct that his short legs *were bound to result in* his never being a great dancer. He turned into the narrow alleyway, *intending* to take a shortcut home. His life no longer seemed to have any *purpose*.

There is no good reason to demand of a theory of meaning that it give an account of every kind of meaning. It *may* turn out that there is some underlying unity to the uses of 'mean' (or 'means', 'meant', 'meaning') on display here, but that is not something we should insist on.

In view of the plethora of meanings of 'meaning', Grice proposes to set aside those that are not his immediate concern and to focus on understanding the nature of those that are. One kind of meaning that is left over is defined by Grice in terms of the speaker's intentions. This is a good candidate for being the kind of meaning *we* are interested in, i.e. the meaning utterances have that accounts for the role they play in communication. But before coming to what he says about this kind of meaning, we need to see which kinds of meaning he sets to one side as confusing distractions.

Grice begins his paper (Reading 1) by making an important distinction between two species of meaning that it is particularly easy to confuse, which he labels *natural meaning* and *non-natural meaning*. The kind of meaning he later defines in terms of speakers' intentions is non-natural meaning. Natural meaning is the kind being attributed in claim (a):

(a) 'Those spots on your face mean *you have measles.*'

This claim could be true only if the italicized sub-sentence is true, i.e. only if you really do have measles. If you had spots but you didn't have measles, the spots would not mean that you had measles. They would have to have some other source. Contrast this with claim (b), which uses 'mean' in its non-natural sense:

(b) 'The spots in the arrangement below mean *you have measles.*'

This whole assertion would be true even if the italicized sub-sentence was false. That is, an assertion of (b) would still be correct even if you did not have measles. Generalizing, the difference between the two kinds of meaning is this: it is consistent with something's having non-natural meaning that what it non-naturally means is false; but it is not consistent with something's having natural meaning that what it naturally means is false. (In the paper, Grice notes other differences, but this is the main one.)

Grice's purpose in making this distinction is merely to avoid confusion. He sets natural meaning (or 'meaning$_n$' as he calls it) to one side and moves on to developing a theory of non-natural meaning ('meaning$_{nn}$'), the kind he is more interested in. His partiality has to do with the fact that examples of meaning that involve language are typically cases of meaning$_{nn}$, and no one has so far come up with a good theory of meaning$_{nn}$. Natural meaning, by contrast, does not really have much to do with the meaning of words or utterances, and is in any case relatively non-mysterious. 'X means$_n$ that p' can be understood as a substitute for one or other of various simple phrases, including:

> X causes it to be the case that p
>
> X is conclusive evidence for p
>
> X is not possible unless p is true
>
> X entails that p

Natural meaning is mentioned later in his paper, but only in order to clear up potential confusions, not because Grice is especially interested in it.

ACTIVITY Read part I of Grice's paper, 'Meaning' (Reading 1). As with several of the Readings associated with this book, the original paper is not actually divided into parts; they are my addition (indicated by the square brackets) to facilitate guided reading. Grice distinguishes natural from non-natural meaning. He also rejects an attempt (by C.L. Stevenson) to define non-natural meaning in terms of natural meaning, prior to offering his own theory of non-natural meaning in the rest of the paper.

Which of the following claims about meaning are most plausibly interpreted as claims about natural meaning, and which are most plausibly interpreted as claims about non-natural meaning?

(i) John is sneezing. This means he has a sinus infection.

(ii) The French sentence, 'Pierre aime les chats', means that Pierre likes cats.

(iii) In saying what he did, John meant that he would be late.

(iv) Failure to bring an accurate map with him meant that John would be late.

(i) Natural. If John has no sinus infection, his sneezing could not possibly mean that he had a sinus infection. If it means anything, it would have to mean something else, e.g. that there is pepper in the air.

(ii) Non-natural. The sentence would mean what it does even if Pierre hates cats.

(iii) Non-natural. John's utterance (whatever it was – perhaps it was 'I will be late' or 'start without me') would have had this meaning even if he in fact ends up arriving on time.

(iv) Natural. Suppose John arrived on time. This would lead us to reject the claim that his failure to bring an accurate map meant that he would be late.

The distinction between natural and non-natural meaning is, Grice notes, not always clear cut. The same entity can sometimes have both natural and non-natural meaning. Here is an illustration:

> The canyon-dweller's shout of 'here comes an echo' meant that we would hear an echo a few seconds later.

This is plausible on both readings of 'meant'. But in most cases the distinction seems to be reasonably easy to apply. Let us move on, then, to Grice's theory of non-natural meaning. (Henceforth in this chapter, 'meaning' should be read as 'non-natural meaning' unless specified otherwise.)

The meaning of expressions versus the meaning of individual utterances

I drew a contrast at the beginning of the chapter between those approaches to the meaning of utterances that look to the meaning of the words used, and those approaches that look instead to the content of the mental or psychological states of speakers. Grice belongs to the second camp. He aims to show that the meaning of an expression (e.g. a word or a sentence) is derivative, definable in terms of how that expression is typically used in meaningful utterances. The meaning of individual utterances is, he concludes, more fundamental than the meaning of expressions. More fundamental than both, though, are the contents of the speakers' minds, and in particular the intentions that give rise to the production of utterances.

With this agenda in mind, Grice draws a distinction within the category of non-natural meaning. What an utterance means 'timelessly' is tied to the meaning of the words and sentences used in making it. The word 'timeless' is used to allude to the fact that expressions can be used over and over again with the same meaning, but we can follow standard practice and talk of *expression meaning* – the meaning of the sentences and words that occur in utterances. But more fundamental than expression meaning, in Grice's view, is another kind of non-natural meaning: the meaning of an individual utterance (or, as he sometimes puts it, of an expression as it is used 'on a specific occasion'). This more fundamental notion can be defined (Grice thinks) in terms of the psychological states of the speaker. Grice's working hypothesis, then, is that both kinds of meaning ultimately have their source in the content of psychological states, something he seeks to show in two steps:

> *Step One:* give a definition of the meaning of single, isolated utterances couched entirely in terms of *what the speaker intends to bring about*.
>
> *Step Two:* give a definition of expression meaning ('timeless meaning') couched entirely in terms of the definition of the meaning of single isolated utterances given in Step One.

ACTIVITY Read part II of Grice's paper. This is where he sets out the agenda just described. The crucial phrase is 'this might reasonably be expected to help us with'. Grice is asserting the priority of the meaning of individual utterances (or of expressions as used by someone on 'specific occasions' as he puts it) over the meaning of expressions (used 'timelessly'). He will go on to define the former in terms of the intentions of the utterer (what I have called his Step One) and the latter in terms of the former (Step Two).

Why intentions?

Most of the rest of Grice's paper is dedicated to spelling out a way of identifying the meaning of an individual utterance 'on an occasion' with the content of the utterer's intentions (Step One). The hard task he faces is to say what type of intention creates meaning. If someone shouts 'I saw a film last night' extremely loudly at their brother with the intention of making this brother fall off his bike, this 'utterance' (if that is the right word) does not thereby mean *fall off your bike, brother*. So Grice must distinguish between different kinds of intentions. To appreciate his efforts it will help to understand what is driving Grice's choice of the utterer's *intention*, rather than some other type of psychological state, as the source of an utterance's meaning. The motivation for this choice is important but is left largely implicit in this early groundbreaking paper.

Many of the examples Grice gives of events with (non-natural) meaning are non-linguistic. Ringing the bell on a bus is a case in point. The existence of non-linguistic but meaningful acts leads Grice to the view that it is *as acts* that linguistic acts have meaning – their being linguistic is something of a side issue. Grice even goes so far as to stretch ordinary usage of the term 'utterance' to include *any* event that has (non-natural) meaning. But what is it about meaningful acts, linguistic or otherwise, that gives them the meaning they have? One thing all acts seem to have in common is that they are performed with an intention, even if that intention is not always fulfilled. Grice's hunch is that it is the intention behind the production of a meaningful act, linguistic or non-linguistic, that gives it its meaning.

He attempts to vindicate this hunch by spelling out in detail the precise form the intention must take. Merely being intended does not make an act meaningful since all acts are intended but not all acts are meaningful. When a tree surgeon saws off a branch, this does not normally have any meaning. There must be something special about the intention behind utterances (i.e. meaningful acts) that sets them apart from acts that lack meaning. But what is that special something?

Which intentions?

Grice makes three attempts to answer this last question. The second builds on the first; the third, which he proposes to adopt, builds on the second. In the next three activities, you will be asked to extract these attempts in turn, and appreciate the alleged shortcomings of the first two.

Read part III of 'Meaning', in which Grice makes a first attempt to specify   **ACTIVITY** which form an intention must have if the resulting act is to be meaningful. He then quickly dismisses the attempt. What is the definition, and why does he find it wanting?

According to Grice's first suggestion, an utterance means whatever it is that the utterer is trying to get his or her audience to believe. (He is talking only about assertions, setting aside questions and orders.) Call this first definition 'Grice 1'.

> *Grice 1*: A specific utterance U means that p if, and only if, in performing U, the utterer intends an audience to come to believe that p.

Grice quickly dismisses this as insufficient. Doing something with the intention merely of getting one's audience to believe that p does not amount to meaning that p. He gives a simple example to show this. The example is a non-linguistic one, which fits with his hunch that the source of an individual utterance's meaning is not, ultimately, the words used.

The example involves someone, call them A, secretly leaving B's handkerchief at a murder scene with the intention of getting the detective to believe that B is the murderer. Intuitively, we would not really say of A's act that it *means* that B is the murderer. (It certainly doesn't mean$_{nn}$ this, anyway, and this is the only kind of meaning Grice is interested in. But in fact it does not really seem to mean$_n$ this either. At most, the detective may be led to *think* it means$_n$ that B is the murderer.)

A common reaction to this counter-example is that leaving a handkerchief at a crime scene is not verbal, so is not an utterance, so is irrelevant. But Grice's use of 'utterance' is meant to be stipulative and artificial. Using 'utterance' in this self-consciously broad way is a reminder of the fact that verbal utterances are not the only kind of meaningful act. (Think of nodding, or miming breaststroke behind a boss's back to mean that a co-worker should not cave in.) But in any case Grice's counter-example could easily have been a verbal one, where by 'verbal' is meant something like 'involving use of the voice'. Suppose that, for some reason, C wants D, a monolingual English-speaker, to believe that D's house is haunted by the ghost of the Russian émigré who used to live in it. At night, from inside a cupboard in D's bedroom, C produces Russian-sounding nonsense using a guide to Russian enunciation. We would not say that C's utterances mean that D's house is haunted as Grice 1 requires. They do not mean anything, not even in Russian.

Grice uses the failings of this first definition to develop a better one.

Read part IV of 'Meaning', in which Grice modifies his earlier definition. He also argues that the modified version still falls short. What is the modified version?

The new element, required for meaning but missing in the handkerchief scenario, is *openness of intent*. *A* placed *B*'s handkerchief secretly, since if the detective was aware that *A* had put it down, he would not have been led to suspect *B*. If we add an openness requirement to Grice 1, it should rule out this example and others like it. Grice incorporates this new element into his second attempt at a definition, which we can express as follows:

> *Grice 2*: A specific utterance *U* means that *p* if, and only if, in performing it, the utterer intends:
>
>> (a) that an audience will come to believe that *p*, and
>>
>> (b) that this audience will recognize intention (a).

The new clause, (b), is not met in the handkerchief case or in the haunted-cupboard case. This lends support to this formulation of the Gricean proposal.

But even Grice 2 is inadequate. In one of several counter-examples, Grice imagines himself supplying Mr *X* with a photograph of Mr *Y* 'showing undue familiarity to Mrs *X*'. (Note: Grice was writing before the manipulation of photographs became commonplace.) He supplies it with the intention that Mr *X* will come to believe that 'there is something between Mr *Y* and Mrs *X*'. If we take '*U*' to be the act of supplying the photo to Mr *X*, and '*p*' to be that there is something between Mr *Y* and Mrs *X*, clause (a) is satisfied. Suppose moreover that Grice, in this imaginary scenario, wishes his intention to be recognized. Perhaps he wishes this because Mr *X* is powerful and supportive of those who are loyal to him. So rather than posting the photo anonymously, Grice hands it to Mr *X* in person. This means that clause (b) is also satisfied. But we would not really want to say that Grice's act *means* that Mr *Y* and Mrs *X* are joined in some illicit union. We might be tempted to say that this is what the photo itself means, but that is at best meaning$_n$, not meaning$_{nn}$, the kind we are interested in. The photographic image is evidence for the existence of an illicit union, in the same way that red spots on a person's face are evidence of measles; if there were no illicit union then the claim that this is what it meant would have to be withdrawn, and this is the mark of meaning$_n$. (This is where the danger of confusion between the two kinds of meaning is at its greatest, which is why Grice was keen to make the distinction explicit early on.)

Read part V of 'Meaning'. In this passage, Grice adds a further clause to get to what we can call Grice 3. What is the new requirement?

The problem with Grice 2, illustrated in the photograph case, is used by Grice to draw a moral. Even though clause (a) and clause (b) are both met in the photo scenario, there is *no connection between* the intention required by clause (a) and the intention required by clause (b). In particular, the prospects for success of intention (b), i.e. the intention to be recognized as having intention (a), is inessential to the prospects for success of intention (a). Grice (in the photograph scenario) could easily have succeeded in intention (a) without succeeding in intention (b). The photo, so to speak, tells its own story without Grice's (b)-intention playing any essential role. To see this, suppose for contrast that the 'undue familiarity' were represented by a drawing by Grice of matchstick figures rather than by a photo. Such a drawing could serve as a warning, or as a strange fantasy, or as a reminder of what is happily not the case, or any number of purposes other than as the recording of a witnessed event. What would settle which of these possible messages was the drawing's actual meaning would turn on Grice's (b)-intention – his intention to be recognized by Mr X as producing the drawing for a particular purpose. That, thinks Grice, is why drawings have meaning$_{nn}$ and photos have mere meaning$_n$. This thought feeds into his final theory of the meaning of individual utterances. What would rule out the photo case, thinks Grice, is the requirement of a connection between intentions (a) and (b).

> *Grice 3*: A specific utterance U means that p if, and only if, in performing it, the utterer intends:
>
>   (a) that an audience will come to believe that p, and
>
>   (b) that this audience will recognize intention (a), and
>
>   (c) that the recognition in (b) will cause the belief in (a).

This final version is complex, but that is unsurprising given the implausibility of the crude version of the approach advanced by Humpty, according to whom what the speaker means is just what the speaker chooses to mean. We will have to decide shortly whether Grice's theory is a genuine improvement over Humpty's or merely hides the same basic misconceptions behind increased complexity.

Expression meaning as defined by Grice

Recall Step Two in the Gricean agenda: to define the meaning of expressions in terms of the meaning of individual utterances. Carrying out this strategy successfully would lend strong support to the thought that it is the mental states of speakers, rather than the meaning of expressions, that are the ultimate source of utterances' meaning.

Read the rest of Grice's paper (part VI). Pay particular attention to (1)–(3) on pp.185–6, which state his overall theory. (1) and (2) are a summary of his theory of the meaning of individual utterances. (Be warned: Grice is not kind to his readers here. For example, his theory of the meaning of utterances is given twice over. He gives a definition of what it is for a speaker ('*A*') to mean something by producing an utterance. He then gives a definition of what it is for of an expression ('*x*'), as it is used by a speaker to produce an utterance 'on a specific occasion', to mean something. But according to him these notions are equivalent. That is why, in an effort to simplify his position, I represented him as offering a theory of the meaning of just one thing, the utterance itself, *U*.) (3) is his theory of the meaning an expression ('*x*') has 'timelessly', i.e. independently of the meaning it has in the context of any particular utterance. (This is what I have been calling 'the meaning of an expression'.)

ACTIVITY

Before coming to (1)–(3), Grice extends his account to cover utterances that are not intended to convey information, for example questions or orders; after (1)–(3) he attempts to deal with some potential problems with his overall account.

What is expression meaning, according to Grice (i.e. how does he define the meaning an expression, *x*, has 'timelessly')?

DISCUSSION

The meaning of an expression is defined by Grice in a way that takes for granted the meaning of individual utterances made using it, since this notion is already given in his (1)–(2). He claims (though he is not very clear at this point) that an expression – a sentence, in effect – means that *p* within a loosely circumscribed linguistic community if, and only if, members of that community tend to use that expression in utterances that mean that *p*. So, for example, the expression 'the train is late again' means what it does among the people of Britain, America and so on, because they tend to use it in individual utterances that mean the train is late again.

The theory of the meaning of expressions in (3) on page 186 comes to this:

> Sentence *s* means that *p* in the language of a specific population if and only if most utterances of *s* by members of that population mean that *p*.

Unfortunately, there seems to be an important lacuna in Grice's account of expression meaning: at best it defines sentence meaning, since it says nothing about word meaning. Words are typically uttered meaningfully only in combination with other words, typically within sentences. (There are a few exceptions, such as 'Fire!' or 'Help!') But they can appear in many *different* sentences, associated with *a huge variety of distinct* communicative intentions. So even if Grice is right to claim that a sentence means what it does because of a regularity in the meaning of the utterances made using it, the meaning of a word cannot be defined in terms of such a regularity.

But there is a problem with this definition even as it applies to just sentences. Some sentences have never been uttered before. Consider:

> It is easier to dry-clean umbrellas that have been soaked in giraffe saliva than it is to inhale freshly plucked Namibian goose down.

If Grice is right that a sentence's meaning is a matter of how it is regularly used, then this novel sentence, never used (I presume) before I wrote it down just now, ought to be meaningless. But that seems not to be the case. Its meaning is unusual, but it has one.

This second problem seems to have its source in the first. If we had a theory of word meaning, we could attempt to see how the meaning of a novel sentence is built up from the meaning of the words it contains. Grice's predicament is not quite as desperate as it appears. We will see a theory of word meaning that is in keeping with Grice's ambitions towards the end of this chapter.

The Gricean Programme

Before considering any further potential criticisms of Grice's position, let us step back and consider his wider importance to philosophy: his contribution to what is often called *The Gricean Programme*. Grice himself was not really a Gricean in this sense, since he was not committed to all elements of the programme that bears his name. But Grice's influence has been as great as it has in part because of the way in which his ideas have been co-opted into this broader programme.

The goal of the programme is to show that all species of representation (including the various kinds of meaning associated with language, as well as mental content) are reducible to the natural sciences. That is to say, Griceans aim to restate all uses of phrases like 'means', 'represents', 'stands for' and so on using only phrases drawn from the language of science. As it is sometimes put, the aim is to 'naturalize' the notion of representation. Grice (according to Griceans) shows us how to reduce the meaning associated with language to the content of mental states, and if the content of mental states can be reduced in turn to the natural sciences, the programme will have succeeded. One motive behind this reductionist enterprise is to give science a comprehensiveness it would lack if the notion of representation, very useful in its various guises, fell outside the main fold of science; another is to confer legitimacy on the notion itself by integrating it with the rest of science, much as biology, chemistry and physics have been increasingly integrated with one another.

The structure of the Gricean Programme is reflected in Figure 2, which I discuss below, starting at the top and following the arrows in order. The diagram looks complex, but most of it is already familiar.

We have seen already that Grice makes a plausible case for the existence of an ambiguity in the word 'meaning' between natural meaning and non-natural meaning (arrows 1 and 2). Natural meaning, we saw, can be thought of as a causal relation or necessary or lawlike connection (p.18), where these are notions that sit happily with the natural sciences (arrow 3). If we want to know whether a particular cloud configuration means$_n$ that rain is on its way, our best bet is to ask a meteorologist.

Non-natural meaning – the kind still left mysterious after natural meaning is set aside as definable in terms of causal connections, etc. – can be distinguished into two sorts (arrows 4 and 5). This is the familiar distinction between the meaning of expressions and the meaning of individual utterances. We have just seen how Grice proposes to define the former in terms of the latter, and this is captured in arrow 6. (The outstanding matter of accounting for word

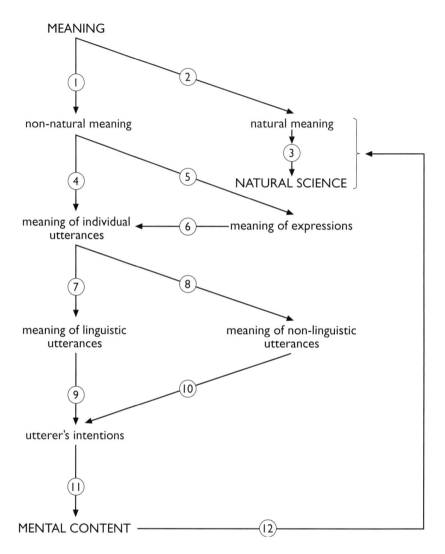

Figure 2 The Gricean Programme. Arrows represent the direction of flow in the analysis of representational notions (meaning and mental content) into, ultimately, properties belonging to the natural sciences.

meaning as opposed to sentence meaning will be returned to at the end of the chapter.)

We saw that Grice uses the term 'utterance' in a broad and slightly artificial way to mean any action with non-natural meaning. Utterances in this sense can include not only linguistic actions but many other kinds of non-linguistic action, such as the ringing of a bell on a bus. The distinction between linguistic and non-linguistic meaningful acts is, he thinks, misleading if it is taken to be a fundamental one, since all meaningful acts have something in common: the source of their meaning is the agent's intention. In the diagram, this is why the downward flow bifurcates temporarily into linguistic and non-linguistic utterances (arrows 7 and 8) but immediately comes together into a single point (arrows 9 and 10), the intention of the utterer. The content of intentions is but one kind of mental content (arrow 11).

Everything recounted so far is more or less resonant with Grice's position as it is manifested in his 1957 paper. But if the Gricean Programme stopped here it would be incomplete. For what, in scientific terms, is mental content? The final piece in the jigsaw would be a theory of mental content (including the content of intentions) in terms that are familiar from other areas of science (arrow 12). This final part of the programme – following the course of arrow 12 – will be a main theme in the second part of this book (chapters 4 to 7), and we can ignore it here. But perhaps worth noting is that one approach to the content of mental states, examined in chapter 5, involves trying to define it in terms of what Grice has called *natural meaning* (hence the bracket in the diagram at the end of arrow 12).

How successful is Grice's theory of the meaning of utterances?

I turn now to difficulties for Grice's account of the meaning of utterances, beginning with a concern over his methodology. By focusing on examples, real or imagined, Grice attempts to draw out our intuitions and so lead us, as he has been led, to Grice 3. But perhaps our intuitions are wildly inaccurate, or wildly irrelevant. We need to check that Grice's notion of meaning, mined out of his and our intuitions, delivers what we were after when we turned to him for a theory of the meaning of utterances.

In fact, the definition Grice arrives at does seem to be well suited to our needs once we consider the model of communication we get when Grice's final statement of what it is for an individual utterance to mean what it does (p.24) is plugged into the simple theory of communication (p.13). Think of a communicative predicament. *A* is with *B* in the jungle, and sees a leopard nearby, hidden from *B*'s view. *A* wants *B* to appreciate the leopard's presence but is not able to point it out. *A* must therefore communicate the leopard's presence to *B*. By uttering an appropriate sentence, *A* intends that *B* will come to believe there is a leopard nearby. Moreover, it is through *B*'s recognition of this intention that *A* intends this to come about. When *B* hears *A*'s utterance and recognizes it as having been performed with the intention that *B* believes there is a leopard nearby, *B* obliges by forming just this belief, exactly as anticipated by *A*. This elaborated version of the simple theory seems to go a long way towards capturing what is going on in the communication of knowledge. And unlike the unelaborated version, it does not rest on an unanalysed notion of meaning that can be compared unflatteringly to the *virtus dormitiva* in Molière's satire (see chapter 1). So, Grice's theory is a reasonable candidate for being what we want from a theory of the meaning of utterances. But before celebrating, we need to consider other potential weaknesses.

One is the extreme structural complexity of the intentions we would need to have for Grice 3 to be correct. This structural complexity seems to be at odds with the ease with which we speak. If Grice is right, every time we open our mouths or pick up our pens to communicate, we form a complex triple-parted intention. Is this plausible as a description of our psychology as speakers? Ordinary speakers would be hard pressed to give a verbal statement of the content of the intentions that Grice is saying they form at high speed in everyday conversation. Such complex intentions also seem to be far more than we are capable of recognizing in others in the real-life communication of knowledge.

Whether we have these complex intentions is a difficult topic. In his paper Grice does say something in his own defence (pp.186–7), denying that the intentions he is describing are 'explicitly formulated linguistic (or quasi-linguistic) intentions'. The fact that these communicative intentions – unlike the intention to, say, hail a taxi – cannot be verbalized does not show that they do not exist, he is suggesting. But the problem seems to go deeper than he realizes, even if he is right to insist that there can be unverbalizable intentions. The communicative intentions Grice posits are not only unverbalizable, they are unconscious. When we speak we are aware of an intention to produce a particular sentence or to communicate in some loose way, but we are not aware of ourselves as having complex triple-parted intentions. (Or at least I am not. You are invited to decide for yourself the next time you communicate.) But the idea of an unconscious intention has struck many as an odd one. Grice could reply that intentions *can be* unconscious. He could draw an analogy with

Freud's claim that we have unconscious drives, or with the way in which learning to type or to play a musical instrument is deliberate and conscious at first but gradually becomes unconscious and fluent. But many are left with a nagging doubt that this is an account of utterance meaning that fails to do justice to our actual experience of using and understanding language.

A different worry turns on the adequacy of the content of the intentions rather than on their structural complexity. The development of Grice 3 out of Grice 2 and, before that, Grice 1 involved *adding* clauses. But there are some reasons to worry that the first clause, (a), demands too much, not too little. There are plenty of meaningful utterances in which there is no intention to get an audience to believe anything, for the simple reason that there is no audience.

Are communicative intentions of the kind set out in Grice 3 (or Grice 2 or   **ACTIVITY**
Grice 1 for that matter) genuinely necessary for an utterance to be meaningful? Think about this question in relation to:

(i) writing a diary;

(ii) talking to a dog – not as in 'Fetch!' but as in, 'Oh Rover, how I wish I were just a dog like you, with no worries';

(iii) Hamlet's 'To be or not to be' soliloquy.

In each of these cases, Grice would have to demonstrate that, contrary to   **DISCUSSION**
appearances, there is an intended audience. Perhaps he could reason as follows. (i) The intended audience of a diary is often the wider world, since not all diaries are intended to be secret. For the secret ones, Grice could say that the audience is just a future version of oneself, as it is with shopping lists. For (ii) the audience might be some constructed fantasy, a dog that understands English. (i) and (ii) could each also be thought of as involving an element of soliloquy like (iii). Soliloquy might be understood as an attempt to communicate with a god, or with posterity in the abstract.

The Humpty objection

The Humpty objection to the Gricean position can be formulated as the charge that Grice is too much like Humpty for his own good. Humpty, we saw, seems to be advocating the following thesis:

What we mean when we utter a word or sentence is under our own control; we can mean whatever we want and choose.

The charge against Grice can be formulated in a two-premise argument:

Premise One: Humpty's thesis is false.
Premise Two: Grice's position entails Humpty's thesis.
Conclusion: Grice's position is false.

To assess this charge, let us first consider Premise One. There does seem to be something terribly wrong with Humpty's thesis, but before getting to what is wrong with it, it is as well to appreciate why it could be attractive, to us and not merely to a self-important egg. Words do not have their meaning intrinsically. What they mean is *arbitrary*. The word 'dog' might have meant what the word 'cat' in fact means, and vice versa. Equally, nothing about the letters 'i', 'm', 'p', 'e', 'n', 'e', 't', 'r', 'a', 'b', 'i', 'l', 'i', 't', and 'y' requires that, taken together, they must mean what they do – roughly, a lack of susceptibility to physical infiltration. They could easily have been combined to mean something quite different. What is wrong with assuming that this arbitrariness is resolved by a decision of the utterer to mean one thing rather than something else? Nothing at all, Humpty would no doubt insist (see pp.14–15).

He could support his case by pointing to the benign practice, common in philosophy as in any sphere of life, of deciding to introduce a new term with a specific meaning laid down in a definition, or else of taking an old term and stipulating that it will be used in a novel way, or with one from among several established usages. We have an example of this in Grice's potentially insightful departure from the normal usage of 'utterance'. Is this practice of stipulation not proof that we can choose to use a term however we want and to bestow on it any meaning whatsoever?

Against this, there are strong reasons for thinking that Humpty's thesis is mistaken, as Premise One asserts. A quick reason for thinking this is to follow Grice's own methodology of appealing to intuitions. Suppose Humpty were to utter: 'There's glory for you.' We would judge that his utterance means that some salient object or event is glorious. Humpty, following his own thesis, regards it as meaning that he has just given a nice knockdown argument. So, our considered intuitions do not accord with Humpty's thesis.

A second and more sophisticated reason for denying that meanings are entirely in our control depends not on any appeal to brute intuitions but on consideration of the role of meaning in the communication of knowledge. Utterer-controlled meaning, unless it is accompanied by uptake on the part of the audience, would not lead to communicative success. Evidence for this is provided by Alice's confusion when Humpty uses a word in a particular way without announcing to Alice beforehand that he is going to use it this way. What our utterances mean must be available to the audience if this meaning is to be any use. To that extent, what words mean is *not* entirely up to the speaker. Grice himself seems to be working towards this point when he writes, 'the intended effect must be something which in some sense is within the control of the audience' (Reading 1, p.186).

Moreover, Humpty's thesis is not clearly supported by the phenomenon of stipulation. When we depart from common usage we generally have to announce this beforehand, using terms whose meaning is already familiar. Humpty fails to make a prior announcement, which is why Alice is left confused. It is only because he falsely believes his thesis that he is led to suppose that he can mean whatever he wishes with no prior announcement.

The falsity of Humpty's thesis can also be reconciled with the arbitrariness of language. There are other ways than individual legislation for words to come to mean what they do. Perhaps they mean what they do because we have beliefs about what they mean, not because we *decide* what they mean. So let us accept Premise One – that Humpty's thesis is false – and turn to the second premise, which is that Grice's theory entails Humpty's thesis. This is where the Humpty objection looks vulnerable.

Humpty's thesis asserts that our utterances and the words in them mean whatever we want or choose them to mean. Grice's theory is that what our utterances mean is a matter of what we intend to communicate. Intending, wanting and choosing may sound as though they come to much the same thing, but reflection suggests that they may be quite different.

Are any of the following states of mind equivalent?   **ACTIVITY**

(i)   Wanting to deposit $8,000,000 in US Government bonds in your bank vault.

(ii) Intending to deposit $8,000,000 in US Government bonds in your bank vault.

(iii) Choosing to deposit $8,000,000 in US Government bonds in your bank vault.

(i) seems to be possible without either (ii) or (iii). (i) might well be true, but I can only intend something if I expect that I will be successful when I act on that intention, and I have no reason to expect that I will ever successfully deposit bonds of this value in my bank vault, even if I had one. Similarly, I can only choose to do something that is in my power, and depositing valuable bonds in my personal vault is, sadly, outside my power. (ii) and (iii) seem to differ from one another, too. I could mistakenly believe that I am in a position to make a large deposit and go to the bank intending to do just this; but I can only choose to make a deposit if I genuinely have the funds available.

If the subtleties noted in the previous activity are taken seriously, the second premise in the argument against Grice looks weak. Humpty's thesis is about choosing and wanting, neither of which is the equivalent of intending.

The main difference between Grice and Humpty seems to be this. Intention formation, the notion at the heart of Grice's theory but not Humpty's, requires an expectation of success. This was a lesson of the bank vault example: in general, we cannot form intentions to act unless we expect there is some chance that acting on the intention will lead to its fulfilment. In Grice's theory, the intention is to bring about a change of belief in an audience, and to bring it about through having them recognize this very intention. If we selected words according to personal whim, there would be no reasonable expectation of success. When Humpty used 'impenetrability', he had no reason to think that he would be successful in getting Alice to recognize him as meaning what, after the fact, he insists he did mean. After all, he had not warned her beforehand that he would be ascribing this unusual meaning to the word. With no such reason, he could not *even have formed the intention* to communicate using those words with that meaning. So Grice would not allow that Humpty meant what he later claims he meant.

Premise Two, then, seems to be false. Humpty's thesis may be mistaken, but Grice's theory looks like it is consistent with this falsity. In fact, once the distinctions between choosing and intending and between wanting and intending are granted, Grice's theory even seems to *explain* why Humpty's thesis is false. Because we cannot expect to be interpreted however we wish, we cannot intend to be interpreted however we wish, and so cannot mean whatever we wish.

These considerations may see off the Humpty objection, but they should also remind us that Grice still owes us a viable theory of what expressions mean. Grice, unlike Humpty, does not hold that what our utterances mean is entirely up to us. This is because what our utterances mean is a matter of what we intend to communicate, and we cannot intend to communicate that *p* unless we expect to succeed in communicating that *p*. This expectation of success is clearly tied to our choice of words. A speaker will have to feel that she has chosen *appropriate* words, words that her audience will interpret accordingly. For example, she will choose 'tiger' rather than 'apricot' if she intends to communicate information about a tiger (unless she and her audience have a special code). But to talk of 'appropriate' words, here, is to talk of words that *have a particular meaning*, i.e. ones that accord with what the speaker intends the audience to come to believe, etc. Grice's theory of the meaning of utterances therefore needs to be supplemented with a theory of the meaning of expressions that is more plausible than the one he provides in Reading 1. We saw earlier (p.26) how that theory does not extend to words or novel sentences.

The meaning of words, and of the sentences built out of words, also figures in the next objection, due to John Searle. In the subsequent discussion of Searle's objection I will sketch a theory of word meaning that seems to be compatible with Grice's project. This theory, which has in fact been around since long before Grice wrote his paper, is discussed in detail in the next chapter.

Searle's objection

In 'What is a speech act?', John Searle introduces a memorable example of an utterance in which Grice's conditions are all met for it to mean one thing, but where the words used suggest that the utterance means something quite different, if it means anything at all. The conclusion Searle invites us to draw is that what our utterances mean is not exhausted by the speaker's intentions alone. An additional consideration is the meaning of the expressions used. If they don't match the intention, then nothing is meant.

Read the extract from Searle's article, 'What is a speech act?' (Reading 2). **ACTIVITY** Searle summarizes Grice's theory and then offers what he claims is a counter-example, the example of a captured American soldier in wartime Italy. Why is Searle's example a potential problem for Grice?

In the example, the American soldier's utterance of the German sentence does not mean what, according to Grice's theory, it should mean. On Grice's account, the utterance means *that the speaker is a German officer*. This is what the American soldier intends his Italian captors to believe, and he intends them to arrive at this belief through recognizing his intention that this is what the Italians will come to believe. But intuitively either the American soldier's utterance means nothing at all, or else it means just that the speaker wishes to know whether his Italian captors are familiar with the land where the lemon trees blossom (i.e. what the German sentence he uses means).

What should we make of Searle's American soldier example? Grice could just dig in his heels and insist that what the American soldier's utterance means *really is* that he is a German officer, notwithstanding any intuitions we may have to the contrary over this interpretation. In philosophy we are often called on to reject the pre-theoretical intuitions we have about situations. But it is usually better to avoid doing so unless forced.

Searle's own response is to suggest that Grice has overlooked the importance of community-wide linguistic conventions, the 'rules of language', to the meaning of an utterance. Searle proposes that the speaker's intentions are *the main* source of what our utterances mean, but he adds a further condition: these intentions must accord with the meanings of the expressions we use, where this is fixed by community-wide conventions, the rules of the language from which the expressions are drawn.

Searle thinks of himself merely as extending the Gricean analysis, correcting it for an oversight. He does not think he is overthrowing the Gricean project. But it may be that adding this new constraint – that what the speaker means depends on community-wide conventions – would in fact leave Grice's project deeply damaged. This would depend on whether the meanings of expressions, fixed as they are by community-wide linguistic conventions, can be reduced to the mental states (the beliefs, intentions, etc.) *of those who make up that community*. If they can, then the reduction of linguistic meaning to mental content will have succeeded, albeit not quite in the way Grice envisaged. On this new picture, but not on Grice's original picture, the meaning of an individual utterance would depend on more than the mental states of the speaker alone. It would depend also on the mental states of those in the speaker's community, since these fix the meanings of the expressions used, and these meanings in turn are a factor in the meaning of the individual utterance.

Two questions arise at this point. It is clear that following Searle's suggestion or persisting with Grice's original theory will require a viable theory of how the meaning of expressions reduces to the content of mental states. So what is that theory? A different question is whether the relevant mental states are those of the speaker alone, or whether they also include those of members of the wider linguistic community as Searle implies. Let us start with this second question.

Grice could endorse a slightly weakened version of Searle's additional requirement, and in doing so persist with his claim that only the individual speaker's mental states are relevant to what an utterance means. Searle requires that the speaker's intentions *actually* accord with the community-wide meaning of the sentence used. But Grice could require merely that the speaker's intentions accord what the speaker *thinks* is the community-wide meaning of the sentence used – or even with what the speaker thinks the specific audience takes the sentence's meaning to be. Adding such a weak requirement is enough to explain our intuitions about the American soldier example. The American soldier does not think that the established meaning of 'Kennst du das Land, wo die Zitronen blühen?' is that the speaker is a German officer, so Grice would not be committed to saying that this is what the utterance means. Moreover, Grice's attempt to define the meaning of utterances in terms of the individual speaker's psychological states would still be on track. The weakened condition, unlike Searle's condition, is couched in terms of the beliefs of the individual utterer alone.

We might wonder whether this weaker condition deals with counter-examples as well as Searle's condition does. For example, suppose the American soldier really did believe that 'Kennst du das Land, wo die Zitronen blühen?' meant the same as 'I am a German officer'. Perhaps he was told this in military training. Would it now be fair to say that the American soldier's utterance meant that he was a German officer? Grice's new condition (and all the old ones) would be met but Searle's condition would not, so an affirmative answer would favour Grice's weaker condition and a negative answer would favour Searle's stronger one. I will not try to settle this issue here, except to note that people's intuitions about this new version of the scenario differ. Some think that the American soldier's utterance *does* now mean the same as 'I am a German officer'. They are likely to be happy with the weaker condition.

Others deny that it means this. They are likely to be sympathetic to Searle's stronger condition.

Now consider the challenge, facing both Searle and Grice, of how to reduce the meaning of expressions to the meaning of mental states. Even adopting the weaker condition leaves this challenge in place. Grice could not treat beliefs about what expressions mean as fundamental, because 'what expressions mean' is itself a kind of non-natural meaning, and as such needs to be reduced to the content of mental states.

The next chapter considers (among other things) the viability of a theory of expression meaning that promises to provide what both Grice and Searle need: a theory that reduces the meaning of words to the content of the mental states either of the individual speaker or of the members of the wider linguistic community. (The theory can be adapted to either perspective.) The theory takes the meaning of a word to turn on a condition the speaker (or their linguistic community) associates with that word. If someone associates 'tigers' with a condition that happens to be met by tigers and nothing else – for example, the condition of having black and orange stripes, sharp claws and fangs, being feline, being dangerous to humans, and so on – then for that person the word 'tiger' means tiger. *Associating a condition with a word* is a matter of having a belief, so the meaning of words seems to be a matter of the person whose word it is being in a mental state.

The next chapter will examine this theory in more detail, and consider whether what expressions mean really can depend entirely on the content of mental states. But if the theory works, notice how well it gels with Grice 3, the final version of Grice's theory of the meaning of utterances. If a person wishes to pass on her knowledge that a tiger is nearby, she can do this by producing an utterance that means there is a tiger nearby. According to Grice 3, this amounts to her producing a sound or signal with the intention that her audience comes to believe there is a tiger nearby through recognition of this very intention (see p.24). To form such an intention, she must expect her audience to recognize her intention. This requires that both she and her audience attach the same meaning to the words she chooses. If both attach the same condition to 'tiger', this expectation is likely to be met because each will be led to think about the same object in the world.

Chapter summary

After setting aside 'natural' meaning as largely irrelevant to language (pp.16–19), Grice attempts to define the (non-natural) meaning of utterances in terms of the content of the speakers' psychological states, and in particular in terms of their intentions in performing those utterances. He reaches a final definition, which we called Grice 3, after two false starts (pp.21–4). The meaning of expressions, or of sentences at least, is derivative, defined by him in terms of the meaning of typical utterances (p.24).

Several problems confront Grice's proposal, including the phenomenon of apparently meaningful but audience-less speech (p.31), and the massive complexity of the intentions Grice attributes to ordinary speakers (pp.30–1). Another common objection is that he seems to be committing the same errors as Humpty Dumpty (pp.31–5). Replies to each of these objections are available, though whether these replies are ultimately successful was not resolved here.

Perhaps the most complex issue in Grice's discussion in 'Meaning' concerns the place in it of the meaning of expressions. One source of difficulty is that he provides no theory of the meaning of words or novel sentences (p.26). And Searle thinks that he pays insufficient notice to the contribution of community-wide linguistic conventions to the meaning of expressions and hence of utterances (pp.35–6). At the very end of the final section, prompted in part by Searle's example, I briefly introduced a theory of word meaning couched in terms of the mental states of the person whose word it is. Combined with Grice 3, this theory promises to provide an explanation of how two people could communicate (p.38). This theory is taken up and considered in the next chapter.

One thing we have learnt in the course of this chapter is that the key debate is not as simple as was implied in the introduction to this chapter. The core debate over the source of the meaning of utterances is not between those who look to the mental states of the speaker and those look to the meaning of the expressions used. It turns out that everyone, even those who look to the mental states of the speaker, must provide a theory of the meaning of expressions. Moreover, Searle and others claim that the community-wide meaning of the expressions used is a key factor in what an utterance means, but they often wish to claim that the meaning of expressions itself reduces to the content of mental states – not the mental states of the individual speaker but the mental states of members of the linguistic community. The real debate is between those who think that all species of linguistic meaning – the meaning of utterances and the meaning of words and sentences – reduce to the content of the mental states of those who use the language, and those who deny this. Searle and Grice are on the same side on this matter, even if they disagree over strategy. Hilary Putnam, as we will see in the next chapter, claims that what our words and utterances mean depends on factors that go beyond anything 'in the head' of either the speaker or of anyone in her entire linguistic community. His surprising argument for this position has had far-reaching implications in the philosophy of mind.

Further reading

Grice's writing on the philosophy of language, including the 1957 paper 'Meaning', is collected in Grice 1989. Discussion of the issues raised in 'Meaning' can be found in Avramides 1997 (the most accessible), Blackburn 1984, Miller 1998, and Taylor 1998. A defence of the Gricean Programme can be found in Schiffer 1972, later retracted in Schiffer 1987. Searle's position is developed at length in Searle 1969.

CHAPTER 3

'Meanings ain't in the head'

In chapter 2 we looked at Grice's attempt to trace the meaning of utterances and expressions back to the content of the psychological states of speakers. In this chapter we will look at Hilary Putnam's influential argument for the claim that 'the psychological state of the speaker does not determine' what their words are about (Reading 3, pp.195–6). What our words pick out in the world when we utter them is instead determined, in part at least, by factors that are independent of the psychological states of the speaker, and perhaps independent even of the psychological states of everyone in the linguistic community. Exactly how far these arguments are genuinely incompatible with Grice's own position, or with the Gricean Programme that grew out of his writings, is something to be considered. But there is certainly an *apparent* tension between the Gricean approach and Putnam's slogan that '"meanings" just ain't in the *head*' (Reading 3, p.196).

An interest in Putnam's discussion goes beyond the challenges it poses for Grice. Many take Putnam to have shown something quite unexpected and radical: that the content of our psychological states and not merely the meaning of our speech – mental representation and not merely linguistic representation – depends on factors that are in a certain sense 'outside' us as individuals. These external factors are alleged to include, for example, the hidden structure of our physical environment and the existence of sub-communities of experts to which we may not belong and which we may not even know exist. We will examine *mental externalism* (as this radical thesis is known) only towards the end of the chapter. The focus up to that point will be on Putnam's argument for *linguistic* externalism, the thesis that what we are talking about when we speak depends essentially on such external factors.

Putnam does not mention Grice's theory among those he is criticizing. His explicit target is what he calls a 'traditional doctrine' (Reading 3, p.192) that has since come to be known as linguistic internalism. Linguistic internalism is simply the denial of linguistic externalism, and holds that what a word means when it is used by someone in normal discourse, and hence what it refers to when so used, depends entirely on the psychological states of the speaker. (Actually, a specific kind of psychological state is meant, called a 'narrow' psychological state. But this qualification can safely be ignored until later in the chapter.)

After some preliminaries in the next section, I will present the case for linguistic internalism in detail. We will then turn to Putnam's famous Twin Earth thought experiment, which he uses to argue against linguistic internalism (Reading 3). Our evaluation of this argument will include a response to it by Tim Crane (Reading 4). The chapter will close by considering the radical thesis of mental externalism. Here is where the implications of Putnam's arguments for Grice's theory are considered explicitly.

Sentence meaning and word meaning

Linguistic internalism is normally expressed as a thesis about word meaning, so before becoming embroiled in Putnam's case against it we should pause to ask why we need a theory of the meaning of words in the first place. The answer is not hard to find. What we mean by our utterances depends on what the sentences we utter mean; and what a sentence means depends in turn on what the words within it mean. So without word meaning, we could not ever mean anything when we speak.

UTTERANCE MEANING
depends on
SENTENCE MEANING
depends on
WORD MEANING

The top dependency claim – the claim that what our utterances mean depends on the meaning of the uttered sentence – is plausible, because if the sentence did not have a recognized meaning, the meaning of our utterances of them would not be recognizable in the way communication requires.

The lower dependency claim, of sentence meaning on word meaning, is also quite plausible. It is captured in what has become known as the compositionality principle.

The compositionality principle

The meaning of a sentence depends systematically on ('is composed out of') the meaning of the words within it and on how they are strung together.

There are several reasons for accepting this principle. Here are two.

First reason: the systematicity of understanding

You probably do not understand either of the following sentences, both of which contain a deliberately obscure word chosen from a dictionary:

Jennifer doesn't like mazagans.

The mazagans in the bag are fresh.

But suppose you were to learn that the first means that Jennifer does not like eating a specific variety of broad bean that grows wild in Morocco. Under these conditions, you would also understand the second (as would anyone competent with the more familiar words in both sentences). This 'systematicity' in our understanding is predicted by the compositionality principle. That principle treats the meaning of the obscure word as a component in the meaning of both sentences, so one would expect appreciation of the meaning of that word to be key to understanding both sentences.

Second reason: the productivity of understanding

One might think that we pick up the meaning of a sentence from previous usage. But many sentences have never been uttered before. For example:

I would like 29 kilos of mole poison for Christmas.

The meaning of such novel sentences could not be extracted from earlier uses of it, since there are none. And even if a sentence *has* been uttered many times before, there is a question of how speakers understood them on these earlier occasions: every sentence was novel once. What enables us to understand novel sentences, to 'produce' their meaning without recourse to earlier uses of the same sentence? A promising answer is that we rely on our knowledge of the meaning of the words they contain. But this requires exactly the dependency relation between the meaning of sentences and the meaning of words that the compositionality principle asserts.

Both these reasons point towards a single idea: that word meaning is important because knowing the meanings of the words used allows participants in a conversation to arrive at the meaning of the sentence used and thereby to understand the utterance itself. If the meaning of the sentence:

John kissed Mary

is a product of, or composed out of, the meaning of the words 'John', 'kissed', and 'Mary', then by knowing the meaning of these words, speakers are able to generate, or compose, the meaning of the sentence without having to remember the meaning of sentences individually. Word *order* matters, too, which is why the compositionality principle contains the phrase '... and on how they are strung together'. A person who knew the meaning of the three words but did not know anything about the significance of word order would not be able to distinguish the meaning of the sentence above from the meaning of 'Mary kissed John.'

So much for why word meaning matters. We turn now to the account offered by linguistic internalists of what word meaning actually is.

The case for (a version of) linguistic internalism

When someone says something using the word 'water', they will typically be saying something about water and not milk or vodka. The task of providing a theory of word meaning can be reduced to a question: what is it about words that enables us to use them to pick out and so talk about certain things in the world and not others? What makes it the case that 'water' refers to the stuff that comes out of our taps, and not to milk or vodka? The word 'water' considered by itself is just an arbitrary sound or string of letters. Something must give it its power to be about water when it comes out of our mouths during speech (or from our pens when we write or fingertips when we type). What is that something? In this section I will outline a typical linguistic internalist answer, explaining why many have found this answer plausible.

Linguistic internalists typically preface their answer by claiming that there is an ambiguity in the word 'meaning' as it applies to words, an ambiguity that is only dangerous if we fail to notice it. In one sense, what a word like 'water' or 'Winston Churchill' means is the very stuff or thing that the word refers to. We say that 'water' means the actual liquid out there in the world's oceans, lakes and kettles. The thing or stuff that a word refers to is often called the *extension* of the word or, equivalently, *what it is true of*.

But the meaning of 'water' might instead be given as a list of attributes, such as *colourless liquid, freezes at 0° C, boils at 100° C, falls from the sky a lot, comes out of household taps, quenches thirst*, and so forth (Figure 3). The attributes in such a list can be used to generate an intension for the word. The intension of a word is the condition something must satisfy to be referred to by the word, i.e. to be in the word's extension. So, one might hold that to be what 'water' refers to, something must be colourless, a liquid, freeze at 0° C, and so forth. Linguistic internalists claim that 'meaning' is ambiguous between meaning-as-extension (i.e. what the word refers to) and meaning-as-intension (i.e. the condition something must meet to be referred to by the word).

The meaning of a word as it appears in a dictionary entry is closer to the word's intension, thought of as a list of attributes, than to its extension, an actual thing or actual stuff. The meaning of 'water' one finds in a dictionary entry could hardly be its extension, since a dictionary would then have to contain actual samples of water. A typical dictionary entry will instead express the word's intension by giving a short description of water.

Jonathan Swift's eighteenth-century satire, *Gulliver's Travels*, contains an entertaining warning to philosophers against forgetting that words have an intension and not merely an extension, though he does not put it in these terms. When Gulliver visits the Grand Academy of Lagado, he is introduced by the philosophers and scientists working there to several wildly misguided inventions. One of these is a language with no words. The assumption that

- colourless liquid
- freezes at 0°C
- boils at 100°C
- quenches thirst
- falls from sky
- etc.

Extension
The stuff that the word 'water' is true of, i.e. what it actually refers to.

Intension
A list of attributes associated with the word, where the word's extension is unique in possessing all of those attributes.

Figure 3 The meaning of 'water': extension versus intension. Photo: © Jurgen Freund/ naturepl.com.

gives rise to this invention is that the meaning of a word is its extension and nothing else. The reasoning used, in Swift's own terms, is this:

> Since Words are only names for Things, it would be more convenient for all Men to carry about them, such Things as were necessary to express the particular business they are to discourse on.
>
> (Swift 1726, 76)

The result is, needless to say, highly impractical, as the 'speakers' of this language are weighed down with the objects they wish to 'talk' about with their colleagues by showing them to one another in silent 'conversations'. But the mistake is not just that this 'language' is impractical. The invention seems to miss the whole point of language, which is to be able to talk about something in its absence. The association between a type of mental sound and an intension, a list of attributes, is more portable than a sample of actual water, and it is just as good for communication because the word's intension serves to pick out the word's extension. The philosophers being mocked seem not to have noticed the ambiguity in the word 'meaning' between meaning-as-extension and meaning-as-intension. It is true that what a word names is its meaning in the former sense. But the meanings that people 'carry about' are not extensions but intensions.

The idea that a list of attributes associated with a word generates a *description* of its extension, and that this description is the word's intension (i.e. the condition something must satisfy to be referred to by the word), is sometimes called 'descriptivism'. Not all linguistic internalists think of intensions as descriptions. I have just given linguistic internalism a descriptivist flavour because it is a simple and intuitive version of the position. In any case, disagreement among linguistic internalists need not detain us. The broad picture *all* linguistic internalists are committed to can be summarized into two principles:

Linguistic internalism

1   Words have intensions that are known by (i.e. reflected in the psychology of) those who use and understand them.

2   The intension of a word specifies the condition something must meet if the word is to refer to (or 'be true of') it.

The second of these claims is simply a matter of definition, and so cannot be quarrelled with. The first is more substantial. It asserts that the intension of a word, i.e. the condition something must meet to be what a word refers to (as set out in a description, perhaps), is fixed by the mental states of the person who is using it.

To see why this position has been so popular, consider how well it makes sense of our use of words to communicate knowledge about the world around us. Suppose A wishes to pass information to B about, say, water. If there is water is present, A can let B know what he is talking about by pointing to it. But if no water is present, A can instead use a word. It doesn't matter what the word is so long as A and B associate the word with an intension (clause 1) – where associating is a psychological state, akin to knowing the meaning of the word – and this intension is a condition that is met by water and nothing else (clause 2). That way the word will be taken by both to refer to the actual liquid, water, and they can exchange knowledge about that liquid. Both clauses are critical. Their net effect is that what a word refers to is determined by the psychological make up of the person whose word it is.

This is what Putnam denies. He claims that what our words refer to depends on more than what is going on inside our heads. Since clause 2 is true by definition, he rejects clause 1. When he says meaning 'ain't in the head', what he is denying is that meaning-as-intension is in the head. Before turning to his reasons, the next section presents two arguments in favour of linguistic internalism, especially in the descriptivist guise I presented it in earlier. They go some way to explaining the widespread surprise at and resistance to Putnam's position when Reading 3 first appeared in 1975 .

Two considerations in favour of descriptivism

The first consideration has to do with words that, though meaningful, do not refer to anything. Take the word 'Santa Claus'. This word cannot be meaningless, because it is used across the English-speaking world to say meaningful things – if nothing else it is used to deny that Santa Claus exists. But unlike 'the Pope', its meaning cannot consist in its referring to an actual person, because there is no Santa Claus whereas there is a Pope. So what does it mean? Descriptivists have an easy answer. They say that 'Santa Claus' has an intension, which is why we are able to communicate using it, but no extension. What people know when they know the word's meaning is a list of attributes, a description along the lines of *has a beard, laughs a lot, wears a red suit, and lives in the North Pole*. To be the extension of the word, something must satisfy this description. Since no one satisfies this description, the word simply lacks an extension, i.e. is not true of anyone.

This way of thinking about the meaning of 'Santa Claus' seems to deal particularly well with sentences used to deny existence. According to an old puzzle, anyone who utters 'Santa Claus does not exist', or 'God does not exist', is contradicting themselves. They are using a name ('Santa Claus' or 'God') in an effort to pick out something that, if they are correct in adding 'does not exist', *cannot* be picked out. If it does not exist, how could it be picked out? This reasoning seems to show that it is impossible to deny the existence of God, or even of Santa. Descriptivists are able to resist this perverse conclusion. They can say of the word 'Santa Claus' that it has an intension, and its having this intension is enough to allow us to deny existence. No extension is needed. To utter 'Santa Claus does not exist' is tantamount to uttering, 'The word "Santa Claus" does not have an extension', or 'There is nothing that has a red suit and a beard, lives in the North Pole, etc.' These sentences avoid the embarrassment of attempting to use a word to refer to something at the same time as saying that there is nothing for that word to refer to.

A second consideration in descriptivism's favour has to do with word pairs like 'Eric Blair' and 'George Orwell', which both refer to the same person, the author of *Nineteen Eighty-four*, *Animal Farm* and various other novels. 'Eric Blair' is his birth name while 'George Orwell' is his nom de plume. (Another example, mentioned by Putnam in the upcoming reading, is the pair of phrases 'has a heart' and 'has a kidney'. Every creature with a heart has a kidney, and vice versa, so these two phrases, like the pair of names, have the same extension.) Like non-referring names, co-referring pairs give rise to a puzzle that descriptivism helps to solve. The puzzle is this. If the meaning of a word is identified with its referring to some particular thing in the world, then 'Eric Blair' and 'George Orwell' should share the same meaning. On intuition alone this is hard to accept. But beyond simple intuition is an argument for why they *must* count as differing in meaning. The meaning of a sentence containing the word 'George Orwell' does not remain the same if we replace it with 'Eric Blair', since the sentences would communicate different information to someone who did not know that they referred to the same person. If the compositionality principle is right, and it does seem plausible, this difference in the meaning of the sentences is possible only if the two words differ in their meaning.

Descriptivists deal with this second puzzle by allowing that words can differ from one another in intension even if these distinct intensions both fix on the same extension. The attributes in the intension of 'Eric Blair' might include *son of Mrs Blair, raised in India, born in 1903, etc.* but exclude anything about writing novels. The attributes in the intension of 'George Orwell' might include *author of several novels, fought in the Spanish Civil War, etc.* Someone could perfectly well know these intensions without realizing that both intensions pick out the same person. That is why which word is used affects what information is communicated.

Putnam's Twin Earth thought experiment

Putnam's case against linguistic internalism revolves around a simple thought experiment. In this thought experiment a word is associated in the mind of one person with a specific list of attributes, and is associated in the mind of a second person with exactly the same attributes. When used by the first person, however, it does not refer to what it refers to when used by the second person. According to linguistic internalism, such a situation ought to be impossible. Putnam claims to show from this that facts about a person's mental make up do not always suffice to determine the extension of their words.

The thought experiment involves imagining a planet far away from Earth but very similar to Earth. In fact, it is a physical duplicate of Earth in all respects save one: the seas and lakes of Twin Earth (as he calls it), instead of containing a colourless and odourless liquid with chemical structure H_2O, contain a colourless and odourless liquid with a complex chemical structure given by a long formula that Putnam abbreviates to 'XYZ'. On this planet are people like us who speak a language that sounds exactly like English. It even contains a word pronounced like our word 'water'. Just as we call the stuff in our lakes and taps 'water', so speakers of Twin English call the stuff in their lakes and taps 'water'. The only difference between the two planets is the difference in the underlying chemical structure of the respective liquids. With this scenario in place, Putnam asks about our word 'water' and what it refers to. The answer he gives, which he expects we will agree with, seems to show that linguistic internalism cannot be true. Let us see why.

Read parts I–II of Reading 3 (pp.191–6). Putnam outlines the traditional view **ACTIVITY** that he is going to criticize. He does not call it 'linguistic internalism', but you should find what he says here familiar. Note that his '1' and '2' in part I correspond to the (1) and (2) of linguistic internalism on p.46 above, even if the precise wording is slightly different. Part II contains the Twin Earth case.

(i)   What, according to Putnam's interpretation of his own Twin Earth scenario, is the condition something must meet in order to be referred to by our word 'water'?

(ii) What, according to Putnam, is the condition something must meet in order to be referred to by the Twin-Earthian word 'water'?

(iii) Why does he take this to show that linguistic internalism (the 'traditional picture') is wrong?

DISCUSSION

(i)   According to Putnam, our word 'water' refers to any substance with the chemical composition H_2O, and to nothing else.

(ii) In contrast, the Twin-Earthian word 'water' refers to any substance with the chemical composition XYZ, and to nothing else.

(iii) This shows that linguistic internalism is wrong, Putnam claims, because the difference in extension between 'water' as used by us and 'water' as used by Twin Earthlings is not reflected in any psychological difference. After all, the people on Twin Earth are exact physical duplicates of us, so are bound to be in exactly the same psychological state as we are.

Instead of using the example of the word 'water', Putnam could have used a proper name. Suppose that in the seventeenth century in Twin France there was a philosopher, a physical duplicate of our own René Descartes, who wrote a book called *Meditations* in which he made the inference from 'I think' to 'I exist', and later died of pneumonia in Twin Sweden. His name, even, was 'Descartes'. Everything that has been said by Putnam about the word 'water' seems to apply to the proper name 'Descartes'. The Earthling word 'Descartes' and the Twin Earthling word differ in what they refer to, since Descartes and Twin Descartes are distinct individuals. And yet Earthlings and Twin Earthlings are in identical psychological states. This is incompatible with linguistic internalism. The two clauses of linguistic internalism entail that what a word refers to is determined by the psychological state of the person using it. (Putnam does not rely on the example of proper names because he is keen to show that linguistic internalism is wrong across the board. It would be too easy to dismiss an example involving proper names as nothing more than the familiar phenomenon in which different people have the same name, e.g. 'John Smith'. That is why he turns to terms for what are known as *natural kinds*: water, gold, elm tree and so forth.)

Since linguistic internalism is false, according to Putnam, we must reject at least one of its clauses. Since clause 2 is true by definition, he rejects clause 1: it is not true that the meaning of a word (its meaning-as-intension, i.e. the condition something must meet to be what the word refers to) is a matter of the psychological states of the person whose word it is.

The structure of Putnam's argument is simple: *psychological states do not determine extension*, as linguistic internalism requires. But beneath the surface, disguised by his informal style, are three assumptions that are essential to the argument. Putnam's various scenarios are carefully constructed to deliver intuitions in their favour.

Three assumptions needed by Putnam

First assumption: we and our twins are in the same psychological states (we have the same beliefs and so forth).

Second assumption: our word 'water' does not refer to both H_2O *and* XYZ.

Third assumption: neither our word 'water' nor the twin word 'water' have changed their extension since 1750 (i.e. when the chemical structure of water began to be appreciated).

Only on the first assumption is the linguistic internalist formula, that *same-psychological-state* $\Rightarrow$ *same-extension*, threatened. But in Putnam's example, an Earthling and her twin are only said to share the same *physical brain* state. Why assume that they are therefore in the same *psychological* state? Putnam allows that there may be a sense of 'psychological state' in which two people with identical brains states could nevertheless differ in psychological state. He is opposed only to those versions of linguistic internalism that think *narrow* psychological states determine intension (and hence extension), where a narrow psychological state is a state that does not depend on anything in the surrounding physical environment – e.g. the chemical composition of the transparent liquid that falls from the sky. Psychological states that depend on the external physical environment are called *wide* psychological states. Given this, Putnam's first assumption is acceptable. But it does force a qualification to the definition of linguistic internalism. The psychological states in clause 1 are narrow psychological states. (This is explicit in the glossary entry for 'linguistic internalism'.)

The second assumption is also needed if the *same-psychological-state* $\Rightarrow$ *same-extension* formula is to be challenged. If our word refers to XYZ (as well as H_2O) and the twin word refers to H_2O (as well as XYZ) then there would be no difference in extension between our word and the twin word, so the sameness of our (narrow) psychological states would not be a problem. Many find Putnam's intuition that XYZ is not water (in our sense) unintuitive. But in Putnam's support we can vary his original example a little in an effort to make his assumption more intuitive. Imagine Earthling explorers arriving on an *unpopulated* planet, Mars say, and finding a transparent substance that looks a lot like water, forms large lakes and so on, but which, on inspection, turns out to be no closer in chemical structure to H_2O than it is to vodka. The explorers soon discover its disappointing chemical structure. It is unlikely that they would claim that it *is* water, even water of a different kind from our water. Rather, they would say that it looks like water but isn't. Most people find this judgement easy to accept given the lack of a native population that uses the word 'water' to refer to this liquid. But really, the presence of a population that uses the word 'water' to refer to it should not make a difference. If the population of France suddenly started using the English word 'water' to refer to milk, that would not mean milk was a kind of water. Or consider the fact that speakers of British English and American English use the same spoken noise, 'robin', to refer to the birds depicted in Figures 4 and 5 respectively. We do not say of any use of 'robin' that all members of both species belong in its extension. It can only be used to refer to one or other of the two species.

The point of the third and final assumption is far more subtle. Most Earthlings nowadays *do* know the chemical composition of the liquid that falls from their sky. Their counterparts on Twin Earth are in the same position, so it is

Figure 4 *Erithacus rubecula* ('British/European robin'). Photo: © Colin Varndell/naturepl.com.

Figure 5 *Turdus migratorius* ('American robin'). Photo: © Dr David Blevins/blevinsphoto.com.

implausible to suppose they would make the same assumptions about what their word refers to as we do about what ours refers to. To deal with this complication, Putnam changes the example, transporting everything back in time to 1750, before the discovery by Cavendish and others that water is H_2O (and by Twin Cavendish that twin water is XYZ). In 1750, Oscar and his twin are the same narrow psychological state with respect to the liquids in their respective environments, but what their use of 'water' is true of is not the same. But this transportation back in time only works if the third assumption is accepted. Otherwise a linguistic internalist could claim that Oscar's word 'water' didn't refer (as it does now) to H_2O and only H_2O. Because of his ignorance, they could say, it referred to anything that was odourless, colourless, etc. – including XYZ. Likewise for Twin Oscar's word. So today, 'water' has a different extension on Earth and Twin Earth, but the psychological states of Earthlings differ from those of Twin Earthlings; and in 1750, there was no difference in psychological state between Oscar and Twin Oscar, but nor was there in what they referred to when they used 'water'. Either way, the *same-psychological-state* $\Rightarrow$ *same-extension* formula survives.

In a difficult passage you have already read (p.194), Putnam defends this third assumption by offering an account of what words like 'water' refer to. 'Water' is true of anything that bears the relation *is-the-same-liquid-as* to typical samples of 'water'. What would be counted as a typical sample is unchanged since 1750. A typical sample, for us as for Oscar, might be something like the liquid used in tea or found in lakes. What would count as being the same liquid as these typical samples has not changed, either, and has to do with important but possibly hidden nature. Oscar may have not known what the underlying nature of the samples was, but he would happily have accepted the possibility that something could look like these samples but not be the same substance, because of an important difference in underlying nature. And since he made his tea with H_2O (not that he would put it that way), and since nothing could be importantly similar to a sample of H_2O without itself being H_2O, it follows that 'water' as used by Oscar referred to H_2O and nothing else, and in particular not to XYZ.

Is Putnam, in using the methodology of thought experiments, relying too much on very strange scenarios? Perhaps language breaks down in extreme conditions. Travelling to distant planets only to discover near duplicates of ourselves with an apparently identical language is an extreme condition if anything is. But if language itself breaks down, it would not be surprising that linguistic internalism, even if perfectly accurate in what it says about actual language in ordinary circumstances, fails to apply in the Twin Earth scenario. Putnam attempts to short-circuit this thought by introducing a far more mundane example that does not involve Twin Earth or time travel: his own use of 'elm' and 'beech'. (This comes after his 'aluminium' example, which, like the 'water' example, involves imaginary space travel.)

ACTIVITY

How is the beech/elm example supposed to undermine linguistic internalism?

DISCUSSION

Putnam admits to not being able to tell the difference between beeches and elms. All he really knows about either is that they are large deciduous trees. The intension associated by Putnam with the word 'elm' is indistinguishable from that associated by him with the word 'beech'. Despite this similarity in intension, the two words differ in extension: when he uses the word 'elm' he is talking about elms not beeches. This is reflected in our judgement that, were he to utter the sentence, 'Elms have a reddish tint', what he has said would not be true unless *elms* have a reddish tint (which they do not). It is irrelevant to the evaluation of his utterance that beeches have a reddish tint (as they do).

Putnam on how referring is possible

We have so far been considering only the negative aspect of Putnam's discussion, his case against linguistic internalism. But the failure of linguistic internalism gives rise to a puzzle: how *do* words like 'water' (or 'elm'/'beech') manage to pick out what they do pick out when we use them, if not by being associated, in the minds of the speaker or audience, with a particular intension?

The crisis generated by the Twin Earth examples and the beech/elm example suggests – to Putnam at least – that something other than what is going on in our heads *must* enter into what we are referring to. In the next two extracts from his paper Putnam is more positive. He identifies what he claims are two external contributions to the determination of a word's reference or extension:

(i) a social contribution, which depends on the existence of division in linguistic competence and authority within our speech community;

(ii) a physical contribution, which depends on the existence of facts about the physical world around us.

The social contribution is introduced by Putnam in the context of a discussion of the word 'gold', a discussion that does not involve Twin Earth at all. It gives rise to his *deferential theory* of reference determination. As Shakespeare noted, all that glisters is not gold. But not everyone is in a position to distinguish gold from, say, fool's gold (see Figure 6). How is it possible that when non-experts use the word 'gold', their word is true of gold but not of fool's gold? Linguistic internalists are not in a position to answer this question satisfactorily, since nothing in the list of attributes associated with the word by non-experts has the necessary discriminatory precision. Putnam's hypothesis is that non-experts 'borrow' the reference of 'gold' from experts by being linguistically deferential to them.

Figure 6 Is it gold? Virtuous Lady Mine, Buckland Monochorum, Devon, Thorman collection, BGS RC1234/054. Reproduced by permission of the British Geological Survey. Photo: © NERC. All rights reserved.

ACTIVITY

Read 'A socio-linguistic hypothesis' (part III of Reading 3). Suppose that I, a non-expert, utter, 'My wedding ring is made of gold.' My utterance is correct if the ring is genuine gold and mistaken otherwise. It would not count as correct if the ring is pyrite ('fool's gold'). So despite being a non-expert, my word 'gold' has gold, and only gold, in its extension. How, according to Putnam, can a word like 'gold' in the mouth of a non-expert like me can have this highly specific extension?

DISCUSSION Putnam's answer is that we are able to refer to gold because there are experts in our linguistic community who can discriminate between real gold and apparent gold. Having experts in their midst means that even non-experts can use a word to refer specifically to gold. So long as they are deferential to experts in their own use of 'gold' – as long as they are willing to stand corrected – then they inherit the referential potential of those they are deferential to. Putnam describes this arrangement as a *division of linguistic labour*, suggesting that it is a phenomenon found in all languages.

One way of making Putnam's division-of-linguistic-labour hypothesis seem plausible is to reflect on what happens if we use a word on a topic about which we know very little, only to discover later that there are no experts to fix the reference of the word we have been using, and never have been. For example, suppose I come to think that 'wingetter', like 'carburettor', is the name of an item in a car engine. I use it confidently, telling my bank manager that I need a loan 'for a new wingetter'. But unlike 'carburettor', there is no corresponding practice among car designers or garage mechanics of using 'wingetter' to pick out any part of a car. I simply invented the word 'wingetter' without realizing it. Of such an example it feels natural to say that, though I may *think* I am talking about a car part, in fact I am not talking about anything whatsoever. The necessary network of experts does not exist and never did.

But the social contribution to reference determination cannot be the whole story. It accounts for the beech/elm example and the 'gold' example, but it does not account for the example of 'water' in 1750. If the intuitions eked out in the discussion of that example are right, 'water' as used by Earthlings at that time referred to H_2O, and 'water' as used by Twin Earthlings referred to XYZ. This difference in reference cannot be accounted for in terms of deferring to experts. Although there are now experts who could quickly tell H_2O from XYZ, in 1750 there were not. *The whole community* on Earth at that time, like the hypothetical community on Twin Earth, lacked the ability to distinguish the two chemicals.

This leads Putnam to a second theory, the *indexical theory* of reference, to complement the deferential theory. According to this theory there is a further external factor at work in reference fixing: the contribution not of a linguistic sub-community of experts, but of the physical world itself. What explains the capacity of people in 1750 to be talking about H_2O and not XYZ, even when neither they nor anyone in their community know anything about modern chemistry, is *the structure of the world around them*. It is in part because the stuff on Earth is composed of H_2O that being composed of H_2O is a condition of being part of the extension of 'water'. This was true even when the word was being used centuries before the birth of modern chemistry.

Some people find this suggestion perfectly reasonable. Others find it quite unnerving. Still others think it is plainly absurd. Which category you fall into probably depends on how sympathetic you initially are to the internalist perspective. Certainly, the orthodoxy that prevailed in the 1970s when Putnam wrote his paper made this suggestion sound even more peculiar than the suggestion of a social contribution. The structure of the physical world is no doubt relevant to whether our assertions about it are correct or not; but how, many asked, could it influence what these assertions are actually asserting?

Read the final part from Putnam's paper ('Indexicality and rigidity', part IV).   **ACTIVITY**
Putnam's discussion here is quite dense. He outlines his suggestion that there is a physical contribution to the determination of reference: the physical structure of the world around us contributes to the intension of our words and hence to what it is correct to apply them to. He also suggests that 'water' is in some ways more like an indexical term (such as 'I' or 'now' or 'here') than had previously been realized.

(i)   What is unusual about indexical terms?

(ii) In what respect is 'water' like indexical terms?

(i)   Indexical terms are peculiar in that what they refer to depends on the   **DISCUSSION**
      context in which they are uttered, which can vary. For example, uttering
      'now' yesterday picks out a different time than uttering it today. Similarly,
      my use of 'I' refers to the person who wrote this book, while your use of it
      refers to the person reading it.

(ii) 'Water' is like an indexical term, according to Putnam, because its
      extension seems to depend in part on the context in which it is uttered, just
      as the extension of an indexical term depends on the context in which it is
      uttered. Something belongs to the extension of 'water' if and only if it is
      similar in important underlying physical properties to paradigmatic
      samples *in the speaker's environment*. 'Water' is a bit like 'here', in that what

it refers to depends on whether it is spoken by an Earthling or a Twin Earthling.

To summarize Putnam's position: for some words, there is no condition (i.e. no meaning-as-intension) that is both (1) associated in the mind of a speaker with that word and (2) descriptive of exactly that which the word refers to when it comes out of that speaker's mouth. To understand what goes into picking out what the word refers to, Putnam says, we must look to factors external to the (narrow) psychology of the speaker such as the existence of social structures that underpin our linguistic practices. Sometimes we must look beyond the psychology even of the experts in the linguistic community to the structure of the world around us, and recognize that words like water are like indexicals.

ACTIVITY   Cement your understanding of Putnam's argument in place by reading the concise and very clear summary of it in Tim Crane's paper (Reading 4, part I). This summary is offered by Crane as preparation for his two criticisms, to be considered in the next section.

Two criticisms of Putnam's argument against linguistic internalism

No consensus has emerged over what to make of Putnam's objection to the traditional picture, i.e. linguistic internalism, since it was first published in 1975. In this section and the next I will explore some of the reactions his examples have generated. This section looks at two responses to Putnam's argument, both due to Tim Crane.

Various commentators on Putnam's article have suggested that the intuitions supposedly generated by his Twin Earth scenario are not very robust. In the first part of the extract you are about to read, Crane argues just this. In particular, Putnam cannot allow that H_2O and XYZ are merely two kinds of water. This is just the judgement that Crane defends. He rejects what I called Putnam's second assumption (pp.51–2), supporting his case by pointing out that chlorine has two kinds or isotopes. (Though this is not important to the analogy, the atoms of one isotope contain 19 neutrons while those of the other contain just 18.) When we use the word 'chlorine' we are not referring to just one of the isotopes. Why should it not be the same with water? Crane also notes that water itself contains distinct isotopes. (Again the details are unimportant, but mixed up with the H_2O that comes out of our taps is an isolatable substance called 'heavy water', D_2O. D[euterium] is just H [ydrogen] with an extra neutron.)

H_2O and XYZ are far more divergent from one another than distinct isotopes are. Crane concedes this and considers instead a case involving substances that differ more extensively from one another than mere isotopes: Putnam's own example of aluminium and molybdenum, which are superficially similar to one another but are in fact radically different in chemical structure. Crane draws a very different conclusion from Putnam, claiming that the extension of the word 'aluminium' uttered on earth, as on Twin Earth, includes both metals.

ACTIVITY

Read part II of Reading 4. Crane claims that the word 'aluminium' in the mouth of a non-expert here on Earth expresses the concept *molyminium*, a concept that is true of anything that is either aluminium or molybdenum. The word 'aluminium' in the mouth of a non-expert therefore refers to anything that is either aluminium or molybdenum. (Crane allows that in the mouth of an expert metallurgist here on Earth it expresses the concept *aluminium*, and is true just of aluminium.) Do you agree with Crane or with Putnam?

DISCUSSION

Crane's claim seems to generate difficulties of its own. Suppose that Arnold, a non-expert on Earth, sees a lump of molybdenum ore in a rock while walking in a mountain range. He utters, 'Look, that rock is made of aluminium ore!' Crane seems to be committed to saying that Arnold has made a correct statement, since 'aluminium' includes both aluminium *and molybdenum* in its extension. This seems very counterintuitive.

Crane could possibly reply by saying that Arnold's 'error' consists merely in the discrepancy between his usage of 'aluminium' and that of an Earthian expert, since the extension of the word in the mouth of an expert is more specific. But what Arnold says is not literally false. The details of how this reply might develop are left open here, except to note the oddity of the idea that becoming an expert is a matter not of getting to know more about the same thing but of one's words coming to mean something different.

In his second criticism, Crane considers the positive proposal Putnam makes about how reference succeeds, the indexical theory and the deferential theory. He claims that the indexical theory (i.e. the theory that the physical world around us contributes to what our words refer to) can be used to undermine Putnam's conclusions because it is compatible with linguistic internalism.

To appreciate this criticism it helps to know more about words that can be classified uncontroversially as indexical expressions, such as 'I', 'here', or 'yesterday'. A standard view of these words is to say that they have a constant intension. The constant intension of a *non*-indexical word like 'Winston Churchill' is something like:

> 'Winston Churchill' refers to the individual who smoked cigars, was British Prime Minister in the Second World War, etc.

The constant intension of indexicals can be given by:

> 'Here' refers to the *place in which it is uttered*.
>
> 'Yesterday' refers to the *day prior to the time it is uttered*.
>
> 'I' refers to the *person who utters it*.

Unlike 'Winston Churchill', the extension of an indexical varies according to the context in which it is uttered. (Assume that there is only one person called 'Winston Churchill'.) But the intension itself remains constant 'in the heads' of different speakers at different times and in different places. That is why indexicals are not really a counter-example to the two clauses of linguistic internalism ((1) and (2), p.46). But if 'water' really is an indexical term, as Putnam insists, exactly the same point could be made of it, undermining his entire thesis.

ACTIVITY

Continue to the end of Reading 4 (part III), in which Crane claims that Putnam's indexical theory of 'water' inadvertently provides a way of responding to the Twin Earth examples.

(i) If a linguistic internalist were to adopt this response, what would they say is the intension of 'water'?

(ii) Why, according to Crane, would this intension satisfy the two clauses of linguistic internalism?

(Note that Crane does not himself agree with the indexical theory of 'water'. He is just pointing out that the indexical theory is incompatible with Putnam's objective of overturning descriptivism.)

(i)   The intension of 'water' for both Earthlings and Twin Earthlings could be given as follows: DISCUSSION

> 'Water' refers to the colourless, odourless liquid that comes out of taps *in the utterer's vicinity*, and anything that resembles this liquid *in its underlying physical characteristics.*

(ii) On this reading of the intension of 'water', clause 1 of descriptivism is still satisfied: this intension is something that both Earthlings and their twins, now or in 1750, could be said to know. Moreover, this intension establishes a condition something must meet in order to qualify as part of the extension of the word on any occasion on which it is uttered. So clause 2 is satisfied.

A parallel move could be made with the deferential theory. Someone who lacks the expertise necessary to distinguish gold from non-gold could, by giving it the following intension, pick out gold by borrowing the extension from an expert:

> 'Gold' refers to the substance that experts (i.e. metallurgists, jewellers, and anyone else in the linguistic community with the relevant discriminatory capacities) are referring to when they use 'gold'.

Once again, this intension can easily be thought of as part of the psychological make-up of a non-expert, so it satisfies clause 1 of linguistic internalism. And it successfully establishes a condition something must meet in order to qualify as part of the extension of 'gold' (clause 2).

Mental externalism

This final section considers whether Putnam's argument might not be extended to show that mental content, and not merely the intension of our words, depends on external factors. If this mental externalist contention is true, then there is a sense in which our minds reach out into the external world – or perhaps better, a sense in which the external world reaches into our minds. What we are thinking about depends on factors we know nothing about. Moreover, once mental externalism is recognized as a possible position, Grice's and Putnam's claims can be seen to be less obviously at odds with one another than they appeared to be at the beginning of the chapter.

The argument for mental externalism is in fact quite simple. It is reached from linguistic externalism by the adoption of a single premise: that when we 'give voice' to our mental states we do so accurately, in the following sense: the content of the psychological state we intend to express in an utterance is, typically, identical with the meaning of that utterance. When I utter, 'The shops close in five minutes,' for example, what I am expressing is a thought whose content is the meaning of the utterance: namely, that the shops close in five minutes. Call this the assumption of *expressive transparency*. It is quite plausible. The very function of language is, after all, to allow us to express our thoughts, desires and needs to one another. According to linguistic externalism, what our words – and hence utterances – mean depends on external factors like the hidden physical structure of the world around us or the presence within our linguistic community of experts who determine the extension of our words for us so long as we are appropriately deferential. Adding the assumption of expressive transparency to this view about what our words and utterances mean delivers the conclusion that our mental states – what we actually think, not merely what we say – depends on this hidden physical structure and on such communities.

We will come in a moment to the question of whether this inference from linguistic externalism to mental externalism can be allowed to stand. But consider first what it shows about the apparent stand off between Grice and Putnam. It was more or less assumed at the beginning of this chapter that Grice and Putnam could not both be right. Grice is committed to reducing linguistic meaning in its various guises – utterance meaning, sentence meaning, word meaning – to the content of the speaker's mental states. Putnam seems to be denying exactly this in denying that either the intensions or the extensions of words are determined by psychology. Of course, if we had a genuine inconsistency, the next step would be to consider which of the two is correct. But rather than following that agenda, let us consider whether these seemingly contradictory positions might not in fact be consistent.

The key is to recall a concession made earlier. The first assumption Putnam needs for his argument to go through (p.51) was that two physical duplicates share their psychological states. This cost of making this assumption was that 'psychological state' could be used only in its narrow sense. Narrow psychological states are states that depend entirely on the intra-cranial physical properties of the subject of those states. The thesis Putnam is criticizing, then, needs to be expressed more specifically as: narrow psychological states determine extension. And perhaps Grice is not really committed to this thesis at all. Perhaps Grice is committed only to the thesis that linguistic meaning reduces to psychological states *of some sort*, narrow or wide. The mental externalist argument just introduced is useful because it shows that wide psychological states are a real possibility. Indeed, it shows how Putnam's own position entails their coherence, once it is married to the assumption of expressive transparency.

Here is what we have found so far: mental externalism seems to follows from linguistic externalism via a plausible bridging premise, the thesis of expressive transparency. This raises the possibility that psychological states, or some of them at least, are wide: their content depends on the subject's external environment. Putnam's argument shows only that linguistic meaning is not determined by *narrow* psychological states. So Griceans may not be obliged to find fault with Putnam's Twin Earth argument after all. They could simply relax their position into the thesis that linguistic meaning reduces to the content of mental states – intentions, beliefs – where this mental content *might be wide*. For example, were you and I to communicate about water or gold (I'm assuming you are not from Twin Earth) we would do so by uttering words with particular intentions, intentions of the kind Grice describes in Reading 1. But the content of such intentions could be sensitive to factors such as our shared linguistic community or the physical structure of our shared environment. What we *have in mind* when we speak of 'water' – whether we realize it or not – is H_2O, not just any old colourless, odourless liquid that boils at 100° C.

Quite apart from its implications for Grice and Putnam, mental externalism is a surprising thesis. We are used to thinking of our minds as private, closed-off places, our exclusive domains. Mental externalism suggest that we don't know all there is to know about them. This possibility has had a huge impact on philosophy, and on the philosophy of mind in particular, over the past few decades. We will come back to the topic of mental externalism in Part Two, but I will close the present discussion by raising two concerns some have had about it. Both are alluded to in the final sentence of the following passage. It is from Putnam's essay but was omitted from Reading 3. In it he explicitly assumes mental internalism:

> In order to show [that linguistic internalism is false using the Twin Earth examples], we need first to clarify the traditional notion of a psychological state ... When traditional philosophers talked about psychological states (or 'mental' states), they made an assumption which we may call the assumption of methodological solipsism [equivalent to mental internalism]. This assumption is the assumption that no psychological state, properly so called, presupposes the existence of any individual other than the subject to whom that state is ascribed. (In fact, the assumption was that no psychological state presupposes the existence of the subject's *body* even: if *P* is a psychological state, properly so called, then it must be logically possible for a 'disembodied mind' to be in *P*.) This assumption is pretty explicit in Descartes, but it is implicit in just about the whole of traditional philosophical psychology.
>
> (Putnam 1975, 225–6)

The first reason for adopting mental internalism (and so against mental externalism) can be labelled *the argument from knowledge of our own minds*. Descartes supposed that, in thinking that we have bodies and that there is a world around us, we could be being fooled by an evil demon. A modern variant of this possibility (due to Putnam himself in fact) is that we could be 'brains-in-vats', kept alive in a tank of nutrients and tricked by a scientist into thinking that we are embodied humans with our own homes to go to. Many people find it intuitive that, if we were in either of these scenarios, we would still *have the same thoughts* as we are having now. It is just that many of those thoughts would be mistaken. This suggests that the content of our thoughts (though not their accuracy) is independent of the world outside of us.

A different way of phrasing this first argument does not involve fantastic scenarios. It relies instead on the simple and uncontroversial observation that we are very much better at knowing what *we* think than at knowing what *others* think. Knowing what others think requires making all manner of inferences from how they are behaving, from how we would feel if we were in their position, from what they say, and so on. Knowing what we think is much easier: we just reflect. There are exceptions, of course. If Freud was right, many of us are unaware of our real thoughts about, say, our parents. But exceptions seem to be far rarer than supporting instances. If you think you have not made dinner yet, you generally know that this is what you think; if you want dinner, you generally know this, too; if you take the decision to make dinner, you know that this is what you have decided. But this ease of 'self-knowledge', as it is called, sits uncomfortably with the mental externalist claim that what we are thinking about is determined by factors such as the physical structure of the world around us or the opinions of experts we have never met.

A second common reason for resisting mental externalism can be called *the argument from psychological explanation*. It is this reason that Putnam has in mind when he calls his assumption 'methodological solipsism' in the passage above. An alleged methodological principle of scientific psychology is to consider as part of the mind only what is in the head. For suppose we wanted to explain why a man suddenly confronted by an angry bull ran away. The fact that there *really was* an angry bull in front of him is, strictly speaking, superfluous to the psychological explanation of his running away. What matters is only the occurrence of a bull-like image on his retina (assuming that it is through his visual system that he comes to know of the bull). He would have run away even if the bull was not there, so long as exactly the same retinal image was transmitted to his brain; and he would not have run without the retinal image even if there was a bull. If 'psychological state' is defined as the 'state that enters into the explanation of behaviour', and the world beyond the skull of the behaving individual is, as the bull example suggests, explanatorily redundant, the world beyond the skull must be unimportant to the determination of the content of psychological states. Worrying about the world beyond the skull of the behaving individual is a pointless distraction.

We have found one consideration in favour of mental externalism – it follows from linguistic externalism and expressive transparency – and two considerations against – it threatens to undermine the 'direct access' we ordinarily assume we have into the content of our own mental states, and it is incompatible with the plausible thought that what goes on outside a person's skull is irrelevant to the psychological explanation of their behaviour. Part of what makes mental externalism such a contentious thesis is the way it highlights possible inconsistencies between otherwise plausible assumptions.

Chapter summary

Putnam criticizes the view, nowadays known as linguistic internalism, that what our words refer to depends on our psychological states. Linguistic internalism is, more precisely, the view that the condition for something's being what our words refer to is psychologically determined (p.46). Putnam argues against the position using both fanciful examples involving a far-away and near duplicate planet (p.49), and examples based on everyday ignorance, about the difference between gold and fool's gold, for example (pp.54–5).

We looked in some detail at Putnam's arguments against linguistic internalism (pp.49–54), and also at his alternative 'externalist' theory of how our words pick things out in the world (pp.54–8). We also looked at criticisms of Putnam's position due to Crane (pp.58–61). We ended by considering a radical extension of Putnam's linguistic externalism into the realm of thought: perhaps mental content depends on external factors about which we know very little (pp.61–5). This extension is made possible by the plausible thesis that what we utter matches what we think in its content. If it goes through, Grice's and Putnam's positions may be more consistent than they seem. But there seem to be problems with mental externalism, as this extension of linguistic externalism is known. It appears incompatible both with self-knowledge and with the independence of behaviour from external factors.

Further reading

The linguistic internalist position outlined at the beginning of this chapter is a simplified mixture of views in two influential but difficult papers: Frege 1892 and Russell 1905 (see also Russell 1919). A modern survey of the prospects for descriptivism can be found in Taylor 1998 (chapters 1 and 2). A second source of arguments for a very similar anti-descriptivist position to Putnam's can be found in Kripke 1980, based on lectures delivered in 1972. Though not easy, these lectures should be accessible to you now you have worked through the present chapter. Putnam's position is used as the springboard for an argument for mental externalism by Tyler Burge (Burge 1979). A more accessible statement of Burge's arguments can be found in the full-length version of Reading 4 (Crane 1991). Segal 2000 contains an overview of the topic of externalism which is also a defence of mental internalism. The case for mental externalism of different though still broadly anti-Cartesian varieties can be found in Heil 1992 and Clark and Chalmers 1998.

It should probably be noted that Putnam himself is a mental externalist, and not merely an externalist about the meaning of linguistic terms. This is not explicit in 'The meaning of "meaning"', partly because he was wrestling with the issues for almost the first time, but also because the adoption of methodological solipsism is a strategy designed to demonstrate some of the difficulties it generates in combination with other elements of what he calls the 'traditional picture'.

Part Two
Representing in thought

CHAPTER 4

Rationality as symbol manipulation

The mental representation question

Philosophers have a long-standing reputation for worrying about whether they are justified in their ordinary assumptions about the external world. René Descartes (1596–1650) envisaged an 'evil spirit, who is supremely powerful and intelligent, and does his utmost to deceive me' ('First Meditation', Descartes [1642] 1970, 65). Before him, Pyrrho (c.360–270 BC) is described as having lived his life according to a principle of suspending judgement on everything. This, according to Antigonus, led to his never guarding against anything dangerous in his environment, only the protection of his friends saving him from passing carriages, dogs and precipices (Diogenes, 'Life of Pyrrho', 1853, 402). But prior to the question of whether our thoughts about the world are justified is the question of whether our thoughts are about anything at all. In order for our mental states to represent accurately *or* inaccurately, they must represent. But how is it possible for our mental states to represent, to be about something beyond us? Call this the *mental representation question*. (It is sometimes labelled the 'problem of intentionality' or the 'problem of aboutness'.) Addressing it will be our main concern in this second part of the book.

The mental representation question applies most obviously to the so-called 'cognitive' states such as believing and thinking. But these are not the only mental states to have representational features, and the mental representation question arises also for the 'conative' states. We saw in chapter 2 that Grice's theory of the non-natural meaning of utterances depends on intentions having a specific content. The question of what makes an intention an intention *to do X* rather than an intention *to do Y* is every bit as puzzling as the question of what makes a particular belief a belief *that P* rather than a belief *that Q*. The question arises too for desiring. What makes a desire the desire *for M* rather than a desire *for N*? Some have even made the strong claim that *all* mental states have a representational element.

It is easy to overlook the mental representation question. How it arises, if it arises at all, is sensitive to background assumptions about the nature of mind, metaphysics and even philosophical methodology. Despite a willingness to question just about everything else, Descartes, for example, took the representational character of his own mind – his thoughts, experiences, wishes, etc. – as beyond question. In his First Meditation he considers the possibility that he is merely dreaming. But as the passage below indicates, he seems unwilling to allow that his experiences – dreamt or wakeful as they may be – could lack representational content with the 'likeness' of reality:

> Well, suppose I am dreaming, and these particulars, that I open my eyes, shake my head, put out my hand, are incorrect, suppose even that I have no such hand, no such body; at any rate it has to be admitted that the things that appear in sleep are like painted representations, which cannot have been formed except in the likeness of real objects.
>
> (Descartes [1642] 1970, 62–3)

He goes on to doubt whether the world around him exists, and even whether he exists, but never does he try to doubt the content of his mental states with any seriousness. The closest he comes is when he wonders whether he might not be simply insane, like those 'whose brains are so upset by persistent melancholy vapours' (ibid., 62). But he does not pursue this possibility with any vigour. Instead he moves on to the slightly less radical form of sceptical doubt, in which he imagines himself the plaything of an evil spirit.

In this book we will be approaching the mental representation question by framing it, not as a sceptical concern, but as a problem in contemporary philosophy of mind. Many philosophers today (though not all) are committed in some degree to the assumption that humans are ultimately physical creatures, our characteristics susceptible in principle to explanation by the methods and theories of the physical sciences. Many phenomena, from gravity and lightning to reproduction and biological adaptedness, have moved from being mysteries to being explicable in terms of physics and disciplines that are reducible to physics such as chemistry or biology. Why suppose that human thought is any different? One challenge for naturalism (as this tendency is labelled – it is also sometimes called 'materialism' or 'physicalism', though all these terms are often used in subtly different senses by different authors) is that human thinking is representational: we are able to think about the word outside us, to imagine what the other side of the moon looks like before we have had a chance to see it, to ask ourselves whether there is a God, and to remember the distant past. It is hard to see how a merely physical entity could do this.

This chapter looks at a theory of mind that has shaped much recent discussion of the mental representation question: the *computational theory of mind* or CTM. (The theory is sometimes called the 'representational theory of mind', the 'language of thought hypothesis', the 'symbol manipulation theory of cognition', the 'Mentalese hypothesis', 'computational functionalism', or some hybrid of these. Authors sometimes have slightly different theses in mind, but all are broadly in keeping with the view described in this chapter.) To many of its advocates, CTM promises to show how human rationality is possible in a purely physical system. But to do this, CTM makes essential use of the notion of representing, and philosophers sympathetic to the theory have struggled to say how this use is compatible with the hope that CTM will help to integrate the study of mental phenomena with the physical sciences generally. Although naturalist theories of representation do not have to be phrased in terms of CTM, and frequently won't be in subsequent chapters, many such theories grew out of attempts to reconcile CTM with naturalism, and it is useful to be aware of this.

This chapter will present the main claims of CTM, ask whether its 'tremendous gut-level appeal' (Haugeland, Reading 5, p.207) is warranted or deceptive, and explain why the mental representation question arises so acutely for its advocates. In the next section we will see some puzzles that, according to its supporters, CTM is in a position to solve. What CTM actually claims, and how it purportedly solves these puzzles, will occupy the succeeding two sections. The first of these introduces the main claims of the theory, and the second looks at a specific statement of it by John Haugeland. The final sections of the chapter raise some challenges to the theory – three in total, with one of them being the mental representation question taken up properly in the chapters to follow.

Reason-giving explanations, and two puzzles about them

Intelligence manifests itself in many different ways. The following abilities do not call for an especially high IQ, but each requires mental engagement and, in this mundane sense, each is a symptom of our intelligence:

1   Our ability to do simple arithmetic, e.g. in moving from '3 + 4' to '7'.

2   Our ability to perform valid logical inferences and to avoid committing logical fallacies, e.g. in moving from 'If the universe is deterministic then we lack free will, and the universe is deterministic' to 'We lack free will', but in not moving from 'If the universe is deterministic then we lack free will, and we lack free will' to 'The universe is deterministic'.

3   Our ability to take decisions that are apt relative to our desires and assumptions, e.g. to move from a desire for food and a belief that rustling together a midnight snack will satisfy that desire to a decision to rustle together a midnight snack.

4   Our ability to act on decisions effectively by formulating and then executing a suitable plan, e.g. to move from deciding to rustle together a midnight snack to formulating and executing a plan to go downstairs, locate the bread, open the fridge door, take out the butter, etc., all in a particular order.

5   Our ability to form judgements about the world around us through perception, e.g. in moving from a perception of something red and rectangular getting larger in our visual field to the judgement that a bus is coming.

Extrapolating from this small sample, intelligence seems to consist in transformations in the subject's mental states that are in some sense *appropriate*. Such transformations in human beings are clearly not random. CTM is intended to explain how these appropriate transformations come about.

A common way of explaining the attraction of CTM is in terms of its compatibility with materialism. Materialists about the mind think there is only one kind of stuff, matter, and that therefore all mental phenomena can be explained using the resources of the natural sciences alone. Specifically, their explanation does not require that we posit a mental realm that is separate from the physical realm and somehow outside the explanatory scope of physics and related sciences. But materialism is controversial. A less presumptuous way of motivating CTM is to consider how it relates to ordinary pre-scientific or 'folk' explanations of the kind of intelligent behaviour described in the list above. CTM is not normally advanced as a *replacement* of these folk explanations, but rather as a way of solving a number of puzzles associated with them. CTM's compatibility with materialism – its being a contribution to the 'mechanization of mind' – is very much part of how it is able to solve the puzzles, but framing the attractions of CTM in this way avoids taking materialism for granted.

So what are these ordinary explanations, what are the puzzles they give rise to, and how does CTM purportedly solve these puzzles?

Let us call these ordinary explanations *reason-giving explanations*. In a sense, all explanations involve giving reasons, since to explain an event or a phenomenon is to supply a reason for why that event or phenomenon came about. But not all explanations are reason-giving in the narrower sense intended here. The contrast between reason-giving and non-reason-giving explanations is illustrated in two contrasting explanations for the same phenomenon:

To be explained
Why are mountain rockfalls especially common in early spring?

A non-reason-giving explanation
Water seeps into cracks in the rock face in winter, prior to freezing. Water is an unusual liquid in that it expands as it freezes, with a force that can weaken rock. Repetitive freezing and melting, and the resulting damage to the structural integrity of rock, are more common as the weather warms up, with the result that cliff faces are at their most vulnerable in the early spring.

A reason-giving explanation
Mountain rocks are always anxious to descend to a lower altitude because they think, falsely, that this is where they will find other rocks with which to mate. The urge to mate is at its strongest during the spring, even in rocks. Acting to satisfy one's urges is perfectly reasonable, and the rocks, being reasonable, tumble down.

This second explanation is 'reason-giving' in the sense that the rock is said to *have* a reason for doing something, and is assumed to do it *for* that reason. In the present instance, this form of explanation is absurdly inappropriate. But there are other contexts where reason–giving explanations seem both plausible and unavoidable. The explanation of intelligent transformations (1) to (5) above are just such contexts. It is hard to see how we could explain these transformations in our mental states without attributing reasons. If we want to explain why John concluded that he owed the customer £60 in change after taking £100 for a £40 item, it is overwhelmingly tempting to note that 100 minus 40 is 60, that this *gave him a reason* to conclude as he did, and to assert that this is *why* he did so. When we want to explain why Jane decided to buy a Dalmatian dog for her son when she knew both that he wanted either an Alsatian or a Dalmatian and that Alsatians were unavailable, we find ourselves drawing on the fact that *it is reasonable* for her to infer to 'Q' when she knows already that 'P or Q' and 'not-P', and citing this reasonableness in explaining her decision. Suppose we wish to explain why Nancy stepped on to the bus one morning, given her assumption that getting on the bus will take her where she wants to go. At some point we seem bound to fall back on the fact that Nancy is a reasonable person, and doing what one assumes will lead to one's wants being met is, other things being equal, exactly what a reasonable person will do. If we want to explain why someone has included a fridge raid as part of their plan for a midnight feast, the reasonableness of this inclusion is likely to figure. And the reasonableness of inferring from the bus-like features of an object that is expanding in one's visual field to the judgement that a bus is approaching seems to go a long way towards explaining why people make exactly that inference.

The reason–giving explanation of a transformation X in S's mental states will generally have the form:

> X is a reasonable transformation (for S in his or her context, given background details).
> S is, broadly speaking, reasonable.
> *So:* S undergoes X.

What being reasonable amounts to varies from example to example. But the reasonableness of the transformation, whatever form it takes, is an essential feature of the explanation.

Could we explain a transformation in someone's mental states by pointing to **ACTIVITY** the *un*reasonableness of that transformation (for the individual concerned, given details of their other mental states and their situation)?

No. Instances of the schema below just seem wrong-headed:

> X was an unreasonable transformation (for S in his or her context, given background details).
>
> S is, broadly speaking, unreasonable.
>
> *So:* S underwent X.

For example, suppose that an (honest) supermarket teller gives the wrong change on a purchase of ten 8p items: 12p from £1 instead of 20p. We might try to find a way of explaining why this was in fact a *reasonable* response relative to a mistaken background assumption – e.g. that $8 \times 10 = 88$. But we could not explain her action simply by noting its unreasonableness. (If S is, say, a recalcitrant teenager who takes joy in appearing to be unreasonable, a 'she-did-it-because-it-was-unreasonable' explanation seems at first to be quite plausible. But on reflection, giving the wrong change *would* be being reasonable for such a person, precisely because giving the wrong change is a form of apparent unreasonableness, and appearing unreasonable is what she desires to be. So this is really a 'she-did-it-because-it-was-reasonable' explanation in disguise.)

Reason-giving explanations are very common. But they are also extremely puzzling. Different authors stress different puzzles, but a representative sample might include what I will call the *legitimacy puzzle* and the *surfeit-of-explanations puzzle*. These are puzzles that CTM appears to solve.

The legitimacy puzzle arises because reason-giving explanations seem suspiciously easy. We saw an explanation earlier for the increase in rockfalls in springtime. We could also explain the movement of the planets around the sun by appeal to the fact that such behaviour is utterly reasonable for these planets given their desire to curve perfect parabolas. Reason-giving explanations like these – and parallel explanations could be concocted for any event or phenomenon – are clearly spurious. So perhaps reason-giving explanations *even when used to account for (1) to (5)* are just a way of hiding our ignorance of the proper explanation.

The legitimacy of reason-giving explanations is called further into question by the observation that humans often *aren't* rational. Most of us have made silly arithmetical errors at some point, or taken decisions that, due to factors of which we are perfectly cognisant, were never going to lead to our preferences being met as we hoped. We get confused or behave thoughtlessly, painting ourselves into a corner when redecorating a floor, for example. Indeed, psychological studies have suggested that we make blatant reasoning errors systematically. The next activity contains a typical experiment (based on Tversky and Kahneman 1983).

ACTIVITY

Participants are told that Linda, aged 31, is single, outspoken and very bright, and when studying for her philosophy degree she was deeply concerned with issues of discrimination and social justice, participating in many anti-nuclear demonstrations for example. Participants are then asked to say which of the following is more probable:

Linda is a clerk in a bank.

Linda is a clerk in a bank and active in the feminist movement.

How would you reply to this question?

DISCUSSION

The experimenters have found that 86 per cent of participants attach a higher probability to the second, even though it is logically impossible for this to have a higher probability than the first.

Human fallibility may not matter very much in practical life, but it does matter if reason-giving explanations are to be taken seriously. Reason-giving explanations depend on the generalization that people are reasonable, i.e. on a generalization with exceptions. But why is calling it a generalization 'with exceptions' not just a polite way of calling it false?

The *surfeit-of-explanations puzzle* concerns the relation reason-giving explanations bear to non-reason-giving explanations of the same phenomenon or event. Suppose Nancy stands up as a bus approaches. We could explain this in the reason-giving way, in terms of her desires, her assumptions and her rational character. But there is surely another potential explanation for why she stands up, a *physical* explanation that does not invoke reasons at all. Such explanations are not fully developed, and perhaps never will be. This is why reason-giving explanations are so appealing at a practical level. But most people have a strong suspicion that, in principle, a physical explanation is out there to be had, and that it might go along the following lines: Nancy's standing up is caused by her leg muscles contracting, which is caused by the electrical impulse in the nerves that run from the motor-function part of her brain, caused in turn by some trigger in some other part of her brain, itself caused in part by various other changes in the visual cortex of her brain, changes prompted by electrical impulses from her retina, caused by the impact on her retina of light waves sent out by an approaching bus. The difficulty this physical explanation generates (once it is suitably finessed in light of future advances in the sciences) is that there seem to be two explanations for Nancy getting on the bus. And that is one too many.

It is tempting to reply that reason-giving and physical explanations can co-exist. But such pluralism is undermined by the fact that reason-giving explanations seem to be causal. For if reason-giving explanations are causal, *they are in competition with physical explanations*. Intuitively, events can only have one cause, and the laws of physics purport to give a complete and exceptionless account of the causal goings-on in the universe. If having a reason to get on the bus is what causes Nancy to move, then unless 'having a reason' can be shown to be a property belonging to the physics of the future – which does not seem likely – the completeness of physics is undermined.

But why think that reason-giving explanations are causal? In some ways this is quite intuitive, but we seem positively forced to recognize it by the fact that some reasons are *not* explanatory of subsequent change. Later, Nancy might have a reason for getting off the bus, and might even get off the bus, even though her reason for getting off the bus is not what causes her to get off the bus. Perhaps she gets off the bus because she is daydreaming and not paying attention to what she is doing. In that case we would *not* say that her having a reason explains her action. It is only when her having a reason to get off the bus *causes* her to get off the bus that it explains it. So reasons are explanatory only when they cause.

If purely causal, physical explanations and reason-giving explanations are in competition, then the latter's prospects do not look bright. Reason-giving explanations seem to resemble the purposive explanations that have been progressively phased out in other areas of enquiry, such as physics and biology, for example. Aristotle explained the motion of the sun across the sky by claiming that movement is the sun's *telos* (i.e. 'purpose' or 'end'). The notion of a purpose or end no longer figures in the received explanation of why objects move. Likewise, though once the presence of a physical trait (such as a heart) in an organism was irreducibly explained in terms of the function or purpose it has (to circulate the blood), appeal to a physical trait's purpose has, since Darwin, been understood as no more than a useful shorthand for a non-purposive explanation that invokes heritability and the selective advantage the trait gave to the organism's ancestors. There is a trend, then, away from appealing to purposes in the explanation of observable phenomena. This trend suggests that Nancy's purpose, her reason, for standing up when the bus arrives may eventually have no place in the explanation of her action.

We will see in the next section how CTM supposedly dissolves these two puzzles. But let us first review some difficulties with other approaches that could be taken to deal with them: eliminativism, dualism and materialism.

Both puzzles could be solved in a single stroke by abandoning, or eliminating, the practice of reason-giving explanation. This is not an attractive option, at a practical level at least. It would threaten to undermine our ability to predict other people's behaviour, since dropping reason-giving explanations would entail dropping reason-giving predictions. A reason-giving prediction is a prediction that forecasts what someone will do by looking to what it is reasonable for them to do. But abandoning reason-giving explanations is not a theoretically attractive prospect either, since no worked-out alternative explanation is available of why, say, supermarket checkout clerks return appropriate change nearly every time.

Rather than abandoning the practice of reason-giving explanation, we could follow Descartes and adopt substance dualism. This seems to handle the first puzzle quite nicely. The difference between reason-giving explanations as applied to planetary motion or to falling rocks and reason-giving explanations as applied to human beings is that in the latter case they are applied to fundamentally different kinds of things: minds. Matter has properties that minds lack, such as extension and passivity; and minds have properties that objects composed solely of matter lack, such as having free will, lacking extension, and (pertinent in the present context) *being capable of reason*. So long as we are not tempted to apply reason-giving explanations outside their proper domain, the mental domain, they retain their legitimacy. But substance dualism is not well placed to deal with the second puzzle. This hypothetical separate realm impinges on the physical world, since what we think and decide often leads to bodily movement. This clashes with the common assumption that physics will, in an idealized future, describe the causal goings-on in the world completely and without exception.

A materialist reply to the puzzles might begin with the second. Behaving reasonably – adding up accurately, performing logical inferences, getting on the right buses, forming judgements based on perception – could be thought of just as our going through certain physical changes. The detailed nature of the underlying physical changes may be something of a mystery at present, materialists will allow, but there is no principled incompatibility between the description of the process as a rational transformation and its description as a brute causal change. Compare: 'The reason Kennedy died is that he was shot' with 'The reason Kennedy died is that a bullet entered his skull, working its way through his brain before causing a vein to burst, etc.'. The two explanations are perfectly compatible. Why not assume that the same is the case with reason-giving explanations and purely causal explanations? The problem here is that the underlying purely causal theory is not available, and so the compatibility claim is no more than a matter of faith. Current physics is certainly not up to the task. Moreover, there are some reasons for suspecting that faith in the existence of a simple match-up between reason-giving explanations and explanations couched in physical terminology is misplaced. Reason-giving explanations can be applied to physical systems of widely different types. Reasons, and intelligence in general, are 'multiply-realizable', i.e. can be manifest in creatures differing wildly in physical constitution. Perhaps there is a distant planet populated by intelligent organisms made of zinc and glycerine. This is not an incoherent idea.

It is against this background that the appearance of CTM in recent decades has been welcomed so enthusiastically by so many in so many disciplines, including philosophy.

What is the computational theory of mind?

The core notion in CTM is that of a symbol. A symbol has two kinds of properties, called its *semantic* properties and its *syntactic* properties. To appreciate the difference between these, consider a sign outside a cinema. The sign's semantic properties, broadly speaking, are what it means, expresses, is about, or represents as being the case. The sign in Figure 7 expresses the claim that each day that week the film *The Maltese Falcon* will show at 3:10 and 6:30. The syntactic properties of a symbol are its physical characteristics. We can assume for now that they include *all* its physical characteristics: the fact that it is illuminated, that its component letters weigh a certain amount, are about 20 centimetres tall, and come in a certain order, etc.

Figure 7 The words on a cinema sign are symbols: they have both semantic and syntactic properties. Photo: Alex Barber.

The syntactic properties of a symbol can be described independently of their semantic properties, and vice versa. But an important feature of symbols is that their syntactic properties can be manipulated in a way that affects their semantic properties. The man up the ladder could adjust the order of the letters of our cinema sign so that it announced, instead, that a film called *The Fallom Cane Set* will be showing at 3:30 and 6:10.

Such a transformation would be completely pointless since there is no such film. Anagrams – the rearrangement of the letters in 'The Open University' to give 'I enthuse in poverty', for example – have slightly more of a point to them, even if that point is only to create crossword clues. But symbol manipulation can have a lot of value. Indeed, according to CTM, symbol manipulation is what lies behind all forms of human intelligence, since cognitive activity consists of the manipulation of symbols inside our heads, manipulation that constitutes the rational transformation of mental states. To begin to see how this might be even remotely plausible, we need examples of symbol manipulation that, unlike anagrams or switching the letters on a cinema sign, replicate reasonable transformations.

A simple example is that of adding together small numbers. Here are three transformations of symbols that, given what those symbols mean, are reasonable transformations:

From '6 + 3' into '8 + 1'

From '2 + 5' into '3 + 4'

From '2 + 3' into '5'

The sense in which these particular transformations are reasonable is that the semantic properties of the symbols are preserved under transformation: the initial symbols, '6 + 3', '2 + 5', and '2 + 3', pick out the same numbers as the symbols they are transformed into. But these transformations can be achieved by following a syntactic rule, call it Rule Q, that can be followed without any appreciation of the semantic properties of numerals.

Manipulation Rule Q

The first and second items in the symbol pairs below can be switched at any point.

(a)   '2' ⟷ '1 + 1'

(b)   '3' ⟷ '1 + 1 + 1'

(c)   '4' ⟷ '1 + 1 + 1 + 1'

(d)   '5' ⟷ '1 + 1 + 1 + 1 + 1'

(e)   '6' ⟷ '1 + 1 +1 + 1 + 1 + 1'

(f)   '7' ⟷ '1 + 1 + 1 + 1 + 1 + 1 + 1'

(g)   '8' ⟷ '1 + 1 + 1 + 1 + 1 + 1 + 1 + 1'

(h)   '9' ⟷ '1 + 1 + 1 + 1 + 1 + 1 + 1 + 1 + 1'

Someone could apply clauses (a) to (h) without knowing that the Arabic numerals involved are numerically significant. All they would need to be able to do is recognize and manipulate numerals using visible physical properties.

ACTIVITY Starting with '6 + 3', apply (in order) rules (b), (e) and (g) of Rule Q. What do you end up with? Try to tackle this question by looking at what the symbols *look like* rather than by relying on your mathematical skills.

The transformation of '6 + 3' using (b), (e) and (g) applied in turn yields '8 + 1' (or perhaps '1 + 8').

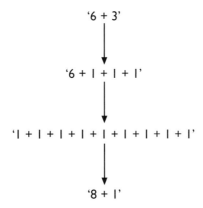

'6 + 3'

↓

'6 + | + | + |'

↓

'| + | + | + | + | + | + | + | + |'

↓

'8 + |'

What you should have appreciated from this activity is a sense of how the 'arithmetically blind' application of rules can result in your doing accurate arithmetic, so long as the rules are the right ones.

In general, whether a transformation of symbols is reasonable depends on the symbols' semantic properties – what they represent – before and after the transformation. The lesson of the example is that a *syntactically*-defined transformation of symbols – that is, a transformation using rules defined solely in terms of physical characteristics of the symbols – can be guaranteed to reproduce only reasonable transformations, relative to a particular system of interpreting the symbols. Of course, the rules of manipulation need to be of the right kind: they need to be *algorithms*. A system of rules for the transformation of a given set of symbols is called an algorithm for a particular intellectual task if it has two features:

(a) the rules are defined solely in terms of the syntactic properties of the symbols;

(b) transformation of the symbols according to that system of rules will solve that task, relative to the semantics of those symbols.

Relative to the ordinary interpretation of single-digit numerals, for example, Rule Q is an algorithm for simple addition. Though it is defined in terms of what the relevant symbols *look like*, i.e. their syntactic properties, applying it will never lead you astray given what those symbols *mean*.

This simple idea inspires CTM's explanation of rational transformation of mental states. CTM holds that the human brain is a massively complex symbol manipulation device, where the rules used to manipulate the symbols it contains are all algorithmic, i.e. meet conditions (a) and (b). Reasonable transformations in our mental states of the kind we are all capable of, such as (1) to (5) (p.73), are said by advocates of CTM to result from this kind of symbol manipulation.

The computational theory of mind

Intelligent processes in human beings are transformations of symbols ('mental representations') found within their brains; these symbols are manipulated according to algorithmic rules.

To illustrate, suppose we are trying to explain how Freddy is able to add up small numbers, for example in figuring out how many apples he owns (Figure 8). That is, we are trying to explain a reasonable transformation from one belief state into another.

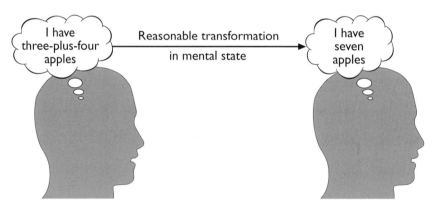

Figure 8 A transformation in Freddy's belief states.

For Freddy to believe something, according to CTM, is for him to have symbols in his head that are subject to manipulation by rules, leading potentially to belief change. Where in his head? This is an awkward question. Obviously they are not in his inner ear or blood vessels. Let us deal with this question with a temporary fix (to be accounted for shortly) and say that they are 'in his belief box'. At the outset the symbols in his belief-box mean *I have three-plus-four apples*. They are transformed into symbols that mean *I have seven apples*. In fact, for still greater simplicity, let us suppose that this comes to the same as saying that he initially has symbols meaning *three-plus-four* in his 'How-many-apples-I-believe-I-own box', and that these symbols are transformed into a symbol meaning *seven* via various intermediate steps involving syntactically-defined rules, such as those in Rule Q (see Figure 9).

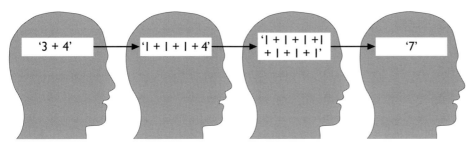

Arrows = syntactically driven transformations using Rule Q

Figure 9 A transformation of the symbols in Freddy's belief box.

Figure 9 is misleading in depicting the symbols being manipulated as numerals. It is extremely unlikely that neurophysiologists will ever find the numeral '4' in a human head. But the example is only meant to give the general idea, and the general idea does not depend on the syntax being exactly as it is in a conventional public language such as English-plus-Arabic-numerals. Strictly, the hypothesis is this: squiggles that mean what we mean by '3+4' are manipulated into squiggles that mean what we mean by '7'. Let us follow others and call the language of these squiggles 'Mentalese'. (It is also sometimes called 'the language of thought'.) So a less misleading diagram is shown in Figure 10.

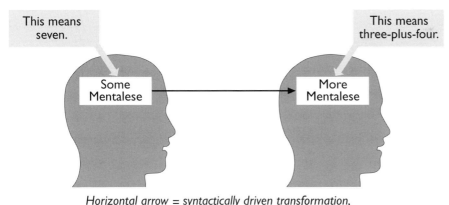

Horizontal arrow = syntactically driven transformation,
probably with intermediate steps

Figure 10 A transformation of the Mentalese symbols in Freddy's belief box.

This may seem an implausible explanation of human intelligence. But CTM gains in plausibility as feats of reason more impressive than adding together single-digit numerals are shown to be reproducible as symbol-manipulation processes. A more sophisticated list of rules than (a) to (h) in Rule Q would allow the addition of larger numbers, and could be used to deal with subtraction, multiplication and division. In fact, children at school *do* learn syntactic rules for symbol manipulation. In principle, someone could learn how to apply the rules of long division to, say, '3,401 ÷ 7' without ever knowing what '÷' means or that the operation they have carried out could help with the task of dividing £3,401 between seven people. Suppose (and this is still a big leap from the examples so far seen) that every rational transformation can be reproduced as a syntactically-defined transformation of symbols, or of 'mental representations' as they are often called. This creates the space for an explanation of rational transformations in humans using CTM.

You may be worried about the man up the ladder outside the cinema and where he fits into the analogy. Don't rules, even rules for the manipulation of symbols, require someone to apply them? If we need to imagine someone applying the symbol manipulation rules, such as Rule Q or its equivalent, to sentences in the head, aren't we presupposing an intelligent being, a rule-applier, rather than explaining how intelligence is possible? This is sometimes put as the charge that this is a *homunculus theory*. The word 'homunculus' was the label used in early biological theories for the pre-formed men supposed to be present in the sperm cell and alleged to be how life is reproduced. In a psychological context, homunculi are small beings inside the head of humans that purportedly explain their intelligence. No one really accepts the homunculus theory (outside comic books – see Figure 11). But to describe a theory as a homunculus theory is to criticize it as in some sense explanatorily circular or regressive, only managing to 'explain' intelligence by secretly presupposing it. Even if there were little beings inside our head, the search for an explanation of human intelligence is simply recast as a search for an explanation of *homunculus* intelligence. The present worry is that the symbol-manipulation view of intelligence is a homunculus theory because it presupposes intelligence enough to apply the rules.

Understanding why this is not a good objection is key to appreciating CTM's attraction. The point of the syntactic rules is that they are (as it is sometimes put) 'stupid rules', rules that can be in place without presupposing an intelligent applier. They are like the rule that a tree develops a new ring every season and the rule that dropped objects fall to earth at a constant rate of acceleration. Setting religious claims to one side, there is no intelligence at work in the rules, or laws, of nature, and in that sense they are 'stupid' rules. What CTM asks us to accept is that the rules governing the syntactic manipulation of the symbols in our head are likewise stupid, the result only of the laws of physics as they operate in our brains. But because our brains are

Figure 11 In the cartoon strip 'The Numskulls', little people inside a man's head are responsible for his actions (upper panel). The flaw in the hypothesis that having Numskulls inside us could explain our intelligence (apart from their never having been seen by brain surgeons) is that the intelligence of the Numskulls would itself need to be explained. There would need to be even smaller Numskulls inside the Numskulls (lower right panel), and still smaller ones inside them, etc. Photo: 1971, 1983 and 1993 'Beezer Book', D.C. Thomson & Co. Ltd, Dundee.

built so that the only physically possible manipulations are algorithms, the overall effect is for only reasonable transformations to occur.

How might forms of intelligence other than arithmetic be accounted for by CTM? Consider, to begin, the performance of valid logical inferences and the avoidance of logical fallacies, in philosophy for example. A valid inference is a transformation in which one belief-state develops into another belief-state, where the truth of the initial belief would serve to guarantee the truth of the resulting belief. On CTM, this can be thought of as a transformation of symbols inside the philosopher's belief-box – a notion that still needs to be unpacked – according to rules defined in terms of the syntax alone, with no loss in truth given the meaning of the symbols (Figure 12).

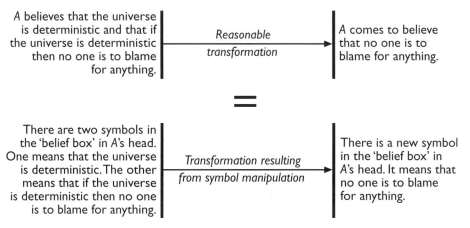

Figure 12 Logical inference as a truth-preserving transformation of symbols in a person's belief box.

This account of what performing valid inferences involves is plausible only if our brains operate according to syntactically defined rules that replicate truth-preserving transformations. But thanks to more than 2,000 years of logic, we know such rules exist, at least in principle. Here are some simple illustrations. The example in Figure 12 draws on the first rule. The Dalmatian/Alsatian example on p.75 draws on the second.

> For any sentences '○' and '□', it is permissible to infer
> from: '○' and 'If ○ then □'
> to: '□'.
>
> For any sentences '○' and '□', it is permissible to infer
> from: '○ or □' and 'Not ○'
> to: '□'

For any sentences '○', '□', and '△', it is permissible to infer

from: 'If ○ then □' and 'If □ then △'

to: 'If ○ then △'

For any sentence-*parts* of the form '♣' '♥' and '•', it is permissible to infer

from: 'All ♣s are ♥s' and '• is an ♣'

to: '• is an ♥'

In contrast, the following transformations are logical fallacies:

For any sentences '○' and '□', it is permissible to infer

from: '○'

to: '○ and □'

For any sentences '○' and '□', it is permissible to infer

from: '□' and 'If ○ then □'

to: '○'

If someone's brain contains algorithms for belief transformation corresponding to the first four rules of symbol manipulation, but does not contain rules corresponding to logical fallacies, then they will only ever perform valid inferences.

The examples of transformations seen so far have led from one belief to another. But transformations are also possible that move from a belief and a desire to a decision. Some such transformations will be reasonable and others unreasonable. Other things being equal, it would be unreasonable to desire to go north, to believe of a particular bus that it is going south not north, and then to decide to get on that bus. By contrast, the transformation in Figure 13 is reasonable.

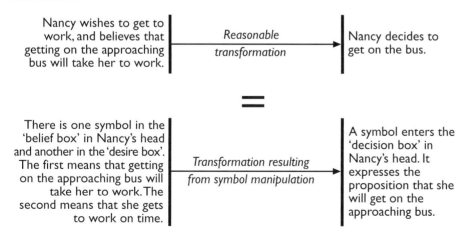

Figure 13 Instrumental rationality as symbol manipulation.

The syntactic rule at work here is:

> For any sentences 'O' and '□', if 'O' appears in the desire box and 'Doing □ will result in O' appears in the belief box, then add '□' to the decision box.

An organism that decides to act in ways that it believes will lead to the satisfaction of its desires is said to be *instrumentally rational*. CTM, by supposing that something like the rule above is at work in the brains of humans, is in a position to explain how we are capable of instrumental rationality. (Of course, it is more complicated than is laid out here. Satisfying one desire may be irrational because that would involve frustrating another. But this and related considerations can perhaps be regarded as wrinkles to be ironed out rather than as fundamental weaknesses.)

The difference between a sentence of Mentalese being 'in your desire box' and its being 'in your belief box' corresponds to the difference (as supporters of CTM construe it) between, say, your wanting it to be the case that you possess cinema tickets and believing it to be the case that you possess cinema tickets. To be in either of these mental states is to have the same sentence of Mentalese in your head but for this sentence to be stored in different contexts. What is the difference between the two contexts? Clearly, it is not literally a matter of being in one or other of two boxes with the labels 'beliefs' and 'desires' on the outside. A standard answer has to do with the different *functions* that believing and wanting have in our lives. If the function of a context is *to contain a sentence representing how things are*, then insertion of a Mentalese sentence, 'I have cinema tickets', into that context constitutes coming to believe that you have cinema tickets. If the function of the context is *to make whatever that sentence represents come about*, then insertion of that same Mentalese sentence into that context constitutes your coming to want cinema tickets. So being in a particular mental state is having some *functionally characterized relation* to a Mentalese sentence with a specific propositional content. (The functional characterizations of believing and desiring just given are intended merely to give the flavour. More sophisticated accounts would draw out the difference between, for example, a desire for something to be the case and an intention or decision to make it the case.)

Another kind of intelligence ((4) on p.73) is planning, subsequent to taking a decision to do something. The algorithm for decision execution is modelled by CTM theorists as a hierarchy of main task, sub-tasks, and sub-sub-tasks, so that at the very bottom are simple, or 'stupid', rules – rules that do not require intelligence to be carried out. Figure 14 is an example of an algorithm for doing laundry, presented in the form of a flow diagram or 'routine'.

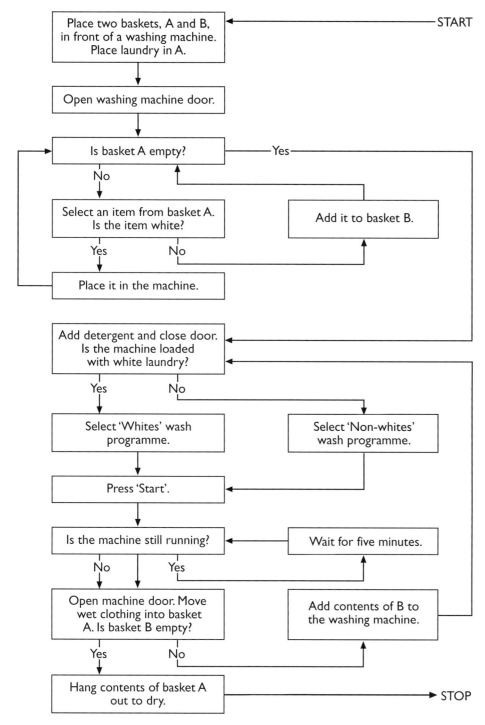

Figure 14 How to do your laundry.

The ultimate aim of artifical intelligence (AI) programmers is to come up with a procedure that could be executed 'thoughtlessly'. For that to be the case, each box would itself need to be associated with smaller flow diagrams corresponding to sub-routines explaining how to open a washing machine door, for example.

In the next section you will be introduced to John Haugeland's more sophisticated presentation of CTM. But even with my simple statement of the basic idea, we are in a position to see how it resolves the two puzzles about reason-giving explanation outlined in the previous section. Its assistance with these puzzles is part of what has attracted many to it.

The legitimacy puzzle concerned the ease with which reason-giving explanations could be generated, threatening to cheapen them. What makes a reason-giving explanation as applied to a human any more compelling than it is when applied to, say, a rock face? An answer to this is available to anyone who accepts CTM.

ACTIVITY

If CTM is correct, why would it be wrong to explain the planetary motions or the falling of a rock along rational lines? In other words, what distinguishes the transformation of planets and rocks from the transformations that constitute intelligent behaviour?

DISCUSSION

Intelligent behaviour, according to CTM, is the result of transformation of inner symbols according to syntactically-defined rules. Changes undergone by rock faces and the solar system are not the result of rules applied to inner symbols, since these objects do not contain any inner symbols. They are just lumps of rock, more or less homogeneous. Human brains, on the other hand, do contain symbols that are subject to rule-governed manipulation. That, at least, is CTM's hypothesis.

The legitimacy of reason-giving explanations was further challenged by the observation that humans are not always perfectly reasonable. Supporters of CTM are in a position to deal with this, too. If a generalization has an exception, that does not *have to* mean that it should not be used in explanation. Suppose we want to explain why James is ill in bed. We could point out that he has a flu virus and then appeal to the generalization that when people have a flu virus they end up in bed. The fact that sometimes people with the flu do not always end up in bed seems to be beside the point. A flu sufferer might not get into bed because he or she does not have a bed, or because a meteorite landed on the staircase, etc. A generalization can accommodate exceptions provided that we can explain *why* those exceptions arise. What is not permissible is to rely on a generalization that has unaccountable exceptions. CTM can account for lapses in rationality by treating them as a mismatch between the underlying syntactic rules of transformation and the rules of transformation that a person would need to follow in order to be rational. This mismatch could be due to the cognitive system being overloaded or poorly evolved.

The surfeit-of-explanations puzzle concerned the relation between reason-giving explanations and physical explanations, given that both are causal. CTM sees the two explanations as working in tandem. Strictly speaking, the causal work is all syntactic: syntactically-defined rules act on the syntactic properties of symbols. But because the rules used are algorithmic, there is no genuine competition between the physical explanation of the transformation and a description of this causal process as reasonable (relative to a particular interpretation of the symbols).

Haugeland on the computational theory of mind

The title of the first reading for this chapter is borrowed by John Haugeland from a metaphor of Daniel Dennett's. 'Semantic engines' are symbol systems driven by unthinking syntactic rules that, because symbols have semantic properties, replicate the rules of reason. Haugeland's explanation of why CTM has 'tremendous gut-level appeal' (p.207) contains some useful repetition of material already outlined in the previous section, but his different emphases reveal potential fault lines that lie beneath CTM's surface. This will be helpful when we turn to criticisms of CTM in the remaining sections.

Different terminologies are a constant menace in this area, though it is usually possible to extract the intended meaning from the context. For example, Haugeland's wording of the CTM thesis is itself superficially different from that given earlier:

CTM (Haugeland's formulation)
Intelligent beings are interpreted automatic formal systems.

Haugeland gives very clear and non-technical explanations of what these words mean, and once his definitions of 'formal system', 'automatic', and 'interpreted' are in place, this amounts to the claim that intelligent beings are systems of symbols governed by syntactically-defined rules that manifest rationality in their transformations.

Haugeland often uses 'formal' instead of 'syntactic', but these are equivalent. (The formal properties of a symbol are so called because they have to do with its appearance or form rather than with its meaning.) The syntactic (i.e. formal) properties were identified, earlier, with all of a symbol's physical characteristics, but a subtle qualification to this is in order. Not *all* physical characteristics of a symbol are, strictly speaking, syntactic properties. Some physical characteristics of a symbol have no bearing on the rules used to define their manipulation. Such characteristics are not syntactic. For example, the order and identity of the numerals used in the addition examples are syntactic because the rules for manipulation were defined in terms of these and a few other properties; the physical composition of the ink used to write these numerals down is irrelevant to their manipulation. The activity you were asked to carry out page 82 could have been performed with chalk, with ink, with pencil lead, or on a computer screen. This narrower understanding of 'syntactic' means that two systems of symbols can be syntactically identical ('formally equivalent' in Haugeland's phrase) despite being made of different physical materials. As Haugeland points out, this allows CTM to deal with the multiple realizability of intelligence, mentioned earlier as a difficulty for traditional materialist theories (pp.80, 209–10).

ACTIVITY

Read Haugeland, 'Semantic engines' (Reading 5). For now, skip part VI ('Interpretation and truth'). Part I begins by outlining the advantages of supposing that human intelligence is identical to the intelligence of a computer. These advantages are different in emphasis from the ones I presented earlier, but you will notice some overlap. He then defines what he means by 'computer', and is led eventually to the main thesis, stated above, that intelligent beings, including humans, are interpreted automatic formal systems. As you work through the article, answer the questions below.

(i)   What is a *computer*? (Attempt shortly after beginning of II.)

(ii) What is a *formal system*? (Attempt at end of II.)

(iii) What is an *automatic* formal system? (Attempt at end of III.)

(iv) What is the control problem? (Attempt at end of IV.)

(v) What is an *interpreted* automatic formal system? (Attempt at the end of V. Remember to skip VI before reading the final section.)

(i) A computer is an automatic formal system.

DISCUSSION

(ii) A formal system consists of uninterpreted symbols (or 'tokens' as Haugeland calls them) that, from a starting position, can be manipulated using rules, roughly like the rules for making a move in a board game. Two formal systems can be made of very different material – wood, marble, bone, silicon – and be essentially the same ('formally equivalent') because they are subject to equivalent rules of transformation. This is how CTM explains the intuition that intelligence is multiply realizable.

(iii) An automatic formal system is a physical device in which the rules apply without external intervention. A chess board and pieces, for example, is a formal system but not an automated one because the pieces do not move on their own. Combining it with a device that moved the pieces in accordance with rules would automate it. (That a formal system is automatic is important if it is to serve as a model of intelligence. Automation gets around the homunculus objection mentioned earlier, p.86, and by Haugeland himself, p.208.)

(iv) The control problem is the second (and difficult) part of the task of automating formal systems in such a way that they replicate, or perhaps constitute, intelligent behaviour. The first part of the task is to come up with rules governing allowable transformations of the symbols of a system. In chess, for example, this would involve saying that a bishop can move diagonally and only diagonally, and so on for the other pieces. For an everyday task such as doing the laundry, it might include 'put the laundry in the tub', 'add two caps of washing liquid to the tray', and 'close the tub door'. The second part of the task will be to determine which of the available rules to apply at any given point. In laundry, it doesn't matter whether one adds the washing liquid before or after putting the clothes in the tub, but it does matter whether one closes the door before or after putting the clothes in the tub. In chess, if one is concerned with winning rather than just with not making illegal moves, it matters a lot which of the legal moves available at any given point in the game is exploited. The control problem is the problem of finding a way of deciding which 'moves' to make, i.e. which transformation rules to apply and when. Solving the control problem even for a simple task like doing the laundry is harder than one might expect. The complexity of Figure 14 (p.91) bears witness to this.

(v) An interpreted automatic formal system is one whose symbols have a meaning. An automatic formal system is just a device that clunks away. Only relative to an interpretation of its symbols could the transformations produced by this clunking be said to be reasonable or unreasonable. The mental representation question as it emerges in the context of CTM is the question of what is responsible for a mental symbol's meaning one thing rather than some other thing. Haugeland addresses the question in part VI of his paper, which you were asked to skip for now.

CTM promises a lot. But to end this chapter I will consider three complications that seem to threaten not only Haugeland's version of the theory but the whole enterprise.

Complication I: the mental representation question

The explanation of intelligent transformations that CTM offers is hopeless without an appropriate interpretation of the manipulated tokens. If the symbols in the post-transformation belief box of the person in Figures 9 and 10 do not mean *seven*, but instead mean *ten*, then we would not have an explanation of how that person adds numbers up correctly. This is why it is important to Haugeland that intelligence be defined as the activity of an *interpreted* automatic formal system. But what gives a symbol its meaning? This is the mental representation question in its CTM guise.

An important opening remark to make here is that Mentalese meaning is unlike the meaning of words of English or other spoken and written languages. The English word 'horse' means what it does because people use and interpret it that way. They could easily have used and interpreted the same sound to mean *cow*. The meaning of a Mentalese symbol, by contrast, cannot depend on the interpretation given to it by the person whose head it is in, in an inner interpretative act. Quite apart from the fact that it does not feel to us that we perform these inner acts, this would be a homunculus answer (see above, p.86). It would simply push the question back one stage: what is the meaning of the symbols used in carrying out the interpretative act? A distinction can be made, then, between *intrinsic* (or 'original') and *inherited* (or 'derived') meaning. On the Gricean picture, for example, words inherit their meaning from the mental states – the intentions – of the person using them. But at some point the interpreting must stop. It can only do so when we have an account of intrinsic meaning. If the CTM picture is correct, they would only do so if the meaning of Mentalese itself is intrinsic.

The two final chapters of this book consider how different authors have taken up the challenge of saying what determines the intrinsic meaning of mental representations. Here we will consider only Haugeland's thoughts on what he describes as 'one of the deepest challenges that cognitive science must face' (1981, 31). He takes a broadly 'interpretationist' approach, though he does not use this (or any) label. An interpretationist will say that a symbol means *three* because that is how we must interpret it if we are to obtain an effective explanation of Freddy's abilities in various domains. If we interpret a symbol as meaning *Tuesday* or *ten*, rather than *seven*, then we would not have an explanation of Freddy's ability to add numbers together successfully (p.85). We would have an explanation of either nothing at all or of his adding numbers together incorrectly. This gives us, *the theorists*, reason to interpret it as meaning seven. Interpretationists hold that there is *nothing more* to a symbol's meaning what it does than that we get good explanations of human intelligence from the assumption that it has this meaning. As Haugeland puts it at the end of part VI, a good explanation will 'make sense' of the subject whose Mentalese symbols are being interpreted. To talk of the meaning of Mentalese as turning on what 'makes sense' of the subject implies that meaning is something *imposed* on the symbols, not as something *discovered* to inhere in them. This is reflected further in his use of 'interpreted' as the description of what makes an automatic formal system intelligent. Being interpreted is something that *happens to* a thing courtesy of someone, the interpreter, who invests it with meaning.

Now read part VI of Haugeland's paper. What, according to him, should guide us in how we interpret someone's inner language?

ACTIVITY

DISCUSSION

The interpretation chosen should 'make sense' of the subject, where this means, in particular, that they should come out having true beliefs. For example, given a choice between interpreting a person's inner sentence as expressing the proposition that there is a horse before them, and interpreting it as expressing the proposition that there is a cow before them, then if there is a horse before them (but not a cow), the first mode of interpretation is to be preferred. In a passage omitted from Reading 5, Haugeland adds that the interpretation should result in the subject having beliefs that are *relevant in the context*, and not merely true. So it would probably be unwise to interpret the sentence as expressing the proposition that it is illegal to make faces at dogs in the town of Normal, Illinois, in the USA, even if that is true.

The maxim that the person (or formal system) being interpreted should come out with mostly true and relevant beliefs has a certain plausibility. After all, if a system of interpretation makes most of what a person believes false or irrelevant, it will probably not be of much use in the explanation of their intelligence. This is not to say that it is only ever legitimate to interpret a person as having true and relevant beliefs. Rather, it is to say that error and irrelevance should be diagnosed only relative to an interpretation that makes most of what the person believes come out true and relevant. This maxim is sometimes called *the principle of charity in interpretation*. It has been used by translators since long before it was advocated by philosophers of mind like Haugeland. Here is John Mitchell Kemble deriding an ex-student, Wilkins, for failing to adhere to the principle when translating '*hwyðer*' in an Old English text.

> [Wilkins] represents it as a Saxon law that 'no man shall kill another man except in the presence of two or three witnesses; and then he shall keep his skin for four days'. Wilkins read '*hwyðer*', and thought it meant other or another, which it does not: ...'*hwyðer*' meant an 'ox' ... [O]ne marvels the utter absurdity of the thing had not struck him at once.
>
> (John Mitchell Kemble, letter to W.B. Donne in 1838, quoted in Thomson 2004, 15)

Kemble prefers to interpret the word as 'ox' because that yields a less absurd interpretation of the author's original assertion. The object being interpreted here is a symbol of language rather than of Mentalese, but it is possible to be an interpretationist about either kind of symbol. Interpretationists say that nothing settles what a symbol means *beyond* what charity in interpretation dictates. If interpreting the symbols of Mentalese in a particular way maximizes the truth and relevance of the person's beliefs, then that is what these symbols in fact mean.

Though it gives us a simple answer to the mental representation question, interpretationism in this form is not accepted by more than a robust minority of authors. One problem with it is that it tells us when it is appropriate for us to interpret a symbol as meaning the same as, for example, the English phrase 'There is a horse before me', but it does so without revealing why its meaning this rather than something else is *causally* significant.

That meaning is causally significant follows from the fact that a difference in what a person believes – their believing *there is a horse before me* rather than *there is a cow before me* – can make a difference in the physical world, and so can cause the world to change. Perhaps believing the first thing would lead to the subject's attempting to sit astride the creature, whereas believing the second would lead to their crouching down to milk it. Since a difference in what a person believes is, according to CTM, just a difference in what their Mentalese sentences mean, a difference in meaning will be causally significant in a way that is not captured in Haugeland's interpretationist suggestion. According to supporters of many competing theories of representation, the conditions on a physical state's representing or being about something should be entirely *physical* (and hence causally potent) ones. What this amounts to is a difficult question, but the general idea is that these conditions should not be stated in a way that invokes properties that are foreign to the physical sciences. Properties like truth and relevance do not look likely to figure in the physical sciences unless they, along with 'meaning', are defined explicitly in other terms. As Jerry Fodor puts it: 'If aboutness is real, it must be really something else' (Reading 7, p.224).

A different way of criticizing Haugeland's answer to the representation question is to ask whether he has provided a theory of intrinsic representation rather than derived representation. His answer to the question, 'What accounts for a symbol of Mentalese meaning what it does?', turns on how he thinks the theorist should interpret the symbol. But how is the theorist able to interpret the symbols? The whiff of homuncularism is in the air. True, Haugeland does not envisage little interpreters inside the head of the subject assigning meaning to the inner symbols. But the source of their meaning is still another mind, the mind of the theorist. This second worry would disappear along with the first if some way could be found of defining representation, the relation holding between mental symbols and objects or features of the external world, entirely in science-friendly language. Chapters 6 and 7 consider efforts in this direction.

Complication II: cognitive architecture

The assertion that the human brain contains symbols that are manipulated in the same way that the letters on the front of a cinema are manipulated by someone up a ladder is often met with wide-eyed incredulity. But this scepticism is perhaps misplaced. Someone brought forward in time from the nineteenth century, asked to figure out how computers do what they do, and encouraged to examine the inside of one, would not suspect that it works through the manipulation of symbols. But that is *precisely* how computers work. The difficulty of seeing how a symbol-manipulation program is 'implemented' in the brain is enormously challenging, but perhaps not in itself a sufficient reason to abandon CTM.

Still, there are facts about our 'cognitive architecture' that may call into question a simple-minded understanding of the relationship between CTM and reason-giving explanation. According to CTM as it has been stated so far, to be in a mental state – to believe something, for example – is to have a mental symbol in your head. Daniel Dennett has suggested that CTM cannot be correct if it is understood so literally, for the simple reason that brains are of limited size whereas the number of beliefs we have is astronomically large. He begins by quoting Marvin Minsky, a pioneer in AI:

> [A] machine will ... need to acquire on the order of a hundred thousand elements of knowledge in order to behave with reasonable sensibility in ordinary situations. A million, if properly organized, should be enough for a very great intelligence.
>
> (Minsky 1968, 26)

Dennett responds:

> If Minsky's estimate were realistic, the brain, with its ten billion neurons or trillions of molecules, would be up to the task no doubt. But surely his figure is much too low. For in addition to all the relatively *difficult* facts I have mastered, such as that New York is larger than Boston and salt is sodium chloride, there are all the easy ones we tend to overlook: New York is not on the moon, or in Venezuela; salt is not sugar, or green, or oily; salt is good on potatoes, on eggs; tweed coats are not made of salt; a grain of salt is smaller than an elephant. ... Surely I can think of more than a thousand things I know or believe about salt, and salt is not one of a hundred, but one of thousands upon thousands of things I can do this with. ... My beliefs are apparently infinite, which means their storage, however miniaturized, will take up more room than there is in the brain. The

objection, of course, seems to point to its own solution: it must be that I *potentially* believe indefinitely many things, but I *generate* all but, say, Minsky's hundred thousand by the activity of an extrapolator-deducer mechanism attached to the core library.

(Dennett 1978, 45)

A distinction between core beliefs that are stored explicitly (e.g. that Kabul is the capital of Afghanistan) and *implicit* (or 'tacit') beliefs that are generated according to need (e.g. that dogs do not have CD collections) seems unavoidable given the finitude of the brain. But that distinction is a difficult one for CTM theorists to negotiate. They must either cease calling implicit beliefs 'beliefs', in which case their theory is not in a position to account for the explanatory potency of such beliefs on those rare occasions when, say, knowing about dogs and CD collections becomes pertinent; or they can call implicit beliefs 'beliefs' but at the cost of contradicting the assertion that to believe that *p* is to have a sentence that means that *p* in one's belief box.

Kim Sterelny, whose sympathies are with CTM, has attempted to see his way   **ACTIVITY** out of this dilemma by defending the first of the two alternatives just described, labelled the 'austere' view in the passage below. Read the passage and consider whether his reply is successful.

> Let us suppose that Boris has an average stock of beliefs and desires. Does Boris believe that worms have no beards? ... It is very likely that Boris does not house within [him] inner sentences that mean that worms don't have beards ... [P]hilosophers like Dennett, Lycan and, apparently, Patricia Churchland [are] most unhappy with the straightforward denial that Boris believes that worms are beardless; [Churchland 1986 calls this] the 'austere' view of implicit belief. She emphasizes the speed and ease with which some beliefs which are not explicitly stored can none the less become conscious. She concludes from this consideration that 'the austere solution looks unacceptable' (1986, 391).
>
> But the alternative to the austere solution is undoubtedly messy. For how obvious do the consequences of our explicitly stored beliefs have to be for them to count as part of what we believe? None of us believe all the logical consequences of our explicit beliefs. There is no principled intermediate place to stop.
>
> So is there anything really wrong with the austere line? I think not. First, the austere line loses no explanatory power. In so far as intentional states [i.e. states like believing, desiring, etc.] enter into the explanation of behaviour, they will [come to] be explicitly represented, though not necessarily conscious. Second, there is no major clash of intuitive judgement with the austere theory. If worries

about hairy worms ... really *never* have crossed Boris's mind, then we have no clear inclination to credit Boris with these thoughts. Perhaps denying that Boris believes that worms are beardless does minor violence to our pretheoretic judgements. But no one planning to integrate folk psychology with serious theory has supposed that folk theory needs no revisions whatever. ... The 'tacit knowledge problem' is not one.

(Sterelny 1990, 162–4)

DISCUSSION A possible reply to Sterelny: the rules followed by the brain when it manipulates Mentalese symbols cannot all be explicit, yet we might still be said to 'know' or 'believe' them. This is sometimes called 'procedural knowledge'. Our knowledge of logical rules is an example. The CTM explanation of how someone manages to infer only in truth-preserving (i.e. logical) ways involves supposing that their brains manipulate Mentalese symbols according to the patterns set out on pages 88–9. But the rules themselves do not have to be listed as explicit Mentalese sentences. In fact, if they were, another rule would be needed to apply these sentential rules when performing an inference. Somewhere in the brain there must be rules that apply to sentences but that are not themselves sentences. It seems easier to think of these rules as procedures, embodied in the structure of the brain but not explicitly set out in the form of sentences. Procedural knowledge is explanatorily potent but not sentential. The austere view defended by Sterelny looks too austere.

Complication III: the frame problem

There is more agreement over the seriousness of the frame problem than over what, precisely, it is. A flavour of it can be had from examples of everyday intelligence that are hard to explain on the CTM model, or indeed at all. Take the case of planning.

Planning

You are planning a midnight snack at your uncle's house. You need to build all and only the relevant information into your plan. You are wondering what is potentially relevant and what isn't. The fact that the fridge is in the kitchen clearly is. At a pinch, your uncle's being a keen photographer is also relevant, since you know that photographers often store undeveloped film in fridges. You build this contingency into your plan. But there is plenty that you do not even bother to consider, including the fact that Kabul is the capital of Afghanistan or that your uncle's dog does not have a CD collection. You act out the plan and manage to get together a midnight snack.

Notice that you do not spend much time assessing the facts excluded from consideration for relevance. This is just as well since, as we know from the previous section, there are innumerably many known facts to exclude. The whole point of excluding something from consideration would be defeated if, before excluding it, you had to consider whether to exclude it from consideration or not. Yet despite this lack of consideration, you manage to exclude only what is irrelevant and include only what is relevant. The proof of this is that you do indeed manage to rustle together a midnight snack. How are you able to determine the relevance/irrelevance in this context of the many different things you know without actually assessing them for relevance?

The frame problem, so-labelled, is normally associated with planning and the problems attaching to planning. But exactly the same difficulties involving the relevance/irrelevance divide arise with attempts to model other cognitive tasks, so the frame problem is in fact quite general. Consider abductive reasoning, or inference to the best explanation as it is sometimes called. The reasoning involved has the following form:

> P is known already and stands in need of explanation; Q provides the best explanation of P available; therefore, it is reasonable to infer that Q.

This mode of reasoning lies at the heart of much of science, but also our everyday thinking about the world. Here is an everyday example of abductive reasoning:

> You are waiting for a friend at a café. She is late. You wonder why. You remember that she has a sister in Argentina; you know, too, that sending parcels overseas can sometimes take several weeks; and you know that Christmas is approaching; and you come to suspect, correctly, that your friend is caught in a queue at the post office.

What similarities do you notice between the abductive reasoning case and the planning case? Answer by trying to identify (i) a requirement for success in abductive reasoning and (ii) a puzzle about how we manage to satisfy that requirement.

ACTIVITY

(i) Somehow you must have homed in on the relevance to your friend's lateness of the fact that she has a sister in Argentina.

(ii) You can't have done this by assessing everything you know for relevance, not even unconsciously. That would have taken too long. Something prompted you to select this belief as a component in a good explanation. How fortuitous that you selected this belief and not, say, your belief that she does not own a yacht, or that she has a birthmark on her ankle, or that dogs do not have CD collections! Did you know already that the Argentinean-sister belief would be a good candidate? How? What led you to exclude the birthmark belief? You presumably did not think as follows: 'On reflection, birthmarks on ankles do not seem relevant, so I'll exclude that belief from consideration.' That would be to have already considered it. The exclusion of the irrelevant must happen, but not at the cost of the question of its relevance itself becoming relevant.

We can attempt to summarize the frame problem in the form of a question. How do we humans manage to exclude irrelevant knowledge:

(a) *at all*, given that if we stop and assess each item of knowledge for relevance to the task at hand we would never get anything done;

(b) *accurately*, given that the only way of getting round (a) seems to be to select items of background knowledge more or less randomly; and

(c) *retrievably*, since a change in circumstances may make the excluded knowledge relevant again?

Despite the fact that our managing to discriminate between relevant and irrelevant knowledge is an essential pre-condition of our intelligent reactions in the real world, CTM does not seem able to explain how we do it. Haugeland's 'control problem' is really another name for the frame problem, and he was right to mention its seriousness. Designing an automated but successful formal system has proven extremely difficult even for relatively sanitized environments and simple tasks. When the complexity of the real world is factored in, coming up with algorithms that come close to mapping human intelligence looks next to impossible.

Critics of attempts to mechanize thinking have long pointed to these and similar difficulties (see Figure 15). In Dennett's discussion of the frame problem, he calls it 'the frame problem *of* AI', not 'the frame problem *for* AI'.

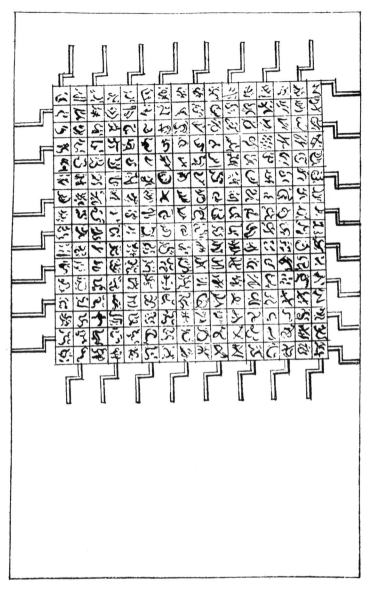

Figure 15 The computational model of the mind has been around longer than one might expect, as too have parodies of it. Gulliver's illustration (in Book III of *Gulliver's Travels* by Jonathan Swift, 1726, p.74) is of the 'engine' used in the 'Project for Improving Speculative Knowledge by Practical and Mechanical Operations' designed by a professor of philosophy at the Grand Academy of Lagado. It is 'composed of several bits of wood, ... linked together by slender wires' on which are written 'all the words of their language'. Describing its operation, Gulliver writes that each of the professor's pupils 'at his command took ... an iron handle, whereof there were forty fixed round the edges of the frame, and giving them a sudden turn, the whole disposition of the words was entirely changed. He then commanded six and thirty of the lads to read the several lines softly as they appeared upon the frame; and ... they dictated to the four remaining boys who were scribes.' By this method of 'computation' – essentially symbol manipulation – he hoped, 'with a little bodily labour, [to] write books in philosophy, poetry, politics, law, mathematics, and theology, without the least assistance from genius or study' (p.73). Swift's point seems to be that mechanical generation could not possibly result in relevant sentences being produced. Only genuine intelligence could be sufficiently non-random.

He accepts that the frame problem is a genuine problem for computational approaches to understanding intelligent behaviour. But he also thinks the problem has always been with us. The computational approach merely forces us to recognize its existence and address it head on.

ACTIVITY Read Dennett's discussion of the frame problem in Reading 6, which focuses on the problem as it relates to planning. He begins with an example that alludes to but does not explicitly name the character of 'R$_2$D$_2$', an intelligent robot in the film *Star Wars*. The designers of R$_2$D$_2$ have overcome the frame problem. But *Star Wars* is a fiction. Dennett imagines some prototypes and the nature of their failings. In part I of the extract, Dennett attempts to say what the frame problem is. In part II he reviews two attempts by workers in AI to solve it and explains why he thinks they are bound to fail.

(i) What is the deductive approach (p.220)? Why does it fail, according to Dennett?

(ii) What is the stereotypes approach (bottom of p.221)? Why does it fail, according to Dennett?

DISCUSSION (i) The deductive approach involves the system (i.e. the robot) storing knowledge about a situation as sentences in its memory alongside other items of general knowledge – the latter being the frame, so-called because it frames, i.e. determines the limit of, what the system will take into account in coming to decisions. When the system needs to assess the wisdom of a proposed plan of action, it derives the outcome from this combined knowledge using logical rules. This outcome is then assessed for whether it matches the desired outcome. The problem with the deductive approach concerns what to include in the frame or 'knowledge base' of the system. If the system has a very small frame, then the absence of knowledge that is critical to successful performance will quickly become salient. The amount of information that is *potentially* relevant outside the artificial confines of a laboratory is apparently unbounded. But if we include in the frame everything that is potentially relevant, the difficulty emerges of understanding how the machine could possible extract the information that is *actually* relevant, as we humans seem able to do.

(ii) The stereotypes approach attempts to capture the human ability to ignore what should be ignored but stay alert to what shouldn't be ignored, not by searching through a list of stored information but by using its experience to build up a repertoire of stereotypical or paradigmatic scenarios to match patterns that exist in the world. When negotiating with the real world, a consideration is treated as potentially relevant only if it is relevant according to a stereotypical scenario. The shortcoming of this approach is just that the world sometimes does not behave at all stereotypically. When this happens, the machine would be flummoxed, but we humans seem able to cope impressively well.

Chapter summary

The mental representation question often arises today as a question about what gives Mentalese, a hypothetical 'mental language', its meaning. This chapter has been concerned mainly with the motivations for hypothesizing such a language rather than with actually answering the mental representation question. The task of saying how a physical state of the brain – for example, the presence of a Mentalese sentence within it – could possibly have content, or be 'about' something, will move centre-stage in the two chapters to follow.

Mentalese is a postulate of the computational theory of mind (CTM), which claims that the rational transformations that constitute our intelligence are in fact physical transformations of meaningful symbols within our brains (pp.80–93). This helps to resolve certain problems that arise for ordinary 'folk' explanations of intelligent phenomena – the legitimacy puzzle (p.76) and the surfeit-of-explanations puzzle (p.77). But CTM explanations face difficulties of their own, including but not only the mental representation question (p.96). Two further difficulties were also raised here: the plausibility of assuming that all mental states involve explicit representations (p.100); and the problem of relevance, particularly in relation to the frame problem (p.102).

Further reading

There are plenty of good introductions to folk psychology and CTM, including (in increasing order of difficulty) Crane 2003, Sterelny 1990, Cummins 1989, and Heil 1998. On some perspectives, computationalism is an alternative to, not a complement of, folk psychology: see Churchland 1984,

Churchland 1986, and Stich 1983. Fodor 1975 and Fodor 1987 are canonical statements of CTM as a 'vindication' of folk psychology. Stich and Warfield 1994 is a collection of papers looking at the mental representation question. Questions about cognitive architecture and explicitness of representation quickly get tangled up with the debate between classical and connectionist models of computation, not discussed here but nicely introduced in both Clark 1989 and Clark 2001, and alluded to briefly by Sterelny 1990 (p.163). The issue of relevance raised here in connection with the frame problem and abductive inference is examined in detail by Fodor 2000, a riposte to the optimism of Pinker 1997. The claim that Descartes does not properly follow up his doubts about his own sanity is developed in Foucault 1961, though the connection with the topics raised in this chapter is minimal.

CHAPTER 5

Representation as indication

Introduction: the naturalization of content

Most advocates of the view that human intelligence is essentially symbol manipulation are drawn to it out of a desire to understand how humans could be both physical creatures and rational at the same time. This desire is often matched by a more general commitment to what is known as philosophical naturalism. There are more and less demanding forms of philosophical naturalism, but the central idea is that human phenomena can best be understood in terms of the methods, theories and ontology of the natural sciences (i.e. of physics plus any other sciences that have been or are expected to become integrated with physics, such as chemistry and biology).

Not all philosophical naturalists are committed to CTM, even if they applaud its aspirations. Most, though, will share the hope that a scientific explanation is available for how a physical entity – a human being – could have thoughts, desires, and other psychological attitudes that are *about* the world beyond it. Supporters of CTM usually interpret this hope very narrowly. They try to say, in naturalistic terms, what it is that gives symbols of an inner language their power to represent. Less restrictively, philosophical naturalists try to say how a physical organism or system, by virtue of being in a particular physical state (whether or not that state involves the occurrence of inner symbols), can count as representing some object or aspect of the external world.

Though it is not immediately easy to see why, representation does not *itself* seem likely to turn out to be a natural property. This thought is evident in the following remarks by Jerry Fodor:

> I suppose that sooner or later the physicists will complete the catalogue they've been compiling of the ultimate and irreducible properties of things. When they do, the likes of *spin*, *charm*, and *charge* [i.e. properties drawn from contemporary physics] will perhaps appear upon their list. But *aboutness* surely won't; intentionality simply doesn't go that deep. It's hard to see, in face of this consideration, how one can be a Realist about intentionality [i.e. how one can

accept that attributions of mental states are objective and often correct] without also being, to some extent or other, a Reductionist. If the semantic and the intentional are real properties of things, it must be in virtue of their identity with ... properties that are themselves *neither* intentional *nor* semantic.

(Reading 7, p.224)

In this chapter and the next we will be looking at attempts to provide exactly what Fodor demands: a theory under which *aboutness* is something that can 'to some extent or other' be described in science-friendly terms. Slightly more precisely, such a theory might be expected to state conditions under which someone is in a mental state *with a particular content*. This statement must be couched in terms drawn from, or amenable in some way to, physics.

The basic question being asked, then, is what representing must be if humans, physical creatures, are able to do it. One does not have to be a philosophical naturalist, still less a supporter of CTM, to find this question interesting. But the undoubted difficulties of giving a naturalistic answer to this question are often interpreted as a sign that naturalism is misguided. Discussions of representation have come to serve almost as a touchstone that separates those inclined to examine all human phenomena only through the lens of science from those who think this perspective is blinkered – about human phenomena, about science, or about both. With this in mind, let us turn to consider one of the most popular approaches to carrying out the task of naturalizing content: the indicator approach.

Simple indicator theories

Since philosophical naturalists wish to treat humans as part of the natural world, many are tempted to look to the natural world for simple examples of rudimentary representation that could serve as a model for the kind of representation manifest in human higher cognition. Consideration of examples of what Grice calls 'natural meaning' has struck many as a good starting point (see chapter 2, pp.16–19, 29). This was the kind of meaning that Grice set aside in favour of non-natural meaning, the sort that really interested him. But non-natural meaning, as it was analysed by Grice anyway, is not really what we want here. His analysis of non-natural meaning was given in terms of the intentions of the speaker, but it is the content of intentions and other mental states that we are hoping to develop a theory of, so a Gricean notion of non-natural meaning cannot be fundamental. Natural meaning, though, could be exactly the notion we want for a naturalistic theory of mental content.

When someone has spots on their face, we describe this as a 'sign' that they have measles, or say that it 'means' they have measles. If tracks in the snow have a particular pattern, we 'read' this as evidence of a passing fox. If a tree trunk has 33 rings, we take this to 'show' that it is in its 33rd season. Our use of 'sign', 'read', 'means' and 'show' in describing these cases is suggestive. Perhaps the simple notion of natural meaning can be built up into a notion of representation of the kind present in human cognition. Unless there were humans around to count them, no one would *take* tree rings to represent tree age. But the relation of correspondence between tree rings and tree age does not depend on anyone counting rings. The correspondence has existed since long before humans noticed it. Perhaps this kind of *correspondence*, independent as it is from human intentions and purpose, could form the heart of a naturalistic notion of representation. This idea is the central claim of what have come to be called *indicator* theories of representation. They are also sometimes called 'information theories' or 'causal co-variance' theories. What is common to all the approaches is not the label but the central place they give to naturalistically explicable causal correspondences.

Natural correspondences of this kind can be distinguished from what, for contrast, we might call 'artificial' correspondences. The representational properties possessed by language and by religious or other cultural symbols seem to derive entirely from the representational capacities of intelligent creatures. Words written down on a page represent what they do only because we *invest* them with significance. Intuitively, if humans did not exist to produce or interpret them, such patterns would not mean anything. A crossed pair of sticks of differing lengths on a wall in a church represent Christ's crucifixion, but they do so only because the practice exists of interpreting such objects in this way. In a dark wood never entered by humans, they would not represent anything in the same sense. If we are interested in understanding mental content, then it is important to distinguish it from representation that is somehow parasitic on mental content. In the terminology of chapter 4 (p.97), we must develop a theory of intrinsic rather than derived representation. The development of just such a theory is what indicator theorists hope to arrive at by focusing on the simple correspondences present in nature rather than on artificial correspondences.

The simplicity of the examples presented so far may not encourage optimism. What reason is there to expect that a correspondence relation found in tree trunks could possibly be enriched into a theory, ultimately, of mental content in humans? It would help, then, if we could find simple, naturally occurring correspondences that involve the representation by organisms of things outside them. A striking example of just such a correspondence is the frog's sensory system. This system goes into a particular state whenever a fly crosses its visual field, but never does so otherwise (in normal circumstances, at least – biologists can trigger the frog to enter the state without using a fly). Call this state F, for 'fly'. Frogs in state F shoot out their tongue towards the fly. The correspondence between a frog's sensory system being in state F and the presence of a fly looks to be no different in principle from the correspondence between the number of rings in a tree and the tree's age. Both correspondences are 'naturalistic' in the sense that we can expect a straightforward scientific explanation of their existence. But the frog's sensory system is, intuitively, more akin to the kind of representation we are interested in, the kind involved in human thinking. It seems perfectly acceptable to say that the frog's visual system is able to represent the presence of a fly. Indeed, the neurons involved are often described by biologists as 'bug detectors' (see Reading 8, p.242).

But what exactly *is* the correspondence relation manifest in these simple examples drawn from nature? The relation is often called 'indication', or sometimes 'causal co-variance' or 'carrying information'. What we might call *simple indicator theories* claim that the notion of representation and the notion of indication are equivalent. But authors differ in how they define 'indication' even while they agree that it consists in some kind of reliable correspondence with a causal basis that is explicable in naturalistic terms and can be used in the development of a theory of mental content.

Indication is usually thought of, in the first instance, as a relation between events, or perhaps between situations. An extremely basic way of understanding the notion would be to stipulate that an event of type A indicates an event of type B if, and only if, events of these two types regularly co-occur: whenever an A-type event takes place, so does a B-type event, and vice versa.

ACTIVITY

On this definition, the presence of 33 rings in a tree trunk would indicate that the tree was 33 years of age. But equally, being 33 years of age indicates that the tree has 33 rings. Why might this symmetry in the definition be problematic for a simple indicator theorist?

Simple indicator theorists identify indication with representation. But representation is, intuitively, a non-symmetrical relation: *x* represents *y* does not entail that *y* represents *x*. In fact, it is hard to think of any examples where it feels right to say of two things that they represent each other.

DISCUSSION

An obvious way to avoid the symmetry in this basic definition of 'indication' is to look to the notion of cause. Cause is non-symmetrical: if one event causes a second event, then that second event cannot be what caused the first. A definition of indication might exploit this by treating only the caused event as an indicator (i.e. representer), and only the causing event as what is indicated (i.e. represented). The age of a tree would not count as representing the number of rings the tree has, because the causal relation is, intuitively, from age to number-of-rings, not the other way around. This gives us what can serve as our basic understanding of the term 'indication' for the rest of the chapter.

Definition of indication

An event of type A indicates an event of type B if, and only if, events of type A are reliably caused by, and only by, events of type B.

For example, suppose that whenever a frog's sensory system is in state F there is a fly nearby causing it to be in that state; and the passing of a fly always results in the frog's sensory system going into state F. In that case, when on a particular occasion the frog is in state F, this indicates (represents) the presence of a passing fly.

The introduction of 'cause' into the definition is in keeping with the naturalistic aspirations of indicator theorists. Although the notion of 'cause' does not occur within actual physical theories, these theories can be thought of as explaining what gives rise to causal processes. So for any actual case of indication in this sense, there should be a physical explanation of its occurrence. In the measles case, spots can be explained scientifically as an effect of the measles virus.

As noted, different authors offer different definitions of the correspondence relation that is central to the indicator approach. For example, the way just suggested of capturing the non–symmetry of 'represents' will, to some, seem too strict. While it seems to work for the frog–fly case, in other cases it is the causing event, and not the caused event, that seems to represent. Clouds on the horizon, for example, can be said to represent, or be a sign of, rain; but it is plausible to say that the clouds are what cause the rain, not vice versa. This matter turns on issues that will be remote to our concerns in what follows. Our definition, which is close to the definition of 'representation' focused on in Reading 7, will serve as well as any for our purposes.

While it is easy to see how the indicator account could be applied to sensory states, and perhaps even beliefs that depend directly on sensory experience, it is not immediately obvious how it could work for other kinds of mental state. Suppose that, as I type this on a dreary day in February, I am *imagining* myself lying on a sunny beach. My imagining this does not (sadly) indicate that I am lying on a sunny beach – that is, it is not caused by my being on the beach. Again, suppose that I *wish* that I were lying on a sunny beach: the representational content of this state cannot be identified with what it indicates, either. This is enough to establish that the simple indicator theory cannot be applied directly to every kind of mental representation.

Nevertheless, if the theory could be applied to certain kinds of representation – to sensory states, for example, and to the beliefs that they generate – this would be an important first step. Indeed, it might turn out that the content of wishes and imaginings depends in some way on the content of the subject's sensory and belief states. Desire content, for example, is often said to be definable in terms of belief content along the following lines:

> *S* desires that *p* if, and only if, *S* acts in a way that, were *S*'s beliefs all true, would tend to bring it about that *p*.

So this simple indicator theory, while it could not be applied directly to all mental states, could perhaps provide a foundation on which we could build a more comprehensive account.

Two characteristics of indicator theories: externalism and atomism

In this section we will be look at Fodor's statement of a simple indicator theory, what he calls the Crude Causal Theory (CCT) of content, and then draw out certain characteristics it shares with indicator theories in general. Before turning to Fodor's discussion, though, it will be useful to take note of how his CCT differs from the simple indicator theory in two superficial ways.

The definition of indication given above is a relation between events or situations. But Fodor's CCT is a theory of the representational properties of *symbols of Mentalese*, not of physical states of the subject. That is because he is committed to the symbol manipulation view discussed in the previous chapter. This gives his CCT the appearance of differing quite markedly from the simple indicator theory defined in the previous section. But this appearance is superficial, and is irrelevant to our concerns in this chapter. A simple way to 'translate' between his CCT and simple indicator theories that are not committed to the symbol manipulation view is to think of the representer, in the CCT case, not as the symbol itself but as an event or situation: *the presence of* the symbol within, say, the subject's visual system or belief box. Fodor's way of putting this is to talk of a particular symbol being 'tokened' in the visual system or belief box, where this is a kind of event. His theory, then, is a theory of what a particular symbol's *being tokened* represents.

Fodor also talks about (tokenings of) symbols as expressing *properties*, such as the property of being a horse, rather than as representing the occurrence of an event of a certain kind. Again, this is a superficial but potentially confusing difference. One can think of him as asking what makes it the case that tokening a particular symbol represents the occurrence of a horse-event rather than of a cow-event – for example, what makes it the case that someone is representing an object in front of them *as being a horse* rather than *as being a cow*.

Read parts I and II of the extract in Reading 7 from Fodor's 1987 book, **ACTIVITY** *Psychosemantics*. In part I he announces his ambition to develop a theory of representation for Mentalese; in part II he sketches the Crude Causal Theory (CCT) of representation. A word of warning: Fodor is writing for specialists. His style is often marked by a combination of informality and the frequent use of technical terms. So, even though these extracts are short, you may need to take some time to digest them.

According to the Crude Causal Theory (CCT), what would suffice for the Mentalese symbol, H, to express the property of being a horse?

According to CCT, H expresses the property of being a horse if, as a matter of **DISCUSSION** nomological necessity, (i) all horse events cause H-tokenings, and (ii) all H-tokenings are caused by horse events. By 'nomological necessity', Fodor means that the causal relations are not the result of a freak accident: they will be explicable by reference to scientific laws. ('Nomological', literally, means 'having to do with laws'.)

Fodor does not endorse CCT; he merely thinks that it is a good starting point. In part III of the same reading we will see his objection to it. Before this, let us note two important features of simple indicator theories, including CCT: their externalism and their atomism.

What a sensory or belief system represents will depend on what is found in the physical environment the subject actually inhabits. This is because the physical environment the subject actually inhabits is the one with which she or he causally interacts. In the environment that human beings actually inhabit, someone's visual system being in state W would represent the presence of H_2O nearby if that is what is reliably correlated with their being in state W. On Twin Earth, by contrast, there will be a reliable correlation between the occurrence of W and the presence of XYZ, so W will represent the presence of XYZ. CCT and the simple indicator theory are, therefore, both committed to mental externalism. What we are seeing and thinking about depends on where the subject is. Here is how Fodor puts it in Reading 7 (pp.224–5):

> ... what makes it the case that (the Mentalese symbol) 'water' expresses the property [being] H_2O is that tokens of that symbol stand in certain causal relations to water samples. Presumably if [the symbol has a different interpretation on Twin Earth], that is all because [on Twin Earth] it's XYZ that bears to ... tokens [of 'water' on Twin Earth] the sort of causal relations that H_2O bears to tokens of 'water' [on Earth].

This apparent commitment to mental externalism can be viewed as either a weakness or a strength of indicator theories, according to how far one is persuaded of the arguments for and against mental externalism (see pp.64–7). Conversely, the availability of the indicator theory might be thought to lend support to mental externalism. The idea that what our thoughts are about depends on the physical structure of the world around us seemed strange when it was first raised by Putnam. But when one comes at this proposal from the perspective of trying to understand how a simple organism could represent the world around it, the dependence of what it represents on the nature of the world around it is welcome and unsurprising.

A second significant feature of indicator theories is that they are atomistic rather than holistic. Holistic theories of representation treat the representational properties of one state (or symbol of Mentalese) as dependent on the representational properties of certain other states (or symbols). But with indicator theories, including Fodor's CCT, this is not so. If a tokening of H would represent the presence of a horse, this does not require that a tokening of C should represent the presence of a cow. The causal co-variance between the symbol and the property it represents is independent of the existence of causal co-variance involving other symbols. According to the CCT and other simple indicator theories, mental states have the content they do in a relatively autonomous fashion. In this sense they are atomistic theories of representation.

We will be examining a holistic theory in the next chapter, but in fact we already have an example: the interpretationist theory outlined by Haugeland. His use of the principle of charity is what gives rise to this holism. Recall how the principle was put to work in the translation of written language. The question at issue (in the letter quoted on p.98) was how to interpret the word left untranslated in the following sentence:

> No man shall kill a *hwyðer* except in the presence of two or three witnesses; and then he shall keep his skin for four days.

The principle of charity dictates that a word should be translated in such a way as to avoid attributing absurd claims to the author, e.g. so as to avoid needlessly rendering the sentence false or irrelevant. By this score, the letter writer is surely correct that 'other [man]' is poorer than 'ox' as a translation of '*hwyðer*'. But notice that applying this methodology requires the meaning of the other words in the sentence to be given already. 'Other [man]' would have been *more* in keeping with the principle of charity than 'ox' if the rest of the original sentence had been translated instead as it is below:

> No man shall borrow from a *hwyðer* except in the presence of two or three witnesses; and then he shall repay his debt after four days.

If the principle of charity is constitutive of the representational properties of symbols – words or mental representations – then representation is holistic. That is why interpretationism, to the extent that it is paired with the principle of charity, is holistic.

We are not yet in a position to say whether being atomistic rather than holistic makes indicator theories more attractive, less attractive, or neither. But Fodor is, in fact, well known for having raised a number of nasty objections to holistic theories. We will meet some of these in the next chapter. In view of this it is unsurprising that he defends an atomistic theory. For now, let us just note that its non-holism is a distinctive characteristic of indicator theories, and potentially an attractive one.

The problem of misrepresentation

In this section of the chapter we will look at the first serious objection to indicator theories, including the CCT: the difficulty they have in explaining how we can *misrepresent*, i.e. represent inaccurately. It seems obvious that we can have false beliefs, or be victims of a visual illusion. But it is no easy matter to see how an event could *misindicate* another event, given our serving definition of 'indication'. This difficulty is, perhaps, to be expected given that the simple examples of representation inspiring the definition were the kind that Grice called 'natural meaning'. For recall that the mark of natural meaning is that something means$_n$ that p only if p is actually the case. Spots on someone's face do not 'mean that they have measles' unless they really do have measles (see p.17).

The frog–fly case can be used to illustrate the difficulty. Suppose state F in the frog's sensory system is causally correlated with the presence of flies. On the simple indicator theory, its being in state F represents the presence of the fly. If, for some reason, the sensory system goes into state F even when there is no fly causing it to do so – because the frog's nerves are triggered by power surges in nearby electrical pylons, for example – and the frog's tongue shoots out in vain, then we would like to be able to say that the sensory system has misrepresented: that it is reporting to the frog's brain that a fly is present even though no fly is present. But we can't say this. All we can say is that, since state F is no longer correlated with flies, being in state F no longer represents flies as present. And if it no longer represents flies as present, it no longer *wrongly* represents flies as present. Misrepresentation is impossible.

It is tempting to dismiss this objection. Can we not just say that it is enough for state F to count as representing the presence of a fly that, *save on exceptional occasions*, the frog's visual system is caused to be in state F by, and only by, a nearby fly? This would seem to require nothing more than changing the definition of 'indicates' slightly. On those exceptional occasions when the frog's visual system is in state F but there is no fly, state F still represents the presence of a fly, but it does so inaccurately: it misrepresents a fly as present.

The difficulty with this dismissive response to the misrepresentation problem is to say in a principled way what counts as an 'exceptional occasion'. A frog under a pylon sticking its tongue out at empty space seems like odd behaviour, which might incline us to treat it as 'exceptional'; but from a naturalistic perspective such judgements of oddity are subjective and thus irrelevant. Why should we not take state F to represent, accurately, *the presence nearby of either a fly or a pylon*? If this interpretation seems bizarre, it is hard to say why that amounts to more than a reflection of our own prejudices. Is it, objectively speaking, any more bizarre than the interpretation of state F as inaccurately representing the presence nearby of a fly?

A defender of the simple indicator approach might respond that being exceptional is simply a matter of not happening very often. If the frog is not under the pylon except in midsummer, then state F continues to represent the presence of a fly even then. But if it is under the pylon as long as it lives, then perhaps state F *does* represent the presence nearby of either a fly or a pylon. But this response is not going to work well for certain other cases, cases in which mistakes happen quite often. Consider a monkey that, whenever its visual system is in state E, is driven by an innate mechanism to hide under a dense bush where monkey-eating eagles cannot see it. E can be triggered by any large bird, since in evolutionary terms it is better to be safe than sorry about extreme risk, and *most* triggerings are not caused by monkey-eating eagles. Yet still we want to say that E represents, often inaccurately, the presence of an eagle, and not simply the presence of large bird.

In order to appreciate the extent of the problem, you are asked in the next activity to look at Fodor's statement of it as an objection to his CCT. His objection takes the form of a worry that has come to be known as 'the disjunction problem'. The example he uses involves someone who normally tokens H of, and only of, horses but, on a dark and rainy evening when he is in a hurry to get home, tokens it of a cow. Intuitively, we want to say that this person is mistakenly representing the cow as a horse. But the CCT has difficulty showing how this could be so.

Read parts III and IV of Reading 7. In part III Fodor presents the 'disjunction problem', which seems to show that it is impossible to misrepresent instances of a property. In part IV he describes how Dretske, in an earlier version of the indicator theory, fails to cope with the problem. Dretske's early theory is similar to the simple indicator theory and to the CCT, but is expressed in terms of one event 'transmitting or carrying information' about another event. Fodor defines this phrase in his exegesis. Part V is optional. In it, Fodor presents his own solution to the disjunction problem. This is included here only in case you are curious; it will not be discussed. Instead, we will look at Dretske's latest, and very different, solution to it.

Why might simple indicator theorists find it so hard to show that the person who tokens H of a cow is representing it inaccurately as a horse?

The problem is that there are no principled grounds for deciding between (i) saying that the person who tokens H of a cow is *inaccurately* representing the cow as a horse, and (ii) saying that he or she is *accurately* representing it as a horse-or-cow. Causal co-variance alone does not seem to offer a way to discriminate between these two competing interpretations of a tokening of H that is caused by a cow.

Many different attempts have been made to overcome the misrepresentation problem, or Fodor's related 'disjunction problem'. Perhaps the most popular involves treating indication as having a function, and defining representation in terms of this function. Misrepresentation, i.e. erroneous representation, can then be understood simply as the failure of the function to be carried out. Theories of mental content that rest on the notion of a function are known as *teleosemantic theories*, from the Greek word '*telos*', meaning *purpose* or *end*. In the next section we will look at Fred Dretske's version of such a theory.

Dretske's teleosemantic theory

In this section we will consider a relatively non-technical statement of Dretske's theory taken from his book *Explaining Behavior: Reasons in a World of Causes* (1988). The simple indicator theory holds that for a state of the frog's visual system to represent the world as being a certain kind of way – as having a nearby fly in it, for example – is for this state to indicate that the world is that way. It does this when the world interacts with the frog's visual system in such a way that the visual system is regularly caused to be in the state when, and only when, the world is that way. Something along these lines is what Dretske held in earlier work, and it was this theory that Fodor criticized in the previous reading (in part IV). Dretske's new theory holds that for a physical state of a certain kind to represent the world as being a particular way is for the state to *have the function of indicating* that the world is that way.

The core notion in Dretske's theory is that of a representational system. Once Dretske's definition of this notion, below, is appreciated, it becomes relatively easy to see how misrepresentation is alleged to occur.

> By a representational system (RS) I shall mean any system whose function is to indicate how things stand with respect to some other object, condition, or magnitude. If RS's function is to indicate whether O is in condition A or B, for instance, and the way RS performs this function (*when* it performs it) is by occupying one of the two possible states, a (indicating that O is A) and b (indicating that O is B), then a and b are the expressive elements of RS and *what they represent* (about O) is *that* it is A (in the case of a) and *that* it is B (in the case of b).

(Reading 8, p.233)

Once 'O', 'A', 'B', 'RS', 'a' and 'b' are translated into an actual example, the definition is highly intuitive. Suppose you are an ostrich farmer. You need to know whether an ostrich you are interacting with is aggressive or benign. You can tell which is the case by virtue of the fact that whenever it is angry it opens its beak and emits a loud shriek, and it never does this save when it is angry (see Figure 16).

The representational system in this case is the ostrich's beak (= RS). Its function, for you at least, is to indicate whether the ostrich itself (= O) is angry (= A) or benign (= B). There are two possible states for O to be in, A and B, and two possible states for the beak to be in, open (= a) and closed (= b). When the RS (i.e. the beak) is carrying out what for you is its representational function, the states of the beak indicate the mood of the ostrich: a co-varies causally with A, and b co-varies causally with B. In other words, the beak is never closed when the ostrich is angry, and never wide open and emitting a squawk when the ostrich is benign.

As well as illustrating Dretske's definition of a representational system, we can also use this example to show how misrepresentation (i.e. inaccurate

Figure 16 The photograph on the left indicates a benign ostrich, while the one on the right shows an aggressive ostrich. Ostrich-with-an-open-beak events are causally correlated with aggressive-ostrich events. Photo: (left) © David Tipling/naturepl.com; (right) © The Natural History Museum, London.

representation) is possible under Dretske's definition. For suppose that the representational system is damaged in some way: the mechanisms linking the ostrich's mood and the state of the beak are broken. Perhaps the ostrich's muscles are in a spasmodic state, so that the beak is closed even though the ostrich is angry. You do not realize any of this. You continue to assign to the beak the function of indicating mood, but it fails to actually do so. Put simply, misrepresentation is what occurs when RS's indicating function goes unfulfilled.

ACTIVITY A frog's visual system is a representational system. How, according to Dretske, could it misrepresent the presence of a fly? Begin your answer by stating what RS, a, b, O, A and B would be in this case; then describe how the visual system could represent inaccurately.

DISCUSSION The variables in Dretske's definition can be adapted in various ways to our example, but something like the following will suffice:

RS: The frog's visual system   *O:* The zone around the frog's head

a: This visual system being in state F   *A:* There's a fly in this zone

b: This visual system not being in   *B:* There's no fly in this zone
state F

The frog's visual system has the function of indicating whether the zone around the frog's head has a fly in it by moving into state F whenever there is, and only when there is, a fly present. It misrepresents when it still has this function but either it is in state F and there is no fly, or this is a fly but it is not in state F.

Dretske's definition of 'representational system', and of what it is for a state to represent, makes it easy to see how misrepresentation could occur. All it takes is for a function to fail to be carried out. In this respect it is a big improvement over simple indicator theories, which *identify* representation with indication. But the hard part comes with trying to show how *purely natural entities* could be representational systems in his sense. The bulk of the extract from his book (Reading 8) is given over to this task. The main difficulty, here, is that functions often depend on humans to assign them, perhaps with some purpose in mind. If what gives a representational system its function depends on an external, purposive intelligence – such as an ostrich farmer – then the notion of representation that arises would be derived rather than intrinsic, akin to the kind of representation that depends on an interpreter behind the scenes – a homunculus, in other words. So this appeal to the function of indication needs to be treated with care.

Still, and as Dretske points out, the idea that purely natural devices have functions is a familiar one. My heart moves blood around my body. This is not something that it just happens to do. It is its function, something it is meant to do. But nor is it the case that this function is 'read into' the heart by an external intelligence. Its function arises as the result of natural selection in the course of the evolution of the species. Similar examples abound. It is the function of the swim-bladder to provide buoyancy; it is the function of a skunk's distinctive markings to warn predators; it is the function of a spider's web to catch flies. But if all these traits have functions, it makes sense to suppose that the representational systems possessed by humans and other animals have functions too. Dretske illustrates the point with a nice example.

> Some marine bacteria have internal magnets, magnetosomes, that function like compass needles, aligning themselves (and, as a result, the bacterium) parallel to the Earth's magnetic field ... Since the magnetic lines incline downward (toward geomagnetic north) in the northern hemisphere, bacteria in the northern hemisphere, oriented by their internal magnetosomes, propel themselves toward geomagnetic north. Since these organisms are capable of living only in the absence of oxygen, and since movement toward geomagnetic north will take northern bacteria away from the oxygen-rich and therefore toxic surface water and toward the comparatively oxygen-free sediment at the bottom, it is not unreasonable to speculate ... that *the function* of this primitive sensory system is to indicate the whereabouts of benign (i.e., anaerobic) environments.
>
> (Reading 8, pp.238–9)

If the function of this system is to indicate the whereabouts of an anaerobic environment, then, according to Dretske, this is what it represents.

Dretske attempts to show how a representational system could have its indicating function without this function necessarily being assigned by an external intelligence. If he is successful in this, he could claim to have given a satisfactorily naturalistic definition of representation that may have general application. He proceeds by classifying representational systems into three kinds, Types I, II, and III. They are distinguished according to how independent their representational operations are from human purpose.

ACTIVITY

Read the extract from Dretske's *Explaining Behavior: Reasons in a World of Causes* (Reading 8). Dretske classifies representational systems into three kinds. They differ in how much their status as representational systems derives from the existence of other representational systems. Type I systems are entirely conventional. They depend on humans (or other mental beings) assigning representational properties to the states of the system. Type III systems do not depend on an external interpreter at all: their capacity to represent is wholly intrinsic, underived, or 'natural' (i.e. unconventional). Type II systems are an interesting hybrid, with a capacity to represent that is in part derived or assigned, and in part intrinsic or natural. To avoid the charge of homuncularism, Dretske must claim that states of the human mind represent in the Type III way. Once he has made this distinction, he shows (in a way that will by now be familiar) how a Type III system, like any representational system, can misrepresent.

You may find it helpful to use Table 1 below as an aid to keeping track of the differences between the three types as you work through the Reading, which is relatively long.

Table 1   Three kinds of representational system

Type of representational system	What it indicates ...	What it functions to indicate ...
Type I	... depends on human beliefs and intentions.	... depends on human beliefs and intentions.
Type II	... does not depend on human beliefs and intentions.	... depends on human beliefs and intentions.
Type III	... does not depend on human beliefs and intentions.	... does not depend on human beliefs and intentions.

Although Dretske writes in a very accessible manner, with suggestive illustrations, there is one trap to beware of. He stipulates that he will use 'symbol' to mean 'conventional symbol' (p.234), whereas throughout the present book, and in the Fodor reading, 'symbol' is used more widely to mean any representational entity, and in particular to include mental representations that by hypothesis are not conventional. Dretske uses 'sign' for this more general notion.

(i)   What is a Type I representational system? Give an example.

(ii) What is a Type II representational system? Give an example.

(iii) What is a Type III representational system? Give an example.

(iv) How do Type III representational systems misrepresent? (This is set out in part V of the extract.)

(v) What are three ways in which misrepresentation, i.e. erroneous representation, can occur in Type III systems?

(i)   Type I representational systems depend on other representational systems – intelligent human beings, usually – for (a) their indicating function *and* (b) for this indicating function to be carried out. Their status as representational systems is, then, conventional, or 'derived', twice over.

DISCUSSION

Type I representational systems neither indicate, nor have the function to indicate, without homunculan assistance.

Dretske's main example is of a popcorn-and-coins tableau used to represent a basketball manoeuvre. Another example might be that of the code word 'SOS'. The function of this word is to indicate distress, and it is *given* this function by human beings; moreover, it *fulfils* the function it has been given because of the fact that humans use it when they are in distress and not otherwise.

(ii) Type II representational systems (a) depend on other representational systems to assign them a function to indicate some aspect of the world; but (b) what ensures that they in fact indicate this aspect of the world (i.e. represent accurately, fulfil their function) is independent of human intervention.

Dretske gives the example of tracks in the snow being *used by human beings* in the wilderness as a *natural* sign (and not a mere conventional symbol) of the earlier presence of a fox. Another familiar example is of red spots on the face of a child indicating (or 'naturally meaning' as Grice would put it) measles, when only the use of this fact by doctors or parents is what gives spots on the face the function to indicate measles.

(iii) Type III representations do not depend on other representational systems *either* (a) for having the function to indicate *or* (b) for fulfilling that function. If there are any systems of this kind, they will be purely natural in their representing. Dretske claims that human mental states are Type III representational systems.

The examples Dretske gives of purely natural representational systems are biological, because it is in biology that natural functions are most readily found. Perhaps the simplest example is of the species of marine bacteria with internal magnets, magnetosomes, whose natural function is to indicate oxygen-free environments. Another example is that of the frog's visual system. This seems to have the natural function of indicating the presence of flies to the frog.

(iv) Type III representational systems misrepresent in the same way that all representational systems misrepresent: their function to indicate is unfulfilled. Any device that *has* a function may *fail to carry out* that function: a damaged heart may cease to move the blood around the body; a broken web may fail to capture flies. The same goes for devices with the function to indicate. Since the frog–fly example is a Type III system, the Discussion in the previous activity already contains an illustration.

(v) Dretske mentions three kinds of situation in which a Type III representational system can misrepresent how things are. The system may come into existence functionally defective; it may become functionally defective over time; and it may be that the system finds itself operating outside an environment in which it can function effectively.

One nice feature of definitions of representation built around the notion of a function is that *widespread* misrepresentation becomes, potentially, easier to understand. We saw an example of this phenomenon earlier: the monkey that is led to hide under a dense bush whenever its visual system is in state E, even though E is triggered by any large bird and not just by monkey-eating eagles. If we want to say that E always represents the presence of an eagle, even though it does so inaccurately most of the time, we may be able to do so. As long as we can claim that E's function is to notify the monkey's escape mechanism of an overhead eagle, the fact that it carries out this function inefficiently is not important. A non-natural example is clearer. The presence on the cover of a tattered manuscript of the symbol below represents the play inside as having been written by William Shakespeare:

Even supposing that the majority of manuscripts with this symbol on their cover are forgeries, the function of the symbol is still to imply that Shakespeare wrote the play inside; and that could be why it is right to say that this is what the symbol expresses.

How could there be natural functions? Dretske does not offer a detailed answer. But he suggests that the heart has the function to move blood around the body because hearts have been selected for carrying out that task in the course of evolution. In the past, the fact that hearts moved blood around their owners' bodies increased the chances that their owners would survive and produce healthy offspring. That is why hearts exist. Likewise, according to Dretske, the sensory system possessed by the magnetotactic bacteria has the function to indicate the direction of an anaerobic environment because it has been selected to serve this purpose over many generations.

But few of our mental states are so primitive that they can plausibly be thought to result from natural selection alone. Consider someone thinking to themselves that the best way to open a jam-jar lid is to run hot water over it. Although it is the function of their mental state to correspond to how things are with jam-jar lids, it is extremely implausible to think that this particular function arose because it gave the person's ancestors a selective advantage. Most of these ancestors never had jam jars. If Dretske's theory is to work for cases it is meant for, i.e. human mental states, the notion of a natural function needs to be extended beyond evolved functions.

Teleosemanticists, Dretske included, usually make this extension by pointing out that one of the results of natural selection is the development of *mechanisms that allow us to learn*. So perhaps functions can be classified as natural not only if they have been naturally selected during evolution, but also if they result from the proper functioning of mechanisms that have been naturally selected because they enable learning. Consider Pavlov's dogs. They were conditioned by him to associate the sound of a bell with the imminent arrival of food, so that when they heard the bell, they began to salivate and get excited. On Dretske's account, the auditory state that is caused by the sound of the bell eventually comes to represent the imminent arrival of food. This is because the fact that it indicates the imminent arrival of food explains the fact that it has come to be used in a certain way – that is, to prompt behaviour appropriate to the imminent arrival of food. More sophisticated theories of learning than this can be integrated with Dretske's theory, and ultimately could be used to show how human beliefs and desires come to represent what they do.

Swampman: a counter-example to teleosemantic theories of content?

Donald Davidson introduced the character of Swampman in 'Knowing one's own mind' (1987, 19):

> Suppose lightning strikes a dead tree in a swamp; I am standing nearby. My body is reduced to its elements, while entirely by coincidence (and out of different molecules) the tree is turned into my physical replica. My replica, Swampman, moves exactly as I did; according to its nature it departs the swamp, encounters and seems to recognize my friends, and appears to return their greetings in English. It moves into my house and seems to write [philosophy articles]. No one can tell the difference.

He introduced the scenario simply as an alternative way of phrasing the Oscar/Twin Oscar example. But others have adapted it into an apparent counter-example to teleosemantic theories. For, intuitively, we would like to say that Swampman has plenty of thoughts, desires and so on, but there is nothing in Swampman's past that could give the states of his brain the functions said by Dretske and many other teleosemanticists to be essential for those states to represent.

Someone holds out a glass of orange juice to Swampman, whose 'sensory systems' (if it is fair to call them that) get into a state identical to the state that Davidson's sensory systems would get into if he were offered a glass of orange juice.

ACTIVITY

(i) On Fodor's CCT theory, can Swampman be described as genuinely sensing the glass of orange juice?

(ii) On Dretske's theory, can Swampman be described as genuinely sensing the glass of orange juice?

DISCUSSION

(i) Fodor's answer would be that if, for nomological reasons, Swampman's sensory states causally co-vary with the presence of the glass of juice then, yes, they represent it. Whether this is the case turns on what is true of Swampman now, not on what has or hasn't taken place in the past (see pp.225–6 of Reading 7). The example presents no particular problem for Fodor's theory.

(ii) Dretske's answer would have to be that, no, Swampman is not sensing the presence of orange juice. Dretske's account of representation has the consequence that the content of a natural representational system has to do with its history. In some cases, content will be determined by the evolutionary history of a particular representational system. In other cases, what will be relevant is the history of the individual organism as it learns to produce certain kinds of behaviour in response to certain kinds of representation. Swampman has not evolved, nor has it had time to learn how to behave in its environment. As a result, none of its states have the function to indicate how things are.

Critical to Swampman's being a potential problem for Dretske's theory is the fact that his notion of a natural function is defined in terms of facts about the past: the organism's learning history, or the evolutionary history of the species to which the organism belongs. As it is often put, natural functions in Dretske's sense are diachronic. *If* it were available, a synchronic notion of natural function, i.e. one defined in terms of present usefulness to the organism, would not be susceptible to the example in the same way.

Is this a serious problem for Dretske? How to answer this depends on one's intuitions and how seriously one takes them. And intuitions about this case differ. You may regard the suggestion that Swampman's state represents orange juice as equivalent to the suggestion that meteors in a desert on Mars accidentally spelling out the word 'Lo, Earthlings!' represent a greeting. That is, we are only even tempted to treat Swampman as perceiving the glass of orange juice because he/it superficially resembles creatures with perceptual states that are genuinely representational. On the other hand, you may be struck by the fact that Swampman is an extremely complicated object, with states, including the states of its 'brain' and 'sensory organs', that bear complex relations to each other and to the environment, with the result that Swampman is able to behave in ways that tend to secure what it needs to survive, and to protect it from being harmed. Swampman will not suddenly empty a glass of orange juice over the floor (assuming that the original Davidson would not). All these characteristics need explaining, and it would be odd if the explanation were of a different order than the explanations we offer for non-Swampcreatures (e.g. the original Davidson). But these latter explanations certainly seem to involve the attribution of representational states to the behaving creature. Many people are led by this kind of consideration to defend the intuition that Swampman is able to sense and to think about how things are in its/his environment, to wish for certain outcomes, and to plan how to achieve them. If this is right, it is a serious problem for teleosemantic theories.

Does Dretske's account solve the misrepresentation problem?

Consider the account Dretske gives of a frog's sensory system. In the frog's usual environment, the signals produced by this system have the function to indicate when a fly is present. If the frog is moved to a laboratory in which it is surrounded by small moving black dots that are not flies, its sensory system will cease to be a reliable indicator of flies. It no longer indicates what it functions to indicate. This is one way in which misrepresentation is supposed to occur (Reading 8, p.242, and (v) in the Discussion on p.127).

However, there is a worry here, as Dretske acknowledges. Why must we say that the function of the frog's sensory system is to indicate the presence of a *fly* in the environment rather than the presence of a *small black dot* in its visual field? After all, even in the frog's original environment, the system was a reliable indicator of the presence of small black dots in its visual field. Flies *are* small black dots. But if we say that, in its original environment, the sensory system functioned to indicate the presence of small black dots, then when the frog is moved to the laboratory its sensory system cannot be described as misrepresenting how things are if Dretske's theory is right. And yet, intuitively, the frog is making a mistake when it goes into state F and shoots its tongue out into a fly-free environment.

How might Dretske respond to this objection?

ACTIVITY

DISCUSSION

Dretske's might answer to this challenge by appealing to the way in which the states produced by the sensory system *are used to control the frog's behaviour*. The states produced by the sensory system cause the frog to shoot its tongue out at the object that triggers the sensory state. This behaviour, it seems, has the function to get flies into the frog's stomach. The frog will succeed in doing this only if there is a fly in the vicinity. The presence of small black dots, as such, will be of no help at all. So, what explains the fact that the frog's sensory states helped to ensure that its behaviour was successful is that, in the frog's usual environment, the sensory states indicated the presence of a fly, not the presence of a small black dot. So their function, and their representational content, is concerned with flies, not with small black dots.

Unfortunately, there are two problems with the response suggested in the Discussion. The first is that it is not clear what obliges us to accept that the helpfulness of the frog's sensory states is explained by their indicating the presence of flies rather than of small black dots. After all, in the frog's usual environment, small black dots *are* flies, so indicating the presence of a small black dot is a useful thing to do in that environment. Second, it is not clear why we should agree that the function of the frog's behaviour is to get flies, rather than small black dots, into the frog's stomach. In the frog's usual environment the small black dots are flies. So, in that environment, getting small black dots into the frog's stomach is a useful thing to do.

It is possible to envisage a similar difficulty arising when we attribute functions to other biological devices: for example, the heart. Is the function of the heart to move blood around the body, or is it just to make squeezing motions of a certain kind? You may think that there is something odd about the claim that the function of the heart is to make squeezing motions; but after all, given the way that heart is placed in the body, making squeezing motions of just the kind that a healthy heart does is a useful thing for it to do in that environment.

Making squeezing motions, you might think, is not the heart's function. Rather, making squeezing motions is how the heart carries out its function. Similarly, perhaps detecting small black dots is not the function of the frog's visual system; rather, this is just the way in which it carries out its function. This could be taken to suggest a diagnosis of the problem. Perhaps Dretske has not yet told us enough about how to assign functions to natural devices. If we could account for why it seems odd to say that the function of the heart is to make squeezing motions, then we might be in a better position to explain why it is wrong to say that the frog's visual system functions to detect small black dots. But others have drawn another, less sympathetic, conclusion and suggested that there is no such account to give: natural devices do not have determinate functions, and so we cannot appeal to the functions of natural representational systems to solve the misrepresentation problem.

Causal relations: a poor foundation for mental representation?

The previous few sections have focused on Dretske's teleosemantic version of the indicator approach to the naturalization of mental content. This detour was prompted by the problem of misrepresentation. It may turn out that an appeal to natural functions solves the problem without raising new and intractable difficulties in the process, but this question will not be discussed any further here. Instead we will close our consideration of indicator theories by asking whether causal relations could ever be a core ingredient of mental content given various features of the latter that are absent from the former.

If representation were simply a matter of causal relations between physical states of the brain and that which these states represent, it is difficult to see how we could ever represent abstract or theoretical objects, properties, or propositions. Take, for example, the concept of conjunction (i.e. the concept expressed in English by the word 'and'). Conjunction is essential to our thinking and reasoning, and we need to be able to distinguish it from, for example, disjunction ('or') or conditionality ('if ... then ...'). But conjunction, disjunction and conditionality are abstract notions. For this reason it is not easy to see how they could be implicated in causal relations that give rise to particular types of physical state in the brain of a human subject. Fodor's CCT, for example, is meant to be a theory of how symbols represent. But how could the tokening of a symbol be caused by the property of conjunction? It is not clear that this even makes sense.

There are plenty of other examples. We seem able to think about numbers, but numbers, too, are usually thought of as abstract objects rather than part of the physical universe. How could the tokening of an inner symbol be caused by *fifteen-ness*? In addition to abstract notions are complex theoretical notions like those of progress, Freudian slips, supply-side economics, or (to take an example close to our present interests) mental content. These concepts seem to be embedded in theories, often very speculative ones, and one picks up the concepts by learning the theory, not by entering into causal relations with actual examples of what they stand for.

Sometimes these speculative theories turn out to be mistaken, and this points to a second feature of representation that is potentially troublesome from the perspective of indicator theorists: our capacity to think about what does not exist. The theory of combustion that preceded the discovery of oxygen is a case in point. Central to that theory was the notion of phlogiston. We know now that there is no such thing as phlogiston. The kinds of properties phlogiston was supposed to have are not possessed by anything in reality. But supporters of phlogiston theory in the eighteenth century were presumably able to *think* that phlogiston had those properties. How could this be explained in terms of causal relations? Only actual events and objects have causal significance. Phlogiston, like Santa Claus, cannot cause any change in the physical state of someone's brain.

A final feature of representation that gives rise to difficulties for causal theories like the simple indicator theory, the CCT, and perhaps Dretske's teleosemantic theory, has been called (by John Searle) *aspectual shape*. When we think about an object, we think about it in a certain way. When you make a judgement about your home, you will think of it *as* a home, or *as* a physical structure, or *as* a financial commitment, etc. Which of an object's many aspects you think of it under will shape the thought itself, and it will do so in a way that is hard to explain as arising out of causal relations between the object and the subject who is thinking of the object.

This is brought out clearly in the myth of Oedipus. Oedipus ends up marrying Jocasta, whose husband he has killed, without realizing that Jocasta is in fact his mother or that the man he has killed is his father. The same entity – the same woman, that is – can be thought of by Oedipus in two different ways, or under two different aspects: as Jocasta and as his mother. As we might put it, it seems possible for him to believe he is marrying Jocasta without his believing that he is marrying his own mother. This difference in content between the two beliefs is critical to the explanation of why Oedipus behaves as he does. But how could this difference be captured in terms of causal relations between the state of Oedipus's brain, on the one hand, and the object he is thinking about, on the other? Any causal relation between his brain and *Jocasta* is also a relation between his brain and *his mother*, since they are the same person, with exactly the same causal properties, even if Oedipus is ignorant of the fact.

These three problematic features of representation have, needless to say, been addressed by both Dretske and Fodor, and whether they are successful in their response is beyond the scope of this chapter. But it is fair to say that these features are widely regarded as raising, at the very least, serious difficulties for theories that treat representation as fundamentally a matter of some kind of causal correspondence between the representing state and what that state represents. The naturalistic theory we will be examining in the next chapter takes a different approach, and has the advantage of being able to explain these features with apparent ease.

Chapter summary

How is it that we are able to think about the world beyond us? Naturalistic theories of mental content seek to answer this question by providing conditions under which a particular physical state of an organism can be said to represent, or be about, an object, feature or situation in the world. In this chapter we have been looking at indicator theories. They are often inspired by simple, naturally occurring organisms or mechanisms that represent – or perhaps proto-represent – by virtue of standing in some sort of causal correspondence with the world.

A simple version of this idea treats representing as nothing other than indicating. But simple indicator theories seem unable to account for the possibility of misrepresentation (i.e. inaccurate representation). What are, intuitively, conditions in which a physical system is representing inaccurately are also conditions in which, if the simple indicator theory were right, it would not be representing at all (pp.118–19). A variant of this difficulty, due to Fodor, suggests that any apparent misrepresentation can be re-described as a correct (but 'disjunctive') representation (pp.119–20).

Dretske's teleosemantic solution to the problem of misrepresentation involves dropping the simple idea that representation is indication in favour of the idea that representation is a matter of having the function to indicate (p.121). Because a physical system can have the function to indicate but fail to carry out that function successfully, it is possible for it to represent inaccurately (pp.122–3, 126–7 (iv)–(v)). Objections to this theory usually centre on the appeal it makes to natural functions. The Swampman example seems to show that tying the notion of a natural function to evolution or learning history is too restrictive (pp.129–31). And the misrepresentation problem may in any case re-emerge as a problem of how to isolate functions precisely (pp.131–2).

We ended by considering some features of representation that call into question the strategy of looking to extremely simple and naturally occurring organisms and mechanisms for inspiration in the search for a naturalistic account of mental content. Mental content has a number of features that causal co-variance – the only species of representation present in simple systems – seems to lack: abstraction, theoretical commitment, existential non-commitment, and aspectual shape (pp.133–5).

Further reading

Indicator and teleosemantic theories are reviewed in many book-length introductions to the philosophy of mind, including (in increasing order of difficulty) Crane 2003, Sterelny 1990, and Cummins 1989.

Fodor's asymmetric dependency solution to his disjunction problem is stated in part V of Reading 7 and elaborated in Fodor 1990. He changes his emphasis and his mind in Fodor 1994.

Dretske's view as found in Reading 8, classified as an indicator theory here for simplicity, is in fact a hybrid of an indicator approach (found in a purer state in Dretske 1981, and criticized in that state by Fodor in Reading 7) and a teleosemantic approach. Distinct teleosemantic theories include the 'success semantics' found in Papineau 1993 (summarized in Papineau 1996), Millikan 1984, and Price 2001. Millikan's position, though not discussed here, has been particularly influential, and is most easily approached through her essay 'Biosemantics' (Millikan 1989, reprinted in Millikan 1993 and in slimmed-down format in Macdonald and Macdonald 1995).

Papineau 1993 and Stalnaker 1984 describe and exploit the apparent inter-definability of belief and desire. The Swampman objection is pressed in Cummins 1989 with an interesting reply in Papineau 2001.

CHAPTER 6

Representation as functional role

Contrasting metaphors: indicator lights versus pictures

The metaphor that drives causal co-variance theories is of representation as an indicator light flashing on and off inside the agent's brain. This light represents because its flashing is in correspondence with (and caused by) the presence and absence in the external environment of some entity, feature or circumstance. Attempts to make this work as more than metaphor, we saw, are not easy. Satisfactory responses to the challenges discussed in the previous chapter may become available. In the meantime these challenges give impetus to a different conception of mental representation, built around a competing metaphor for representation, that of a picture in the agent's mind. The elements of a picture are meaningless by themselves, mere points on a canvas. They are able to represent only in combination with other elements of the canvas. Only by virtue of the relation they stand in *to one another* do the different elements of a picture have meaning.

This is just another metaphor, and no one suggests that the brain literally contains pictures. But many have claimed that the relations a physical state of the brain bears to other actual or possible physical states of the brain are what can give it its power to represent. These various relations, taken together, constitute the state's functional role, and to define representation in terms of these relations is to adopt the functional role perspective. (The notion of 'function' at work differs from Dretske's, as we will see.) This perspective will be our focus in the first half of the present chapter.

To illustrate the functional role approach, suppose that Angela's brain is in state X in the circumstances set out below.

> Whenever Angela's brain is in state X and she is <u>hungry</u>, she is caused to <u>decide</u> to move towards the table.

> Whenever Angela <u>perceives</u> lettuce, tomatoes, eggs, cutlery, crockery, a water jug, etc. on the table, her brain is caused to go into state X.

State X's functional role is the pattern of causal relations it bears to other mental states (underlined). The fact that state X has this causal profile, a functional role theorist might say, is what makes being in state X equivalent to *believing that dinner is ready*. Just as a blob of paint on a canvas only depicts a bird on a lake by virtue of its relation to other parts of the painting and what they mean, so X counts as this belief because of its relation to certain other states and their content.

The functional role for believing that dinner is ready will, on reflection, be far more complex than is suggested by the example above. Angela could be hungry and believe that dinner is ready and yet still not decide to move towards the table. For example, she might decide to wait until the others have sat down so she can rifle through her brother's desk, or she might think that dinner is ready in the garden, not at the table in the dining room. And she might not believe that dinner is ready even though she perceives it, because she might think she is perceiving a hologram. But these considerations do not show that it is wrong to identify content with functional role; they show only that the functional role that makes X the mental state that it is can be, and usually will be, extremely complex.

We saw in chapter 4 (p.90) that the psychological attitudes – believing, desiring, etc. – can be distinguished from one another according to their functional properties. The function of believing is to represent how things are, whereas this is not the function of desiring. The present theory can be thought of as an extension of that idea into a more ambitious principle, one for distinguishing *between* beliefs with different contents (and between desires with different contents), not merely for distinguishing beliefs from desires. It should be noted that many authors – including Dretske and Fodor, for example – endorse the more limited view that the attitudes need to be defined functionally without accepting that content is a functional notion. So 'functional role theory' is being used here to pick out the more ambitious claim.

Before looking at Block's theory it will be helpful to note two contrasts between functional role theories and indicator theories, and one similarity. The first contrast is that functional role theories tend to be internalist rather than externalist. Even if the relations between states of the brain *give rise to* a representational relation that links inner states with external circumstances, functional role is in the first instance a matter of relations between physical states within the agent's head, not of relations between something in the head and something outside it.

The second contrast with indicator theories is that representation from the functional role perspective is holistic rather than atomistic. Atomistic theories of representation, as you may recall from the previous chapter (p.117), hold that the representational properties of one state (or symbol) do not depend on the representational properties of another. Holism treats the representational properties of different states (or symbols) as interdependent. The content of state X in the example above is identified by reference to the content of other states the agent, Angela, might be in. Indicator theories, by contrast, tend to be atomistic.

For all that, functional role theories of the kind that interest us here are similar to indicator theories in that they are intended to *naturalize* psychological content. This is why they, too, tend to be couched in terms of causal relations and laws. It is just that the causal relations appealed to by functional role theorists are not relations between the representing state and the entity being represented. Rather, they are relations between one state and another.

Conceptual role theories

As with indicator theories, the functional role perspective can be stated, as it has been so far, in terms that are neutral over whether being in a mental state consists of having a sentence in the head. Any physicalist, even one who is sceptical about Mentalese, will want to say what it is about a particular brain state that makes it the mental state that it is. Isolating its functional role – its causal relations with other actual and possible brain states – offers one possible way of doing this. But functional role theories are favoured by many who, because they are impressed by the explanatory potential of thinking of brains as symbol-manipulation devices, *do* think that being in a mental state is a matter of tokening a symbol of some kind. The task of assigning representational properties to brain states, for them, comes down to the task of saying what the inner symbols represent.

In this guise, functional role theorists claim that the meaning *of a symbol* is a matter of how it is used, and in particular of how it is tokened in the various representational systems of the individual, in combination with other symbols. Functional role theories that are specifically concerned with a symbol's meaning are commonly called 'conceptual role theories', to distinguish them from the wider class of functional role theories. The main example we will be looking at of a functional role theory, Ned Block's, is of this kind, though most of the lessons we will draw from consideration of his position, since they are lessons about holism, generalize. Holism is, after all, a commitment of all functional role theories.

For conceptual role theorists, whether a symbol, H, means horse or cow depends on what use a person (or rather, their brain) puts the symbol to, most of all in forming beliefs. If H is used in holding the beliefs in list 1 below, it could be said to express the property *being a horse*. If it is used in holding the beliefs in list 2, then it could be said to express the property *being a cow*.

List 1	*List 2*
Hs eat grass.	Hs eat grass.
Hs live on farms.	Hs live on farms.
H milk is often drunk by foals.	H milk is often drunk by humans or calves.
Hs have one stomach.	Hs have four stomachs.
The British monarch rides an H during ceremonies at Buckingham Palace.	The British monarch does not ride an H during ceremonies at Buckingham Palace.

To say that H is 'used in the belief that Hs eat grass' is to say that H is tokened together with certain other symbols of Mentalese, those that could be expressed in English as 'eat' and 'grass', in the subject's belief box. What makes it appropriate to translate these other symbols in this way turns on which beliefs *they* are used in, i.e. on *their* conceptual role.

Suppose list 1 (rather than list 2) captures H's conceptual role for a particular subject. Why is it fair to take this as implying that H is about horses: the actual living, breathing beasts outside this subject's head? In contrast with indicator theories, nothing explicitly requires the existence of a causal link between the symbol and actual instances of horses. What makes H about horses 'out there' is the possibility of converting list 1 into a description that is true of horses and only horses:

Something is an H if and only if it eats grass, it lives on a farm, any milk it produces is likely to be drunk by a foal, it has one stomach, and it is the kind of thing that the British monarch might ride during ceremonies at Buckingham Palace.

There are affinities here with the descriptivist theory of word reference discussed in chapter 3 (pp.44–9). Just as what a *word* refers to according to the descriptivist theory depends on the attributes associated with the word by the speaker, so what a mental symbol picks out in the world depends – according to the conceptual role theory – on which beliefs of the subject it is used in. All the problems that causal links to the extra-cranial world seem to generate, recounted in the previous chapter, appear to slip away. That, at least, is one hope of those who favour this approach.

We saw earlier that functional role theories are holistic about the content of mental states. In the case of conceptual role theories, this amounts to the assertion that the representational properties of a symbol are holistic if understood in terms of conceptual role. Show that this is indeed the case.

ACTIVITY

DISCUSSION

What H expresses depends on which beliefs of the subject it is used in, but which beliefs it is used in depends on what other symbols it is conjoined with in the subject's belief box and, crucially, *what those other symbols express*. For example:

H milk is often consumed by Xs

yields different propositions according to whether symbol X expresses the property of being a human or the property of being a foal:

H milk is widely consumed by foals.

H milk is widely consumed by humans.

Intuitively, only the first of these would make H expressive of the property *being a horse*.

Block's defence of conceptual role semantics

A large part of what draws people to the conceptual role approach is how adapted it seems to be to examples that were troublesome to indicator theories.

Consider the difficulty noted in the previous chapter of adapting the metaphor of indication to abstract concepts, including the concept of conjunction ('and'). Let us suppose that conjunction is expressed by the following mental symbol: &. (Giving it this name is meant to serve as nothing more than a memory aid, just as the symbols expressing the property *being a horse* has been labelled H.) What must be true of & for it to express conjunction? The answer that & must stand in a causal co-variance relation with the property *andness* does not even seem to make sense.

An answer expressed in terms of functional role is more plausible. For someone to use H in a way that characterizes it as expressing the property of being a horse, they must believe the items in list 1, or something like them. So how must someone use & for it to express conjunction? Intuitively, the issue depends on how they use & in making inferences. They would need to recognize that certain inferences are permitted, obligatory even, while others are not. So, for example, they would need to be well disposed towards inferring to either (2) or (3) from (1):

1   William the Conqueror was born in Normandy & Winston Churchill married an American.

2   William the Conqueror was born in Normandy.

3   Winston Churchill married an American.

They would also need to *refrain* from inferring from (2) alone to (1), or from (3) alone to (1). The full range of inferences is given in Table 2.

Table 2   The inferential links that would show & expresses conjunction

Inference	Legitimate?
(1); therefore (2)	Yes
(1); therefore (3)	Yes
(2), (3); therefore (1)	Yes
(2); therefore (1)	No
(3); therefore (1)	No

If someone's brain is constituted in such a way that these inferential patterns are respected for *all* sentences containing & and not merely for 'William the

Conqueror was born in Normandy & Winston Churchill married an American', then & could be said to express conjunction.

Read parts I and II of the extracts from Ned Block's 'Advertisement for a semantics for psychology' (Reading 9). In part I he says what he has in mind by a conceptual role theory (or 'conceptual role semantics (CRS)' as he calls it), asserting that it is a naturalistic theory that gels with the computational theory of mind he also endorses. The central example he uses is of a symbol he calls '→'. He outlines how it must be used if it is to count as expressing conditionality ('if ... then ...'). This parallels the example of &, above. In part II he considers three of its naturalistic ('reductionist') competitors and rejects them, mainly for reasons that will be familiar from earlier chapters.

ACTIVITY

(i)   What must the conceptual role of → be for it to express conditionality ('the material conditional' as Block calls it)?

(ii) Does Block take every single aspect of what a person believes using a symbol to be relevant to what that symbol expresses?

(iii) How does Block argue against Gricean, indicator, and teleosemantic approaches to reducing mental representation to natural properties?

(i)   A symbol's conceptual role depends on its causal relations to other symbols. To express conditionality, → must be such that when a person believes the first two propositions below, for example, they must be causally disposed to believe the third:

DISCUSSION

>   The cat is on the mat → the cat is asleep
>
>   The cat is on the mat
>
>   The cat is asleep

(ii) Yes, for Block, conceptual role is identified with 'total causal role' (p.245). This means that *every single belief (or inferential relation)* involving the symbol is relevant to what the symbol expresses. The significance of this will become apparent when we come to evaluate the theory's strengths and weaknesses.

(iii) Gricean theories cannot be extended to internal languages, he says, because computational transformations are automatic in character rather than intended, deliberated over, or thought out; and mental symbols are certainly not tokened with the intention *to communicate*. Against the other two positions he deploys arguments seen already: Fodor's disjunction argument against simple indicator approaches, and a variant of the

> Swampman example – an accidental physical duplicate of an ordinary baby – against teleosemantic approaches.

The argument Block deploys against teleosemantic theories brings out something that has been left tacit to this point: that when functional role theorists talk of 'function', they mean something quite different from function as it is used in, for example, Dretske's theory. For Dretske, functions that are grounded in human purposes are not naturalistic. He concludes that, to be naturalistic, functions must either be symptoms of natural selection, or they must be the result of the application by the individual organism of learning mechanisms that are themselves the result of natural selection. Functions, for him, are diachronic not synchronic – they require a past. That is why Swampman is a problem case. For Block and other functional role theorists, functional role is not based on either human purpose or past development. It is determined simply by the causal relations *that exist in the present* between the various states of the organism. Indeed, common alternative names for 'functional role' are 'causal role' and 'inferential role'. Because they are operating with a synchronic notion of function, Swampman is not a problem for functional role theorists.

We saw earlier that their facility with conjunction puts conceptual role theories at an apparent advantage over pure indicator theories. Conceptual role seems better placed than causal co-variance to capture other kinds of concept, too. It is hard to see how the concepts expressed by theoretical terms such as 'radiation', 'barometer', 'Freudian slip', 'progress' or 'square root' could be treated in terms of causal co-variation, since these objects do not have a characteristic causal profile. Brains cannot be caused by square roots to token a symbol, $\sqrt{}$, since square roots are abstract objects. As such, they do not have causal properties in any obvious sense. Far worse are concepts like *phlogiston*. Phlogiston does not exist, so cannot cause anything; yet the notion of phlogiston was a central notion in early chemical theories of fire, so it must be possible to *think* about phlogiston. It is more promising to suppose that a mental symbol could represent phlogiston by having a characteristic conceptual role than by supposing it to be in some causal relation to the stuff itself.

As well as logical concepts like *conjunction*, theoretical and abstract concepts like *square root*, and 'empty' concepts like *phlogiston*, Block shows how well placed the approach seems to be to deal with mistaken identity cases. Recall the difficulty for indicator theories that these cases gave rise to (pp.133–4). The causal relations between Oedipus's brain states and Jocasta are identical to the causal relations between those same brain states and Oedipus's mother. That is, since Jocasta and Oedipus's mother are but one person, there is only one person to do the causing. So a theory of representation couched in terms of causal relations between a brain state and what it purportedly represents will not, apparently, be able to capture the difference between Oedipus's believing that Jocasta is alone this evening and his believing that his mother is alone this evening. Yet this difference makes a difference to how Oedipus behaves (given his desires), and hence must figure in the explanation of his behaviour. If a symbol's representing Jocasta and its representing Oedipus's mother can be captured as a difference in conceptual role, then that would be a very attractive feature of conceptual role theories. In the next activity you are asked to read Block's treatment of, among other things, this kind of case.

Read part III of the extract from Block's paper. In the first two paragraphs he **ACTIVITY** outlines how a theory of representation along the lines he favours can be used in psychological explanation. He goes on to demonstrate how flexible it is in dealing with a variety of cases of psychological explanation, including cases of mistaken identity.

(i) When Block says that conceptual role is a theory of 'narrow' meaning, what does mean by this? What is wide meaning? Answer by saying which of the pairs below differ in narrow meaning, and which in wide meaning.

  (A1)   Water is wet (as believed by Oscar).

  (A2)   Water is wet (as believed by Oscar's twin).

  (B1)   Jocasta is alone tonight (as believed by Oedipus).

  (B2)   My mother is alone tonight (as believed by Oedipus).

(ii) Why (according to Block) is narrow meaning relevant to psychological explanation in a way that wide meaning is not? Explain by reference to the examples in (i).

(iii) Why might *total* holistic theories be especially well suited to psychological explanation? (See (ii) in the previous activity.)

(i) Narrow meaning is what (A1) and (A2) have in common but (B1) and (B2) **DISCUSSION** do not; wide meaning is the meaning that (B1) and (B2) have in common but (A1) and (A2) do not. Narrow meaning depends entirely on what is in the head, i.e. on internal physical constitution. It depends (or 'supervenes' as Block puts it) on the physical structure of the brain. Wide content can depend on factors outside the head such as the fact that Jocasta is identical with Oedipus' mother, or that the liquid in the local environment has a particular underlying physical structure.

(ii) Narrow content, i.e. all content that abstracts away from factors outside the subject's head, is all that matters to psychological explanation. That, at least, is the claim made by Block, and in this he is giving voice to the thesis Putnam labelled 'methodological solipsism' (p.64 above). The fact that Jocasta and Oedipus' mother are identical is wholly irrelevant to how Oedipus behaves unless this identity is registered by him. Since it is not, (B1) and (B2) have different implications for how he will act. (A1) and (A2), by contrast, do not differ narrowly, only widely, which is why Oscar and his twin will behave in exactly the same way.

(iii) Every Mentalese sentence involving H, even sentences expressing quite peripheral beliefs, is potentially relevant to the psychological explanation of the agent's behaviour. (For example, imagine that A believes that the British monarch rides an H in a parade outside Buckingham Palace on his or her official birthday. Suppose too that B does not believe this but believes everything else about Hs that A believes. On the monarch's official birthday, A and B may both desire to see an H, but only A will be inclined to head off to Buckingham Palace.) Since conceptual role is meant to be a theory of narrow meaning, and narrow meaning is the kind that enters into psychological explanation (see (ii)), it is tempting to think that even apparently peripheral beliefs must be thought of as part of H's conceptual role, i.e. of what it expresses. This is exactly what total holism insists on. It is also, apparently, why Block identifies a symbol's meaning with its total causal role.

It is possible for Oedipus to desire to be alone with Jocasta without him thereby desiring to be alone with his mother. Without this difference in content between the two desires we could not explain why he behaves as he does. It is therefore an attractive feature of conceptual role theories that, unlike indicator theories, they can easily account for this difference. Conceptual roles are extremely *nuanced*, in the same way that mental content appears to be. A difference in just one single belief involving a symbol can affect that symbol's representational properties. The fact that 'J is my mother' is absent from

Oedipus' belief box is enough for J not to mean what it would have meant if this sentence had been in his belief box. When it does finally enter his belief box, his desires, and his behaviour, change quite radically.

Holism: circularity and idiosyncrasy

The fact that Block's conceptual role theory seems able to deal with examples that are problematic for indicator theories is a good sign, both for it and for the functional role approach in general. But on its own it is not enough. The theory must be independently plausible, not just better than the indicator theory (if indeed it is that). And ironically, most objections to it come back to the holism that allows functional role theories to capture nuances of content – which, we just saw, is part of what makes them attractive. In this section we will see how holistic theories of mental content are vulnerable to the charge of being both *circular* and *idiosyncratic*. If these charges turn out to be warranted, holistic theories are worse than false; they are incoherent.

Let us start with the circularity charge. Suppose we take the representational properties of a symbol to depend on the beliefs it is used in, where the content of these beliefs depends in turn on the representational properties of the *other* symbols used. In our earlier example, part of what makes it the case that H expresses the property of being a horse was said to be its use in believing:

Hs eat grass.

What this use amounts to is that H is tokened alongside two other symbols, call them E and G, where E expresses the relation *eats* and G expresses the property *being grass*. But what makes it the case that E and G express these properties and not the properties *drinks* and *being beer*? That would certainly affect whether H expresses *being a horse*, so it had better not be what they mean. But notice the circularity that would follow from insisting that what rules out E and G from meaning *drinks* and *being beer* is that they are joined together with H, where this means *being a horse*, and horses do not drink beer. That would be to presuppose H's meaning, when H's meaning is what we are trying to establish in the first place. We seem entitled to claim only that the agent believes:

Hs E G

But to say this is to say nothing more than that the agent has three symbols in his or her belief box. It is not to say what those symbols mean.

Responses to this charge of circularity are available, though how convincing they are is not easy to judge. Physical states may depend on one another for their meaning, but if that dependence is not to collapse into circularity there must be some way of pegging their collective content to something real, so to speak. A metaphor for how this might be possible is of meaning as like a spider's web. Most mental symbols mean what they do because of their relation to other mental symbols in a web of beliefs, but the whole web only has meaning because the legs of the web are attached to the input of our perceptual systems (and perhaps also the output of our motor systems, i.e. the systems that mediate between our decisions and our actual actions). In terms of our example, let us assume it is true that E and G depend for their meaning on the meaning of H, and vice versa. But they also derive significance from other symbols they are tokened with, which are tokened in turn alongside still more symbols in other beliefs. Eventually one will come to what might be called 'primitive' symbols, which express concepts like *appearing to be red*. Primitive concepts do not receive their content holistically; rather, what makes a symbol express the property of appearing to be red is its causal association with the mechanisms of the perceptual system. Perceptual systems serve as an interface with the outside world. On this proposal, sketchy though it is, primitive concepts link the whole edifice of semantically interrelated symbols to the outside world – or at least to its perceivable properties.

Whether or not this reply can be made to work, there is another and more startling consequence of holism that still needs to be addressed: idiosyncrasy. If functional role determined what we believe, no two people would ever, in practice, hold the *same* belief about anything. For two people to hold the same belief – that horses eat grass, say – is for them to be in a state that has exactly the same causal relations to every other state; and for this to be so, these other states would themselves need to be related in exactly the same way to yet more states. A difference in *any* belief or desire would mean a difference in *all* beliefs and desires. No one could agree on anything without agreeing on everything, including their own name, what town they were born in, and how many corgis the Queen owns.

In Block's conceptual-role version of the theory, the idiosyncrasy problem can be generated by asking how two Mentalese sentences could ever express the same proposition in the belief boxes of two people, A and B. All symbols in the sentences, including (let us say) H_A and H_B, would need to express the same property. For this to be the case, all the beliefs that A has using H_A must be the same as the beliefs B has using H_B. Suppose A's beliefs are as given in list 1 above (p.140), and B's are the same but without the final item on the list (the belief about the British monarch riding an H during ceremonies). This would be enough to show that H_A and H_B do not really have the same content. And this will create a domino effect, starting with all the symbols that H_A and H_B are tokened alongside, until eventually there is *no proposition whatsoever* that both A and B believe.

It is bad enough that A and B could not share any beliefs unless they share every single belief, something that is practically impossible. But the argument can be adapted to show that we cannot ever believe the same thing from moment to moment. There is nearly always some small matter over which we will change our opinion from one moment to the next – what the time is, what we are seeing, whether it is sunny, whether it is time for a tea break, etc. – and by parallel reasoning, there could be no such thing as a belief with duration, not even the belief that China is in Asia. The idiosyncrasy of content, then, is an extremely counterintuitive consequence, if it is a consequence, of total holism.

Of course, we do think we can say legitimately that two people occasionally believe the same proposition, and that a person can hold the same belief from moment to moment despite small changes in what they are thinking. The problem is how a conceptual role theorist can allow either of these things to be true. Many holists are tempted to talk about beliefs being, if not strictly *identical*, then at least *similar* in content. This is precisely what Block suggests at the end of Reading 9. It is what Fodor and Lepore insist is not an available option in Reading 10.

Finish Reading 9 (part IV), in which Block expresses the hope that a notion of **ACTIVITY** *similarity* of content can replace one of *identity* of content. Though he does not say so, he has the kinds of worries expressed above in mind. Then read Fodor and Lepore's rejection of this move in Reading 10.

(i) Why do Fodor and Lepore (in part I of Reading 10) think that it *matters* that our psychological states have shared contents?

(ii) Early in part II, Fodor and Lepore consider two ways of making sense of similarity in what is believed. What are these, and why are they allegedly beside the point?

(i) If psychology (including but not only folk psychology) is to be a science, which is a background aspiration for all the authors we have read so far on this topic, it needs to trade in 'robust generalizations'. Fodor and Lepore assume that a science must culminate in explanations couched in terms of laws, and the laws of psychology, if there are any, are generalizations *over different individuals*, just as the laws of gravity generalize over all bodies with mass. But if no one ever has the same thought, then the generalizations psychology makes are impossible: idiosyncrasy is incompatible with psychological laws. They point out that even forming generalizations that apply to a single person over time is impossible, since we are constantly changing what we believe.

(ii) The first is that two people have similar beliefs if most of their beliefs are the same but some are different. The second is that similarity requires agreement only over the beliefs each holds with conviction. Fodor and Lepore argue that both miss the point. These two colloquial senses of similarity in overall belief systems both presuppose a notion of belief identity. Take the second, for example. In order to establish that there is agreement even over only the beliefs each person holds with conviction, it needs to be established that they share this conviction towards *the same* beliefs, i.e. beliefs *with identical* content. But what it is for their beliefs to have identical content is precisely what is missing from the holistic picture. What is needed to refute the argument, say Fodor and Lepore, is a notion of a belief state's being similar but not identical in content to some other belief state, where this notion does not tacitly presuppose the notion of two beliefs being identical in content. No such notion is available, they claim.

Holism and error

To say that no two people ever share the same belief certainly sounds odd. But how serious is it really? After all, one alleged attraction of holism is that it is so nuanced. What we believe affects how we behave, and we all behave differently in different circumstances. As the case of Oedipus demonstrates, a single change in belief, a single discovery, can have profound implications for behaviour. So perhaps functional role theorists' commitment to idiosyncrasy is a virtue, not a vice. But there is a third potential consequence of holism, equally serious as idiosyncrasy and circularity. Block mentions error in his paper, but only as a problem for the indicator theories that he rejects (p.247). He does not pause to confirm that his own theory fares any better. But there are reasons to think that total holism is just as incompatible with the possibility of error.

Consider the example of & as an expression of conjunction. Suppose that instead of being disposed to make the inferences one would expect of a trained logician, our subject, Andy, is reluctant to recognize the legitimacy of inferences with the following slightly arcane but apparently valid form:

P & Q

R → not-P

Therefore Not-R

(Compare: 'I am poor and I am quiet; if I were rich then I would not be poor; therefore I am not rich.' The arrow, →, is being used, as in Reading 9, as the symbol for conditionality, i.e. 'if ... then ...'.) Perhaps Andy only resists the inference when the topic of the argument, once the meaning of P, Q and R is specified, reminds him of childhood holidays by the sea. Should we say that he is *wrong* in resisting the inference in these cases? That seems a very reasonable description. But notice that an alternative would be to describe his resistance, not as ever so slightly suspect logical ability, but as a demonstration that & does not, after all, express conjunction (or else that → does not express conditionality). Block gives us no reason to rule this alternative interpretation out. In fact it seems to be *required* by his theory. Because he is a total holist, what & expresses depends on every single aspect of its causal-functional role. So Andy's reluctance to embrace the inference above appears to show that his & symbol does not express conjunction at all. Rather, it expresses something like conjunction-except-that-the-inference-above-is-sometimes-not-valid. This is resonant of the misrepresentation case in the previous chapter, pp.119–20, and the problem of ensuring that H expresses horse and not horse-or-cow-on-a-dark-and-rainy-night.

A parallel argument would seem to show that, if conceptual role semantics is true, it is impossible for someone to believe falsely that horses run on petroleum. How might this argument go?

ACTIVITY

DISCUSSION   If someone believed that Hs run on petroleum, the proper conclusion to draw might be, not that they falsely believed that Hs run on petroleum, but rather that H does not express the property *being a horse*.

One response to this argument for the impossibility of error would be to say that peripheral beliefs involving H are susceptible to error, but central ones are not. So it is possible to mistakenly believe that the British monarch does not ride an H, but it is impossible to mistakenly believe that Hs are not animals, or that they do not usually have four legs. This depends on distinguishing the central beliefs from the peripheral ones, and treating the central ones alone as fixing the meaning of H. Relative to the bedrock of these central beliefs, which could not possibly be mistaken, the peripheral ones could be. So error is possible, but not always so. That is something, at least.

Against this response, there does not seem to be any principled way of saying which beliefs 'count for more' than others. But even supposing a principled answer is available, excluding marginal beliefs would involve abandoning the total holism Block advocates, along with the advantages total holism appears to bring with it. Saying that only some beliefs are factors in the symbol's expressive character may generate a solution to the problem of error, but it would mean losing the nuanced, finely discriminated representations that are part of what makes the functional role perspective attractive. For example, whether someone believes that Hs are ridden at royal ceremonies might be what explains their travelling to Buckingham Palace. And whether Oedipus believes that J is distinct from his mother will affect his behaviour. Since every belief has potential behavioural consequences, every belief will need to be reflected in the content of the symbols used in it. So Block is caught in an apparent dilemma (see Table 3). It is an open question whether he can break free from it.

Table 3

What a symbol represents depends on its ...	Does this allow for the possibility of error?	Does it allow for nuanced psychological explanation?
... total causal role	No	Yes
... partial causal role	Yes	No

Chapter summary

Functional role theorists take the content of a mental state to turn on its causal relations to other states rather than to external objects. On this approach, the content a state has is a holistic matter (p.139). Block's conceptual role version of the functional role approach was considered in some detail. He takes the meaning of a symbol to be tied to its conceptual role – to the different beliefs it is used in or the inferential relations it is implicated in, for example (pp.142–3). What a belief state's content is depends on the meaning of all the symbols in the Mentalese sentence, so the symbols of Mentalese are, on this view, semantically interdependent. This interdependency, or 'holism', is characteristic of all functional role theories, not just Block's, and is claimed by some critics to result in circularity (pp.147–8). A second charge often made against holistic theories of content, pressed by Fodor and Lepore, is that content comes out being far too idiosyncratic, with the result that no one is ever able to share any beliefs with anyone else (pp.148–9), nor even with themselves at an earlier moment (p.149). A third criticism of functional role theories echoes the misrepresentation objection to indicator theories. Functional role theories seem to have difficulty explaining how it is ever possible to be wrong in what one believes (pp.150–2).

Despite these concerns, supporters of the functional role perspective can point out how comfortably they are able to cope with what, for indicator theories, are troublesome cases: abstract concepts like conjunction or Freudian slips (p.144); cases of mistaken identity (p.145); and symbols expressing empty notions like phlogiston (p.144). Functional role theories also treat psychological explanation as a brain-internal matter, a feature that has endeared them to cognitive psychologists (p.146 (ii)–(iii)).

Further reading

Functional role theories are discussed briefly in Sterelny 1990, section 6.8, which focuses on the circularity and idiosyncrasy objection, and at greater length in Cummins 1989, chapter 9. Conceptual role theories take some of their inspiration from accounts of the meaning of theoretical terms in science, such as that found in Kuhn 1962 and Feyerabend 1965. These accounts treat the meaning of scientific terms in a way that embed them in the theories they are used to express. If the theory changes, so does the meaning of the term. Many of the objections to conceptual role theories discussed in this chapter are adapted from criticisms of Kuhn and Feyerabend. The web-of-belief metaphor is developed in Quine 1978. The full article from which Reading 9 was taken (Block 1986) describes many alternative conceptual role theories. It also develops into a two-factor theory, though this was suppressed in the discussion above. He factors mental content into two components, narrow and wide, treating the first in terms of conceptual role and the second with a more indication-based theory. We have only been looking at the first part of the theory. Fodor and Lepore 1992, chapter 6, is explicitly targeted at Block's paper, and criticizes his two-factor approach.

CHAPTER 7

The intentional stance

A rethink

For all their appeal, the two standard approaches to mental representation – the indicator and functional role approaches – face a range of objections. This much we have seen in the previous two chapters. These objections may be surmountable, perhaps by developing a hybrid of the two approaches. But there is a radically different take on the topic of mental representation, due to Daniel Dennett, that appears to avoid these objections completely. His view will be the topic of this closing chapter. I will refer to Dennett's approach as *interpretationist*. It differs from – but has affinities with – Haugeland's interpretationism, the shortcomings of which were used as a springboard to our examination of indicator and functional role theories (pp.97–9). A comparison of Dennett's and Haugeland's positions will be noted in passing, but Dennett's will be introduced here on its own terms, not as a refinement of Haugeland's.

To appreciate Dennett's approach, consider how we got to where we are. We began by noticing how often we explain one another's behaviour by attributing contentful mental states to one another – the belief that it is raining, the desire to stay dry, the intention to take an umbrella, and so forth. This was labelled as the practice of giving 'reason-giving explanations'. For simplicity, let us focus on the attribution *of beliefs*, even though this is but one aspect of the practice. What makes the attribution of a belief that it is raining acceptable as an explanation of taking an umbrella to the front door? There are plenty of *un*acceptable ways to explain this behaviour. We could explain it in terms of the umbrella carrier's star sign and the motions of the planets, for example. Or perhaps we could turn to phrenology. Phrenology was the science of personality based on bumps on individuals' skulls, popular early in the nineteenth century but completely discredited since. Why is the attribution of a belief acceptable when astrological and phrenological explanations are bogus?

It is tempting to try to draw a contrast between bogus explanations and reason-giving explanations by insisting that the motions of the planets, and bumps on a person's skull, have no direct causal influence on personal behaviour, whereas beliefs and other mental states do. We may not be able to see inside the brain when we attribute beliefs, but belief attributions, when they are correct at least, must describe *real, physical goings-on inside the head of the believer.*

This approach to distinguishing reason-giving explanations from spurious explanations generates an obligation to say what makes a particular brain state a belief that p, for some p (e.g. what makes it the belief that it is raining). How could a physical state, a state of the brain, represent the world around it as being a certain way? Those who endorse the symbol-manipulation model of the brain's inner workings will frame this question in a more specific way: 'How could a sentence in a person's belief box express the proposition that it is raining?' Both the more general and the more specific formulations of the question prompt the theories of mental representation of the kind considered in the previous two chapters. These theories attempt to vindicate the hypothesis that beliefs and other representational states are physical states of the brain, hidden from direct inspection from those who attribute them. This hypothesis in turn is intended to vindicate the practice of explaining behaviour by attributing beliefs. It distinguishes reason-giving from astrological and phrenological explanation.

According to Dennett, we do not have to provide a theory of how states of the human brain could have the same propositional content as beliefs do. Belief attributions do not have to describe causally influential states of the brain to be better than astrology and phrenology, he thinks, because there is *another way* of distinguishing 'John believes that it is raining and he does not want to get wet' as a more acceptable explanation of John's picking up the umbrella than 'John is a Leo and Saturn is merging with Venus'. This releases us from the obligation to say *how* a brain state could represent the world outside the skull of the person whose brain it is – an obligation that, as we have seen, is not easily discharged. What distinguishes the attribution of beliefs from the reading of astrology charts and phrenology maps, according to Dennett, is that the attribution of beliefs *works* as a predictive strategy while astrology and phrenology do not. Once we accept that belief attribution is predictively successful, that is enough for the practice of belief attribution to be explanatorily acceptable. We need not equate believing that it is raining with being in a certain kind of causally potent brain state. Nor, therefore, need we develop a theory of how a brain state could have representational properties, as beliefs do.

Dennett provides a definition of what it is for an organism to have a belief, for example the belief that it is raining, and it has nothing to do with internal states of the organism's brain. Roughly, an organism, a human being for example, believes that it is raining if that organism's future behaviour *can be predicted successfully* by attributing this belief (along with a range of other mental states) to it. This is called interpretationism because all there is to your having the beliefs you do is that it is reasonable – because it is predictively useful – for someone to interpret you as having those beliefs.

The reading for this chapter is taken from Dennett's clearest and most explicit statement of his interpretationist position, 'True believers' (Reading 11). As well as presenting his position he attempts to deal with issues that tend to arise for all interpretationist positions. To anticipate one of these, notice that the behaviour of a thermostat could be predicted successfully by interpreting it as having beliefs about the temperature and a desire to fluctuate according to what it believes the temperature is. Does that mean thermostats are intelligent, that they have genuine beliefs? This seems implausible, but interpretationists appear to be committed to saying that thermostats have beliefs.

Dennett's theory of belief

Dennett expresses hesitancy over the label 'interpretationism' in part I of Reading 11. The label has connotations that he wishes to distance himself from. Saying that what someone believes is a matter of interpretation *seems* to be like saying that there is nothing objective about whether they really do believe it. For comparison, notice how saying that beauty is in the eye of the beholder has the same force as denying that there is an objective fact as to whether something really is beautiful. Whether something is beautiful depends on the whims of the observer. Such relativity to an observer may or may not be acceptable when we are talking about beauty – that is a debate for another day – but the view that *what we believe* depends on the whims of an interpreter seems to rob the practice of attributing beliefs of much of its value. In particular, it seems to rob it of explanatory value. If an explanation is a good one, it ought to be acceptable no matter who is offering it. Dennett's ambition in this paper is to show that one can be an interpretationist about beliefs but reject the subjectivist connotations that seem to come with this label.

Read part I of Daniel Dennett's 'True believers: the intentional strategy and why it works' (Reading 11).

What, according to Dennett, would make the attribution of a belief true? For example, under what circumstances would it be correct to say that you believe dinner is ready? Is it a matter of you having a sentence that means 'dinner is ready' inside your head?

To have a belief is to be interpretable as having that belief by someone successfully adopting the intentional stance towards you. (Note that it is interpret*able*, not interpret*ed*. Even Robinson Crusoe had beliefs, because his behaviour *could have been* predicted successfully using the intentional stance.) What this comes to is that, if you were to be thought of as a rational agent with desires and beliefs – including the belief that dinner is ready, for example – then your behaviour would be 'reliably and voluminously predictable'. There is nothing in this that explicitly requires you to have a sentence in your head.

This, incidentally, is what sets Dennett's interpretationism apart from Haugeland's. Haugeland was an interpretationist in that he thought that what a sentence of Mentalese means, and hence what the subject believes, turn on the explanatory value of interpreting the symbol that way. Dennett agrees that what we believe is a matter of explanatory pay off, but he does not think that having a belief reduces to having a sentence of Mentalese in your belief box.

Dennett sets out to show that various notions, including those of representation, belief, desire, rationality, and error – what he calls intentional notions – are drawn from a specific mode of explanation and prediction, which he calls the intentional strategy, or the intentional stance. This strategy is indispensable, in practice at least, for the explanation and prediction of the behaviour of human beings and certain animals. There is, no doubt, something inside our heads that makes explanation and prediction using the intentional strategy work; but the truth of claims made from this stance – a claim that someone has a particular belief, for example – does not consist in there being some way of defining intentional notions in terms of what is in the head.

To appreciate and evaluate Dennett's claim we will need to know more about what is involved in adopting the intentional stance, and how adopting this stance differs from adopting other predictive and explanatory stances.

Read part II of Reading 11, in which Dennett distinguishes the intentional stance from certain other stances one could take towards the prediction of human behaviour?

ACTIVITY

(i) What other stances does Dennett refer to?

(ii) What is involved in adopting the intentional stance?

(i) Dennett mentions what he calls the *astrological stance*, which is an unsuccessful stance for the prediction of human behaviour, plus two potentially successful stances: the *physical stance* and the *design stance*. To adopt the physical stance towards something involves thinking of it as a physical object, explaining and predicting its behaviour using the laws of physics. Infamously, the French astronomer and mathematician Laplace (1749–1827) claimed that in principle the physical stance could be used to predict all future events, including those that result from human action. The design stance uses assumptions about what an entity is designed to do to predict what it will do. This stance has limited use, since plenty of objects have not been designed, and nor do they even behave *as if* they have been designed. But it is closer to the intentional stance than the physical stance since it involves an assumption that the organism or system under consideration is, in some sense, in good working order.

DISCUSSION

(ii) To adopt the intentional stance towards an organism, e.g. a human, is first of all to treat it as rational, that is, to expect it to behave in accordance with what it believes will satisfy its desires; next, it is to attribute to this rational organism certain beliefs and desires; and finally it is to predict its behaviour by working out what it is rational to do given those beliefs and desires. Beliefs are assigned generously: unless one has reason to think this is not the case, one assumes that the organism has true beliefs about perceivable features of its environment – or at least, those features that it would need to know about in order to satisfy its desires. The desires one assigns to the organism are certain basic ones: 'survival, absence of pain, food, comfort, procreation, entertainment', plus others that the organism would need to satisfy in order to satisfy the basic ones.

The key contrast between the intentional stance and the physical stance can be thought of as a difference in starting point. To adopt the intentional stance towards an organism or system is to start with the assumption that it is *successful in pursuing its interests.* Success is a normative notion that has no fundamental place in the physical explanation of anything. Most objects in the universe are such that the prediction of their behaviour is not helped by assuming that they are successful in the pursuit of their interests. To be an intelligent being – a being with mental states and rationality – is to be an exception. It is to be such that one's behaviour *can* be usefully predicted from the intentional stance, with its built-in expectation of successful behavioural outcomes.

Two considerations in support of Dennett's theory

Dennett's account of what having a belief or desire consists in seems to accord well with our actual practice of attributing mental states. If having a belief or desire was a matter of one's brain being in a certain way, then we would seem to need to look inside a person's skull – and to know what we were looking for – before we could comfortably attribute a particular belief or desire to them. But this is not something that anyone has ever done. A graphic way of putting the point is to ask what reaction we would have if, while talking to a friend, their forehead fell loose and inside their skull we saw, of all things, an ant colony. We would doubtlessly be surprised, horrified and concerned for our friend's well being. But would we conclude that this friend lacked mental states? Most would say that we would not conclude this, not if the friend carried on behaving as before anyway. This accords with Dennett's contention that having mental states is a matter of behaving in a particular way, not of one's brain being in a particular state.

A second argument in favour of adopting Dennett's perspective on the nature of mental states has already been touched on in chapter 4 (p.100). We saw there how Dennett thinks that human believers have more beliefs than could possibly be stored as explicit sentences in their brains. If he is right in this – and, in particular, if Sterelny's 'austere' reply is misguided – then he is perhaps also right to claim that what having a belief consists in is entirely independent of the internal architecture of the brain.

The problem of bogus explanations

One attractive feature of the 'sentences in the head' view of belief, a view that Dennett wishes to resist, is that it promises to draw a neat distinction between legitimate psychological explanation – the explanation of other people's behaviour, for example – and pseudo-psychological explanation that we would ordinary treat as metaphorical at best and bogus at worst. Consider how unappealing the following explanation is of the motions of the planets in the solar system.

The planets are rational.

The planets desire to mimic the orrery in the Science Museum in London (Figure 17).

The planets have accurate beliefs about the movements of this orrery.

So, the planets circle the sun in a way that matches the movements of the orrery.

Since planets are not symbol-manipulation devices, they should not be attributed with mental states. That, at least, is what a supporter of the

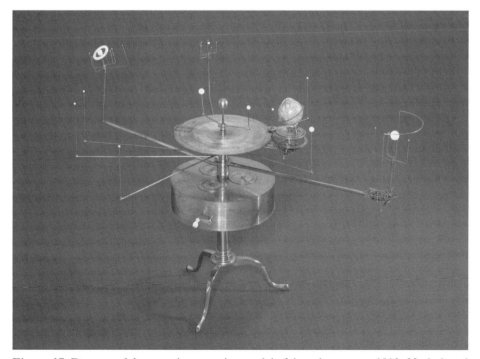

Figure 17 Drum model orrery, i.e. a moving model of the solar system, 1813–22, designed by William Pearson, Science Museum/Science & Society Picture Library, London.

sentences-in-the-head view of belief could say. Unfortunately for Dennett, the explanation above looks like it is a straightforward adoption of the intentional stance towards the solar system. His interpretationist theory seems to allow spurious attributions of intelligence, and spurious explanations of behaviour to match.

How might Dennett respond to the charge that he is lending legitimacy to bogus psychological explanations? He could say that on his view there are no grounds for attributing to the planets a desire to mimic the orrery. After all, mimicking an orrery is not conducive to survival, absence of pain, food, comfort, procreation or entertainment, the basic desires that, he says, 'terminate the "Why?" game of reason giving' (Reading 11, p.262). But these were just the contingent desires of humans, and it would be odd to suppose that they apply to all organisms. An intelligent robot, for example, would not need food. And we could always add to our bogus explanation the assumption that orrery mimicry is, for a planet, both entertaining and comforting. These are the difficulties that arise if one is not allowed to constrain the attribution of belief and desire by reference to the organism's internal workings – exactly what Dennett says we do not need to do.

In the next extract, you will read what Dennett actually says in response to the bogus-explanation charge.

ACTIVITY

Read part III of Reading 11, in which Dennett addresses the issue of whether his account of what being a believer is allows lecterns to count as having beliefs.

(i) Do lecterns have beliefs, according to Dennett?

(ii) Is belief attribution an objective matter?

DISCUSSION

(i) No, lecterns do not have beliefs, according to Dennett. Although one can adopt the intentional stance towards lecterns, and apparently predict their behaviour with considerable success, there is no predictive gain to be had *over* using the physical stance alone. This suggests a modification to Dennett's earlier definition of when belief attribution is appropriate. To his claim that 'what it is to be a true believer is to be an intentional system, a system whose behavior is reliably and voluminously predictable via the intentional strategy', we should apparently add: '... but not, in practice at least, under any other strategy, e.g. the physical strategy'.

(ii) Whether an organism has beliefs is still an objective matter, claims Dennett, since whether adopting the intentional strategy would deliver 'reliable and voluminous' predictions of behaviour is an objective matter – even if the decision to try out that strategy is not.

Has Dennett dealt adequately the faux explanation of planetary motion that attributes beliefs about the orrery to the planets? Adapting what he says about the lectern example to this case, we would expect him to rule out this bogus explanation by citing other predictive strategies that are at least as accurate and probably more so in predicting the future motions of the planets. In particular, he might say, we could use laws drawn from contemporary astronomical physics.

But the flavour of subjectivism remains with this suggestion even after the modification suggested in (i) of the previous Discussion. It seems to be a contingent accident that adopting the physical stance would yield better predictions of the future behaviour of planets, and worse predictions of the future behaviour of humans, than the intentional stance. If physics suddenly improved to the point that Laplace envisaged, would humans all of a sudden cease having genuine beliefs, desires and rationality? And if civilization suddenly went into reverse so that only a left-over orrery and the folk belief that planets enjoy mimicking it allowed us to predict planetary behaviour, would planets suddenly acquire beliefs again? Dennett addressed this in the extract you just read (in his response to Nozick, pp.264–5); his discussion of this issue is less transparent than one would wish.

Nozick envisages Martians whose physics and neuroscience are so developed that they can predict human behaviour without adopting the intentional stance. On Dennett's interpretationist theory, Nozick suggests, humans would lack beliefs from the Martian perspective in the same way that thermostats, planets and lecterns lack beliefs from the human perspective. This possibility appears to show that if Dennett's theory of belief is correct, belief attribution is a subjective practice, undermining its legitimacy in explanation. Dennett replies by insisting that the predictions of human behaviour we make using the intentional stance correspond to objective features of the world that are missed by Martians or anyone else using the physical stance. These objective 'patterns' in the world are what we 'characterize in terms of the beliefs, desires, and intentions of rational agents' (p.265), when adopting the intentional stance; and the success of that stance testifies to the existence of such patterns.

Dennett's appeal to patterns of behaviour – what later in the essay he calls 'real patterns' to emphasize their objectivity – seems to be carrying a lot of weight. This does not necessarily threaten his interpretationist perspective, but it does seem to call at least for a further amendment to his theory, in place of the one proposed in (i) in the previous activity:

> What it is to be a true believer is to be an intentional system, a system whose behavior is reliably and voluminously predictable via the intentional strategy, *where the success of this strategy is grounded in objective patterns in the world that the physical stance ignores.*

Critics have expressed puzzlement over what Dennett has in mind when he talks of 'patterns in human affairs that impose themselves, not quite inexorably but with great vigor, absorbing physical perturbations and variations that might as well be considered random' (Reading 11, p.265). Whether his interpretationism succeeds ultimately turns on what can be made of this notion.

Reductionism, eliminativism and interpretationism

Dennett's core claim, notwithstanding the amendments we have added in light of his own assertions, is that the truth of belief attributions are not to be held hostage to theories of what is happening inside the head. The intentional stance is predictively successful, at least when applied to humans in most situations. That is enough to show that we have beliefs, for that is *what it is* to have a belief (to be a 'true believer' in Dennett's pun). One advantage of accepting Dennett's account is that doing so would free us from any obligation to define intentional notions in physicalist terms – or, as it is sometimes put, to reduce beliefs and desires to the physical sciences. If having a particular belief is not defined as being in some specific kind of internal physical but representational state, then we do not have to provide a naturalistic theory of what *gives* a physical state the representational properties that beliefs have.

Several earlier critics of Dennett suggested that he failed to address the interesting question, which is: what makes adoption of the intentional stance work? The familiar story about an inner language, Mentalese, the symbols of which are manipulated according to algorithmic rules, constitutes one possible answer. But if this is the case, these critics continued, then why not claim simply that belief just *is* a state involving an inner language?

Read the final extract from Dennett's paper (part IV, 'Why does the intentional strategy work?'). What is Dennett's understanding of the relation between attributions of belief and claims about an inner language?

ACTIVITY

DISCUSSION

Dennett is not hostile to the theory that our heads are populated by symbols of a language of thought, which are manipulated in a way that makes intelligent, rational behaviour possible. Indeed, the final paragraph of his paper expresses qualified endorsement of this proposal, including an argument in support. What he resists is the reduction, in the form of a naturalistic definition, of intentional discourse to physical discourse. It may be that having a language of thought is what makes adopting the intentional strategy towards humans rewarding. But it may not be, and it may turn out that other organisms have beliefs but not because they have an inner language. Thinking of beliefs in Dennett's way rather than defining them in terms of sentences in a belief box allows these possibilities to be kept open.

What motivates Dennett is not mere dislike of reductive naturalism about mental states, or pessimism about its prospects. He also wishes to escape the threat of eliminativism. Eliminativism is the view that mentalist discourse is misguided and should be replaced – as an explicit theory of mind at least, if not in ordinary life – by a language that has no term like 'belief'. The commonest form of argument for eliminativism is that psychological explanation in terms of belief and desire attribution is bad science: it yields poor predictions, it is vague and uncorroborated, it does not integrate well with the other sciences, and so on. Dennett addresses this common argument when he states that 'once the intentional strategy is in place, it is an extraordinarily powerful tool in prediction' (Reading 11, p.263). But he also addresses a less common argument for eliminativism. This combines the assumption that to have a belief that *p* is to have a sentence in your head that means that *p*, with the further claim that, as a matter of empirical fact, the beliefs we are typically said to have are not matched by any internal sentences in the head. From these two assumptions it follows that we do not have beliefs.

Against this second argument for eliminativism, Dennett acknowledges that the case for the existence of a language of thought is 'not overwhelming' (p.267). Computational theories that differ quite radically from the traditional 'sentence-in-the-head' model that dominated artificial intelligence in its early years have grown in popularity. This has led many to the conclusion that, since belief attributions do not map on to the underlying physical picture, belief attributions are universally false. By contrast, Dennett refuses to allow that developments in cognitive science could ever show that we do not have beliefs. He takes the possibility of such developments to show only that the reductionist premise, that belief attributions must map neatly on to some physical state of the brain, is a mistake. We undoubtedly *do* have beliefs, he says, because the intentional stance undoubtedly works when it is applied to us, and that is what it is for us to have beliefs. What *makes it possible* for the intentional stance to work, when it works, is a different matter.

Chapter summary

Dennett claims that having beliefs is a matter of one's behaviour being susceptible to 'reliable and voluminous' prediction by someone adopting the intentional stance (p.158). Or, put negatively, believing is *not* a matter of one's brain being in a particular physical (yet somehow representational) state. This interpretationism has seemed, to many, to commit Dennett to subjectivism about belief attribution, an outcome that would undermine the validity of appealing to beliefs when explaining behaviour. Explanations ought to be available to everyone, and not vary according to the whims or circumstances of the explainer (pp.161–4). Dennett attempts to cut the association between interpretationism and subjectivism by claiming that there is still an objective fact about whether adopting the intentional stance rather than the physical stance will result in improved predictive power (p.164).

Dennett's theory, if it is defensible, would show that attempts to provide a reductive theory of how physical states of the brain could represent the external world in the same way that beliefs do are not needed (pp.155–7, 166).

Further reading

Dennett's denial that having a belief is a matter of being in some kind of inner state, let alone a physical inner state, resonates in many ways with Ryle 1949. An accessible early statement of his position is found in the essay 'Intentional systems' (Dennett 1981), and the notion of real patterns is elaborated in Dennett 1991. Dennett's position is criticised in Baker 1989. Clark 2001, chapter 3, is a clear discussion that outlines the relation between Dennett's view and that of reductionists and eliminativists. It includes a response to Baker and an attempt to clarify Dennett's remarks about real patterns. The classic statements of eliminativism are Stich 1983, which is accessible, and Churchland 1979 and Churchland 1986, which are far less so. Churchland 1984, a textbook introduction to the philosophy of mind, covers the topic of eliminativism in a clear if partisan way.

Glossary

algorithm a system of rules for transforming symbols where (a) the rules are defined in terms of the syntactic properties of the symbols and (b) the resulting transformations are reasonable given what those symbols mean.

artificial intelligence (AI) the attempt to mimic or reproduce intelligent processes and behaviours in machines, especially computers.

aspectual shape the way the content of a mental state depends on the subject's viewpoint or background assumptions.

atomism the denial of holism. The theory that what a symbol or state represents does not depend on what other symbols or states represent.

attitude believing, desiring, intending, aspiring, hoping, pretending, etc.

belief box where a Mentalese sentence is when the subject has a belief (rather than a desire, say) with the same content as the sentence. 'Box' is metaphorical for a functional context.

charity principle the maxim that one should interpret an utterance (or attribute mental states) in a such a way as to make the speaker (or the subject) reasonable.

communication knowledge transmission through language, and related processes.

completeness of physics the thesis that, in principle, no cause of a physical event is beyond the reach of physics. (This thesis and variants of it are sometimes called 'closure of the physical'.)

compositionality principle the claim that what a sentence means depends systematically on the meaning of the words that compose it and how they are strung together.

computational theory of mind (CTM) the theory that intelligent processes in human beings involve symbols in their brains being manipulated in accordance with algorithmic rules.

computer a symbol manipulation device. (Haugeland: an automatic formal system.)

conceptual role theories these hold that the content of a mental symbol turns entirely on its causal role in the overall cognitive system.

content (or 'mental content') that which is expressed by the '...' part of 'So-and-so believes (or desires, etc.) that ...'.

deferential theory of reference the theory that sometimes words refer indirectly: the person using them defers to unknown experts in the community, who can pick out the **extension** directly.

descriptivism the theory that a word's intension is a description. (This description is usually said to be built out of attributes the person using the word associates with the word; that is, it is a product of the person's beliefs.)

disjunction problem the problem of how to rule out disjunctive meanings (e.g. 'Horse-or-cow-on-a-rainy-night') for symbols of Mentalese, thereby making misrepresentation possible.

eliminativism the view that **mental states** do not exist and that talk of them is at best a useful fiction.

expression a word, or a sentence composed out of words. (Not the same as the utterance of a word or sentence.)

expressive transparency the content of the psychological state we intend to express in a linguistic utterance is identical with the meaning of that utterance.

extension in this book, the extension of a word is taken to be just what the word refers to. (Putnam says the extension of a word is the set of things the word is true of, but for our purposes this is equivalent.)

externalism see **linguistic externalism** and **mental externalism**.

frame problem the problem of understanding how we are able to select information that is relevant to a task from the total information available to us. (Originally used more narrowly in AI to refer to the problem of judging what information to put into the frame – roughly, the list of background explicit knowledge – of a computational system.)

functional role theories these hold that the content of a brain state turns entirely on its causal role in the overall cognitive system.

Gricean Programme the attempt to reduce all claims about linguistic meaning to claims about mental states, and to reduce these in turn to claims couched in the language of science.

holism the thesis that a symbol or state represents what it does only because at least one other symbol or state in the same representational system represents what it does.

homuncularism the explanation of a mental trait in a way that surreptitiously and illicitly presupposes that very trait. (Note: some authors, though none in this book, use 'homunculus' in a less negative way. When a complex intellectual task is broken down into manageable sub-tasks, these are said to be carried out by homunculi. The homunculi are 'discharged' when the sub-tasks are themselves broken down into what are, ultimately, purely syntactic processes.)

indexical a word whose reference depends systematically on the context in which it is uttered, e.g. 'I', 'now'.

indexical theory of reference the theory that words like 'water' function like indexicals (e.g. 'I', 'now'): what they refer to depends on features of the context in which they are uttered, for example on the hidden physical structure of the local liquid.

indication roughly: an event of type A indicates an event of type B if and only if events of type A are reliably caused by and only by events of type B.

indicator theories theories of representation that rely on the notion of indication. (Simple indicator theories treat representation and indication as identical notions.)

inference to the best explanation e.g. there are small tongue prints in the butter; this is best explained as having been caused by a mouse; so it is reasonable to assume that there is a mouse in the house (often called 'abductive reasoning').

instrumental rationality deciding to do something because one believes doing it will satisfy a desire one has. (Alternative definitions and labels, e.g. 'practical rationality', are also common.)

intension (with an 's') a condition associated with the word; the word refers to something if and only if that thing meets the condition.

intention (with a 't') one kind of attitude; central to Grice's theory of the meaning of utterances.

intentionality a word some authors use as a synonym for 'aboutness', or for the mind's capacity to represent the external world.

intentional stance adopted when explaining or predicting others' behaviour by attributing beliefs, desires, reasonableness, etc. to them. Dennett's label for reason-giving explanation or prediction.

internalism see **linguistic internalism** and **mental internalism**.

interpretationism the theory that a symbol means what it does (or that a person has the mental states they do) comes down to the explanatory or predicative utility of supposing this.

legitimacy puzzle why are reason-giving explanations legitimate when applied to humans, especially given the spuriousness of their use in other domains?

linguistic externalism the view that a word's intension (and hence extension) can depend on more than the narrow psychological states of the person whose word it is.

linguistic internalism the view that a word's **intension** determines what it refers to, and is itself determined by the (narrow) psychological states of the person whose word it is.

Locke's question how is it that the thoughts of men's minds can be conveyed to one another?

mental externalism the view that at least some mental states are wide.

mental internalism the view that all mental states are narrow.

mental representation question what accounts for our mental states having the content they do, especially given the assumption that mental states are, or at least are intimately dependent on, physical states of the subject's brain?

mental state believing that it is raining, desiring not to get wet, intending to take an umbrella, and so forth (equivalent to 'psychological state').

Mentalese a hypothetical language within the brain (equivalent to 'language of thought').

misrepresentation representation that is inaccurate. (Not the same as non-representation, i.e. the failure to represent at all, accurately or inaccurately.)

multiple realizability of the mental in the physical two or more subjects being in the same mental state despite having very different physical make ups.

narrow not wide. Dependent on the subject's internal physical make up, not on the external physical or social environment.

natural meaning it is not possible for something to naturally mean that p unless p is true.

naturalism the thesis that a given phenomenon, e.g. intelligent human behaviour, is best approached through the lens of science. (This definition is deliberately loose. Authors differ over what the naturalistic outlook demands. **Physicalism** as defined below is a relatively stringent form of naturalism.)

nomologically necessary as the result of a law of science (sometimes called 'natural necessity').

non-natural meaning it is possible for something to non-naturally mean that p even if p is untrue.

physicalism as used in this book, the view that semantic properties such as means, represents, expresses, refers to, and so forth can be expressed, or in some other sense captured, using only terms drawn from physics and related disciplines. (Alternative definitions of this term are common.)

procedural knowledge knowledge that involves the application of rules to stored sentences of Mentalese, not simply the presence of such sentences in one's belief box. Some hold that our everyday ability to carry out simple logical inferences involves procedural knowledge.

reason-giving explanation an explanation that cites an agent's reasons (interchangeable with 'psychological explanation').

reductionism the attempt to re-express, or in some other sense capture, the properties associated with one discourse using only terms drawn from some other discourse (e.g. **physicalism** as defined above; as with 'physicalism', authors use this term in different ways).

semantic having to do with what a symbol means, not its physical form.

subject in discussions of mental states, the person whose mental state it is. (Used interchangeably with 'agent' if the emphasis is on action-directed mental states.)

substance dualism the view that physical entities are not the only entities there are. In particular, there are mental entities, perhaps including souls, which are non-physical.

surfeit-of-explanations puzzle how can reason-giving explanations of behaviour co-exist with physical explanations of this same behaviour?

symbol something with both semantic and syntactic properties.

syntactic having to do with a symbol's physical form, not with what it means.

teleosemantic theories these take the content of a mental state to be a matter of its function, i.e. what it is supposed to do. Function is typically understood by reference to evolutionary or developmental history.

tokening producing a symbol, e.g. uttering a word or causing a sentence of **Mentalese** to appear in one's belief box.

utterance a meaningful linguistic act (in Grice's sense: 'linguistic' not required).

wide not narrow. Dependent on the subject's external social or physical environment, not merely on features of their brain.

Bibliography

AVRAMIDES, A. (1997) 'Intention and Convention', in C. Wright and B. Hale (eds) *A Companion to the Philosophy of Language*, Oxford, Blackwell.

BAKER, L.R. (1989) 'Instrumental intentionality', *Philosophy of Science*, 56, 303–16.

BLACKBURN, S. (1984) *Spreading the Word: Groundings in the Philosophy of Language*, Oxford, Clarendon Press.

BLOCK, N. (1986) 'Advertisement for a semantics for psychology', *Midwest Studies in Philosophy*, 10, 615–78.

BURGE, T. (1979) 'Individualism and the mental', *Midwest Studies in Philosophy*, 4, 73–121.

CARROLL, L. (1893) 'Through the looking-glass and what Alice found there', in *Alice's Adventures in Wonderland*, London, Macmillan.

CHURCHLAND, P.M. (1979) *Scientific Realism and the Plasticity of Mind*, Cambridge, Cambridge University Press.

CHURCHLAND, P.M. (1984) *Matter and Consciousness: A Contemporary Introduction to the Philosophy of Mind*, Cambridge, Mass., MIT Press.

CHURCHLAND, P.S. (1986) *Neurophilosophy: Toward a Unified Science of the Mind-Brain*, Cambridge, Mass., MIT Press.

CLARK, A. (1989) *Microcognition: Philosophy, Cognitive Science, and Parallel Distributed Processing*, Cambridge, Mass., MIT Press.

CLARK, A. (2001) *Mindware: An Introduction to the Philosophy of Cognitive Science*, New York, Oxford University Press.

CLARK, A. and D. CHALMERS (1998) 'The extended mind', *Analysis*, 58, 1, 7–19.

CRANE, T. (1991) 'All the difference in the world', *Philosophical Quarterly*, 41, 162, 1–25.

CRANE, T. (2003) *The Mechanical Mind*, 2nd edn, London, Routledge.

CUMMINS, R. (1989) *Meaning and Mental Representation*, Cambridge, Mass., MIT Press.

DAVIDSON, D. (1987) 'Knowing one's own mind', *Proceedings and Addresses of the American Philosophical Association*, 60, 3, 441–58. (Page reference is to the reprint in his *Subjective, Objective, Intersubjective*, Oxford, Oxford University Press, 2001.)

DENNETT, D.C. (1978) 'Brain writing and mind reading', in *Brainstorms*, Hassocks, Harvester Press, 39–58.

DENNETT, D.C. (1981) *Brainstorms*, Cambridge, Mass., MIT Press.

DENNETT, D.C. (1984) 'Cognitive wheels: the frame problem of AI', in C. Hookway (ed.) *Minds, Machines and Evolution*, Cambridge, Cambridge University Press, 129–51.

DENNETT, D.C. (1987) 'True believers: the intentional strategy and why it works', in D.C. Dennett (ed.) *The Intensional Stance*, Cambridge, Mass., MIT Press.

DENNETT, D.C. (1991) 'Real patterns', *Journal of Philosophy*, 88, 1, 27–51.

DESCARTES, R. (1970) 'First Meditation', in *Descartes: Philosophical Writings*, ed. and trans. E. Anscombe and P.T. Geach from the 2nd edn of the Latin text, London, Thomas Nelson for the The Open University (first published 1642).

DIOGENES LAERTIUS (1853) 'Life of Pyrrho', Book IX of *The Lives and Opinions of Eminent Philosophers*, trans. C.D. Yonge, London, Henry G. Bohn (written 230 AD).

DRETSKE, F. (1981) *Knowledge and the Flow of Information*, Oxford, Blackwell.

DRETSKE, F. (1988) *Explaining Behavior: Reasons in a World of Causes*, Cambridge, Mass., MIT Press.

FEYERABEND, P.K. (1965) 'On the "meaning" of scientific terms', *Journal of Philosophy*, 62, 266–73.

FODOR, J.A. (1975) *The Language of Thought* Cambridge, Mass., Harvard University Press.

FODOR, J.A. (1987) *Psychosemantics*, Cambridge, Mass., MIT Press.

FODOR, J.A. (1990) 'A theory of content, II', in *A Theory of Content and Other Essays*, Cambridge, Mass., MIT Press.

FODOR, J.A. (1994) *The Elm and the Expert: Mentalese and Its Semantics*, Cambridge, Mass., MIT Press.

FODOR, J.A. (2000) *The Mind Doesn't Work That Way*, Cambridge, Mass., MIT Press.

FODOR, J.A. and E. LEPORE (1992) *Holism: A Shopper's Guide*, Oxford, Blackwell.

FOUCAULT, M. (1961) *Folie et déraison: Histoire de la folie à l'âge classique*, Paris, Librairie Plon. (English edition translated and abridged by Richard Howard as *Madness and Civilization: A History of Insanity in the Age of Reason*, New York, Pantheon, 1965).

FREGE, G. (1892) 'Über Sinn und Bedeutung', translated into English as 'Sense and reference', *Philosophical Review*, 1948, 57, 207–30.

GRICE, H.P. (1957) 'Meaning', *Philosophical Review*, 66, 377–88.

GRICE, H.P. (1989) *Studies in the Way of Words*, Cambridge, Mass., Harvard University Press.

HAUGELAND, J. (1981) 'Semantic engines: an introduction to mind design', in J. Haugeland (ed.) *Mind Design*, Montgomery, Vermont, Bradford Books, 1–34.

HEIL, J. (1992) *The Nature of True Minds*, New York, Cambridge University Press.

HEIL, J. (1998) *Philosophy of Mind*, London, Routledge.

KRIPKE, S.A. (1980) *Naming and Necessity*, Cambridge, Mass., Harvard University Press.

KUHN, T.S. (1962) *The Structure of Scientific Revolutions*, Chicago, University of Chicago Press.

LOCKE, J. (1997) *An Essay Concerning Human Understanding*, ed. R. Woolhouse, Harmondsworth, Penguin (based on the posthumously published 5th edn, 1706).

LYCAN, W.G. (1996) *The Philosophy of Language*, London, Routledge.

MACDONALD, C. and G. MACDONALD (1995) *Philosophy of Psychology: Debates on Psychological Explanation*, Cambridge, Mass., Blackwell.

MILLER, A. (1998) *Philosophy of Language*, London, UCL Press.

MILLIKAN, R.G. (1984) *Language, Thought, and Other Biological Categories: New Foundations for Realism*, Cambridge, Mass., MIT Press.

MILLIKAN, R.G. (1989) 'Biosemantics', *Journal of Philosophy*, 86, 281–97.

MILLIKAN, R.G. (1993) *White Queen Psychology and Other Essays for Alice*, Cambridge, Mass., MIT Press.

MINSKY, M.L. (1968) 'Introduction', in M.L. Minsky (ed.) *Semantic Information Processing*, Cambridge, Mass., MIT Press, 1–31.

MOLIÈRE, J.B. DE (1879?) *The Imaginary Invalid (Le Malade Imaginaire)*, trans. Roscoe Mongan, London, James Cornish and Sons (first published 1673).

PAPINEAU, D. (1993) *Philosophical Naturalism*, Cambridge, Mass., Blackwell.

PAPINEAU, D. (1996) 'Précis of "Philosophical naturalism"', *Philosophy and Phenomenological Research*, 56, 3, 657–65.

PAPINEAU, D. (2001) 'The status of teleosemantics, or how to stop worrying about Swampman', *Australasian Journal of Philosophy*, 79, 2, 279–89.

PINKER, S. (1994) *The Language Instinct*, London, Allen Lane.

PINKER, S. (1997) *How the Mind Works*, New York, W.W. Norton.

PRICE, C. (2001) *Functions in Mind: A Theory of Intentional Content*, Oxford, Oxford University Press.

PUTNAM, H. (1975) 'The meaning of "meaning"', in K. Gunderson (ed.) *Language, Mind, and Knowledge*, Minneapolis, University of Minnesota Press. Reprinted in R.M. Harnish (ed.) (1994) *Basic Topics in the Philsophy of Language*, London, Harvester Wheatsheaf, 221–274.

QUINE, W.V. (1978) *The Web of Belief*, New York, Random House.

RUSSELL, B. (1905) 'On denoting', *Mind*, 14, 479–93.

RUSSELL, B. (1919) 'Descriptions', in *Introduction to Mathematical Philosophy*, London, George Allen and Unwin. Reprinted in G. Ostertag (ed.) *Definite Descriptions: A Reader*, Cambridge, Mass, MIT Press.

RYLE, G. (1949) *The Concept of Mind*, New York, Barnes and Noble.

SCHIFFER, S.R. (1972) *Meaning*, Oxford, Clarendon Press.

SCHIFFER, S.R. (1987) *Remnants of Meaning* Cambridge, Mass., MIT Press.

SEARLE, J.R. (1969) *Speech Acts: An Essay in the Philosophy of Language*, London, Cambridge University Press.

SEARLE, J.R. (1971) 'What is a speech act?', in J.R. Searle (ed.) *The Philosophy of Language*, Oxford, Oxford University Press, 39–53. Originally published in M. Black (ed.) (1965) *Philosophy in America*, London, Allen & Unwin, 221–39.

SEGAL, G. (2000) *A Slim Book about Narrow Content*, Cambridge, Mass., MIT Press.

STALNAKER, R.C. (1984) *Inquiry*, Cambridge, Mass., MIT Press.

STERELNY, K. (1990) *The Representational Theory of Mind: An Introduction*, Cambridge, Mass., Blackwell.

STICH, S.P. (1983) *From Folk Psychology to Cognitive Science: The Case against Belief,* Cambridge, Mass., MIT Press.

STICH, S.P. and T.A. WARFIELD (1994) *Mental Representation: A Reader*, Cambridge, Mass., Blackwell.

SWIFT, J. (1726) 'A voyage to Laputa, Balnibarbi, Glubbdubdrib, Luggnag and Japan', Book III of Volume 2 of *Travels into Several Remote Nations of the World. By Captain Lemeul Gulliver*, London, Benjamin Motte.

TAYLOR, K. (1998) *Truth and Meaning: An Introduction to the Philosophy of Language*, Oxford, Blackwell.

THOMSON, K. (2004) 'Sacred mysteries: why the *Rigveda* has resisted decipherment', *Times Literary Supplement*, 26 March, 14–15.

TVERSKY, A. and D. KAHNEMAN (1983) 'Extension versus intuititve reasoning: the conjunction fallacy in probability judgment', *Psychological Review*, 90, 293–315.

READINGS

Meaning

H.P. Grice

Source: Grice, H.P. (1957) 'Meaning', *Philosophical Review*, 66, 3, pp.377–88. Edited as indicated. Division into subtitled parts is not in the original.

[Part I: Natural meaning distinguished from non-natural meaning]

Consider the following sentences:

"Those spots mean (meant) measles."

"Those spots didn't mean anything to me, but to the doctor they meant measles."

"The recent budget means that we shall have a hard year."

[...] I cannot say, "Those spots meant measles, but he hadn't got measles," and I cannot say, "The recent budget means that we shall have a hard year, but we shan't have." That is to say, in cases like the above, *x meant that p* and *x means that p* entail *p*.

[...]

Now contrast the above sentences with the following:

"Those three rings on the bell (of the bus) mean that the 'bus is full.'"

"That remark, 'Smith couldn't get on without his trouble and strife,' meant that Smith found his wife indispensable."

[...] I can use the first of these and go on to say, "But it isn't in fact full – the conductor has made a mistake"; and I can use the second and go on, "But in fact Smith deserted her seven years ago." That is to say, here *x means that p* and *x meant that p* do not entail *p*.

[...]

When the expressions "means," "means something," "means that" are used in the kind of way in which they are used in the first set of sentences, I shall speak of the sense, or senses, in which they are used, as the *natural* sense, or senses, of the expressions in question. When the expressions are used in the kind of way in which they are used in the second set of sentences, I shall speak of the sense, or senses, in which they are used, as the *nonnatural* sense, or senses, of the expressions in question. I shall use the abbreviation "means$_{nn}$" to distinguish the nonnatural sense or senses.

I propose, for convenience, also to include [...] under the head of nonnatural senses of "mean" any senses of "mean" found in sentences of the patterns "*A* means (meant) something by *x*" or "*A* means (meant) by *x* that ..." [...]

I do not want to maintain that *all* our uses of "mean" fall easily, obviously, and tidily into one of the two groups I have distinguished; but I think that in most cases we should be at least fairly strongly inclined to assimilate a use of "mean" to one group rather than to the other. The question which now arises is this: "What more can be said about the distinction between the cases where we should say that the word is applied in a natural sense and the cases where we should say that the word is applied in a nonnatural sense?" Asking this question will not of course prohibit us from trying to give an explanation of "meaning$_{nn}$" in terms of one or another natural sense of "mean".

[...]

I want first to consider briefly, and reject, what I might term a causal type of answer to the question, "What is meaning$_{nn}$?" We might try to say, for instance, more or less with C.L. Stevenson,[1] that for *x* to mean$_{nn}$ something, *x* must have (roughly) a tendency to produce in an audience some attitude (cognitive or otherwise) and a tendency, in the case of a speaker, to *be* produced *by* that attitude, these tendencies being dependent on "an elaborate process of conditioning attending the use of the sign in communication."[2] This clearly will not do.

[...] Let us consider a case where an utterance, if it qualifies at all as meaning$_{nn}$ something, will be of a descriptive or informative kind and the relevant attitude, therefore, will be a cognitive one, for example, a belief. (I use "utterance" as a neutral word to apply to any candidate for meaning$_{nn}$; it has a convenient act–object ambiguity.) It is no doubt the case that many people have a tendency to put on a tail coat when they think they are about to go to a dance, and it is no doubt also the case that many people, on seeing someone put on a tail coat, would conclude that the person in question was about to go to a dance. Does this satisfy us that putting on a tail coat means$_{nn}$ that one is about to go to a dance (or indeed means$_{nn}$ anything at all)? Obviously not. It is no help to refer to the qualifying phrase "dependent on an elaborate process of conditioning ..." For if all this means is that the response to the sight of a tail coat being put on is in some way learned or acquired, it will not exclude the present case from being one of meaning$_{nn}$. But if we have to take seriously the second part of the qualifying phrase ("attending the use of the sign in communication"), then the account of meaning$_{nn}$ is obviously circular. We might just as well say, "X has meaning$_{nn}$ if it is used in communication," which, though true, is not helpful.

[...]

A further deficiency in a causal theory of the type just expounded seems to be that, even if we accept it as it stands, we are furnished with an analysis only of statements about the *standard* meaning, or the meaning in general, of a "sign." No provision is made for dealing with statements about what a particular speaker or writer means by a sign on a particular occasion (which may well diverge from the standard meaning of the sign); nor is it obvious how the theory could be adapted to make such provision. One might even go further in criticism and maintain that the causal theory ignores the fact that the meaning (in general) of a sign needs to be explained in terms of what users of the sign do (or should) mean by it on particular occasions; and so the latter notion, which is unexplained by the causal theory, is in fact the fundamental one. I am sympathetic to this more radical criticism, though I am aware that the point is controversial.

[Part II: A strategy for elucidating non-natural meaning]

I do not propose to consider any further theories of the "causal-tendency" type. I suspect no such theory could avoid difficulties analogous to those I have outlined without utterly losing its claim to rank as a theory of this type.

I will now try a different and, I hope, more promising line. If we can elucidate the meaning of

"x meant$_{nn}$ something (on a particular occasion)"and
"x meant$_{nn}$ that so-and-so (on a particular occasion)"

and of

"A meant$_{nn}$ something by x (on a particular occasion)" and
"A meant$_{nn}$ by x that so-and-so (on a particular occasion),"

this might reasonably be expected to help us with

"x means$_{nn}$ (timeless) something (that so-and-so),"
"A means$_{nn}$ (timeless) by x something (that so-and-so),"

and with the explication of "means the same as," "understands," "entails," and so on. Let us for the moment pretend that we have to deal only with utterances which might be informative or descriptive.

[...]

[Part III: A first proposal]

A first shot would be to suggest that "x meant$_{nn}$ something" would be true if x was intended by its utterer to induce a belief in some "audience" and that to say what the belief was would be to say what x meant$_{nn}$. This will not do. I might leave B's handkerchief near the scene of a murder in order to induce the detective to believe that B was the murderer; but we should not want to say that the handkerchief (or my leaving it there) meant$_{nn}$ anything or that I had meant$_{nn}$ by leaving it that B was the murderer.

[Part IV: A second proposal]

Clearly we must at least add that, for x to have meant$_{nn}$ anything, not merely must it have been "uttered" with the intention of inducing a certain belief but also the utterer must have intended an "audience" to recognize the intention behind the utterance.

This, though perhaps better, is not good enough. Consider the following cases:

(1) Herod presents Salome with the head of St. John the Baptist on a charger.

(2) Feeling faint, a child lets its mother see how pale it is (hoping that she may draw her own conclusions and help).

(3) I leave the china my daughter has broken lying around for my wife to see.

Here we seem to have cases which satisfy the conditions so far given for meaning$_{nn}$. For example, Herod intended to make Salome believe that St. John the Baptist was dead and no doubt also intended Salome to recognize that he intended her to believe that St. John the Baptist was dead. Similarly for the other cases. Yet I certainly do not think that we should want to say that we have here cases of meaning$_{nn}$.

[Part V: A third proposal]

What we want to find is the difference between, for example, "deliberately and openly letting someone know" and "telling" and between "getting someone to think" and "telling."

The way out is perhaps as follows. Compare the following two cases:

(1) I show Mr. X a photograph of Mr. Y displaying undue familiarity to Mrs. X.

(2) I draw a picture of Mr. Y behaving in this manner and show it to Mr. X.

I find that I want to deny that in (1) the photograph (or my showing it to Mr. X) meant$_{nn}$ anything at all; while I want to assert that in (2) the picture (or my drawing and showing it) meant$_{nn}$ something (that Mr. Y had been unduly unfamiliar), or at least that I had meant$_{nn}$ by it that Mr. Y had been unduly familiar. What is the difference between the two cases? Surely that in case (1) Mr. X's recognition of my intention to make him believe that there is something between Mr. Y and Mrs. X is (more or less) irrelevant to the production of this effect by the photograph. Mr. X would be led by the photograph at least to suspect Mrs. X even if instead of showing it to him I had left it in his room by accident; and I (the photograph shower) would not be unaware of this. But it will make a difference to the effect of my picture on Mr. X whether or not he takes me to be intending to inform him (make him believe something) about Mrs. X, and not to be just doodling or trying to produce a work of art.

[...]

Perhaps we may sum up what is necessary for A to mean something by x as follows. A must intend to induce by x a belief in an audience, and he must also intend his utterance to be recognized as so intended. But these intentions are not independent; the recognition is intended by A to play its part in inducing the belief, and if it does not do so something will have gone wrong with the fulfilment of A's intentions. [...] Shortly, perhaps, we may say that "A meant$_{nn}$ something by x" is roughly equivalent to "A uttered x with the intention of inducing a belief by means of the recognition of this intention." (This seems to involve a reflexive paradox, but it does not really do so.)

[Part VI: Timeless meaning defined in terms of meaning on an occasion]

Now perhaps it is time to drop the pretense that we have to deal only with "informative" cases. Let us start with some examples of imperatives or quasi-imperatives. I have a very avaricious man in my room, and I want him to go; so I throw a pound note out of the window. Is there here any utterance with a meaning$_{nn}$? No, because in behaving as I did, I did not intend his recognition of my purpose to be in any way effective in getting him to go. This is parallel to the photograph case. If on the other hand I had pointed to the door or given him a little push, then my behavior might well be held to constitute a meaningful$_{nn}$ utterance, just because the recognition of my intention would be intended by me to be effective in speeding his departure. Another pair of cases would be (1) a policeman who stops a car by standing in its way and (2) a policeman who stops a car by waving.

[...]

Perhaps then we may make the following generalizations.

(1) "A meant$_{nn}$ something by x [on a particular occasion]" is (roughly) equivalent to "A intended the utterance of x to produce some effect in an audience by means of the recognition of this intention"; and we may add that to ask what A meant is to ask for a specification of the intended effect (though, of course, it may not always be possible to get a straight answer involving a "that" clause, for example, "a belief that...").

(2) "x meant$_{[nn]}$ something [on a particular occasion]" is (roughly) equivalent to "Somebody meant$_{nn}$ something by x." Here again there will be cases

where this will not quite work. I feel inclined to say that (as regards traffic lights) the change to red meant$_{nn}$ that the traffic was to stop; but it would be vary unnatural to say, "Somebody (e.g., the Corporation) meant$_{nn}$ by the red-light change that the traffic was to stop." Nevertheless, there seems to be *some* sort of reference to somebody's intentions.

(3) "x means$_{nn}$ (timeless) that so-and-so" might as a first shot be equated with some statement or disjunction of statements about what "people" (vague) intend (with qualifications about "recognition") to effect by x. I shall have a word to say about this.

Will any kind of intended effect do, or may there be cases where an effect is intended (with the required qualifications) and yet we should not want to talk of meaning$_{nn}$? Suppose I discovered some person so constituted that, when I told him that whenever I grunted in a special way I wanted him to blush or to incur some physical malady, thereafter whenever he recognized the grunt (and with it my intention), he did blush or incur the malady. Should we then want to say that the grunt meant$_{nn}$ something? I do not think so. This points to the fact that for x to have meaning$_{nn}$, the intended effect must be something which in some sense is within the control of the audience, or that in some sense of "reason" the recognition of the intention behind x is for the audience a reason and not merely a cause.

[...]

Now some question may be raised about my use, fairly free, of such words as "intention" and "recognition." I must disclaim any intention of peopling all our talking life with armies of complicated psychological occurrences. I do not hope to solve any philosophical puzzle about intending, but I do want briefly to argue that no special difficulties are raised by my use of the word "intention" in connection with meaning. First, there will be cases where an utterance is accompanied or preceded by a conscious "plan," or explicit formulation of intention (e.g., I declare how I am going to use x, or ask myself how to "get something across"). The presence of such an explicit "plan" obviously counts fairly heavily in favour of the utterer's intention (meaning) being as "planned"; though it is not, I think, conclusive; for example, a speaker who has declared an intention to use a familiar expression in an unfamiliar way may slip into the familiar use. Similarly in nonlinguistic cases: if we are asking about an agent's intention, a previous expression counts heavily; nevertheless, a man might plan to throw a letter in the dustbin and yet take it to the post;

when lifting his hand he might "come to" and say *either* "I didn't intend to do this at all" *or* "I suppose I must have been intending to put it in."

Explicitly formulated linguistic (or quasi-linguistic) intentions are no doubt comparatively rare. In their absence we would seem to rely on very much the same kinds of criteria as we do in the case of nonlinguistic intentions where there is a general usage. An utterer is held to intend to convey what is normally conveyed (or normally intended to be conveyed), and we require a good reason for accepting that a particular use diverges from the general usage (e.g., he never knew or had forgotten the general usage). Similarly in nonlinguistic cases: we are presumed to intend the normal consequences of our actions.

[...]

All this is very obvious; but surely to show that the criteria for judging linguistic intentions are very like the criteria for judging nonlinguistic intentions is to show that linguistic intentions are very like nonlinguistic intentions.

Notes

[1] *Ethics and Language* (New Haven, 1944), ch. iii.

[2] *Ibid.*, p. 57.

What is a speech act?

J.R. Searle

Source: Searle, J.R. (1971) 'What is a speech act?', in J.R. Searle (ed.) *The Philosophy of Language*, Oxford, Oxford University Press, pp.44–6. Originally in Black, M. (ed.) (1965) *Philosophy in America*, London, Allen & Unwin, pp.221–39. Edited as indicated.

Speech acts are characteristically performed in the utterance of sounds or the making of marks. What is the difference between *just* uttering sounds or making marks and performing a speech act? One difference is that the sounds or marks one makes in the performance of a speech act are characteristically said to *have meaning*, and a second related difference is that one is characteristically said to *mean something* by those sounds or marks. Characteristically when one speaks one means something by what one says, and what one says, the string of morphemes that one emits, is characteristically said to have a meaning.

[...]

But what is it for one to mean something by what one says, and what is it for something to have a meaning? To answer the first of these questions I propose to borrow and revise some ideas of Paul Grice. In an article entitled 'Meaning',[1] Grice gives the following analysis of one sense of the notion of 'meaning'. To say that *A* meant something by *x* is to say that '*A* intended the utterance of *x* to produce some effect in an audience by means of the recognition of this intention'. This seems to me a useful start on an analysis of meaning, first because it shows the close relationship between the notion of meaning and the notion of intention, and secondly because it captures something which is, I think, essential to speaking a language: In speaking a language I attempt to communicate things to my hearer by means of getting him to recognize my intention to communicate just those things. For example, characteristically, when I make an assertion, I attempt to communicate to and convince my hearer of the truth of a certain proposition; and the means I employ to do this are to utter certain sounds, which utterance I intend to produce in him the desired effect by means of his recognition of my intention to produce just that effect. I shall illustrate this with an example. I might on the one hand attempt to get you to believe that I am French by speaking French all the time, dressing in the French manner, showing wild enthusiasm for de Gaulle, and cultivating French acquaintances. But I might on the other hand attempt to get you to believe that I am French by simply telling you that I am French. Now, what is the difference between these two ways of my attempting to get you to believe that I am French? One crucial difference is that in the second case I attempt to get you to believe that I am French by getting you to recognize that it is my purported intention to get you to believe just that. That is one of the things involved in telling you that I am French. But of course if I try to get you to believe that I am French by putting on the act I described, then your recognition of my intention to produce in you the belief that I am French is not the means I am employing. Indeed in this case you would, I think, become rather suspicious if you recognized my intention.

However valuable this analysis of meaning is, it seems to me to be in certain respects defective. [...] [I]t fails to account for the extent to which meaning is a matter of rules or conventions. That is, this account of meaning does not show the connection between one's meaning something by what one says and what that which one says actually means in the language. In order to illustrate this point I now wish to present a counter-example to this analysis of meaning. The point of the counter-example will be to illustrate the connection between what a speaker means and what the words he utters mean.

Suppose that I am an American soldier in the Second World War and that I am captured by Italian troops. And suppose also that I wish to get these troops to believe that I am a German officer in order to get them to release me. What I would like to do is to tell them in German or Italian that I am a German officer. But let us suppose I don't know enough German or Italian to do that. So I, as it were, attempt to put on a show of telling them that I am a German officer by reciting those few bits of German that I know, trusting that they don't know enough German to see through my plan. Let us suppose I know only one line of German, which I remember from a poem I had to memorize in a high-school German course. Therefore I, a captured American, address my Italian captors with the following sentence: 'Kennst du das Land, wo die Zitronen blühen?' Now, let us describe the situation in Gricean terms. I intend to produce a certain effect in them, namely, the effect of believing that I am a German officer; and I intend to produce this effect by means of their recognition of my intention. I intend that they should think that what I am trying to tell them is that I am a German officer. But does it follow from this account that when I say 'Kennst du das Land ...' etc., what I mean is, 'I am a German officer'? Not only does it not follow, but in this case it seems plainly false that when I utter the German sentence what I mean is 'I am a German officer', or even 'Ich bin ein deutscher Offizier', because what the words mean is, 'Knowest thou the land where the lemon trees bloom?' Of course, I want my captors to be deceived into thinking that what I mean is 'I am a German officer', but part of what is involved in the deception is getting them to think that that is what the words which I utter mean in German. At one point in the *Philosophical Investigations* Wittgenstein says 'Say "it's cold here" and mean "it's warm here"'.[2] The reason we are unable to do this is that what we can mean is a function of what we are saying. Meaning is more than a matter of intention, it is also a matter of convention.

Grice's account can be amended to deal with counter-examples of this kind. We have here a case where I am trying to produce a certain effect by means of the recognition of my intention to produce that effect, but the device I use to produce this effect is one which is conventionally, by the rules governing the use of that device, used as a means of producing quite different [...] effects. We must therefore reformulate the Gricean account of meaning in such a way as to make it clear that one's meaning something when one says something is more than just contingently related to what the sentence means in the language one is speaking. In our analysis of [the meaning of acts of speech] we must capture both the intentional and the conventional aspects and especially the relationship between them. In the performance of an [act of meaningful speech] the speaker intends to produce a certain effect by means of getting the hearer to recognize his intention to produce that effect, and furthermore, if he is using words literally, he intends this recognition to be achieved in virtue of the fact that the rules for using the expressions he utters associate the expressions with the production of that effect. It is this *combination* of elements which we shall need to express in our analysis of the [meaning of acts of speech].

Notes

[1] *Philosophical Review*, 1957 [Reading 1].

[2] *Philosophical Investigations* (Oxford 1953), para. 510.

The meaning of 'meaning'

H. Putnam

Source: Putnam, H. (1994) 'The meaning of "meaning"', in Robert M. Harnish (ed.) *Basic Topics in the Philosophy of Language*, London, Harvester Wheatsheaf, pp.221–39. Originally in Gunderson, K. (ed.) (1975) *Language, Mind, and Knowledge*, Minneapolis, University of Minnesota Press. Edited as indicated, with numbering of parts added.

[Part I] Meaning and extension

Since the Middle Ages at least, writers on the theory of meaning have purported to discover an ambiguity in the ordinary concept of meaning, and have introduced a pair of terms – extension and intension, or *Sinn* and *Bedeutung*, or whatever – to disambiguate the notion. The extension of a term, in customary logical parlance, is simply the set of things the term is true of. Thus, 'rabbit,' in its most common English sense, is true of all and only rabbits, so the extension of 'rabbit' is precisely the set of rabbits.

[...]

Now consider the compound terms 'creature with a heart' and 'creature with a kidney.' Assuming that every creature with a heart possesses a kidney and vice versa, the extension of these two terms is exactly the same. But they obviously differ in meaning. Supposing that there is a sense of 'meaning' in which meaning = extension, there must be another sense of 'meaning' in which the meaning of a term is not its extension but something else, say the 'concept' associated with the term. Let us call this 'something else' the intension of the term. The concept of a creature with a heart is clearly a different concept from the concept of a creature with a kidney. Thus the two terms have different intension. When we say they have different 'meaning,' meaning = intension.

Intension and extension

Something like the preceding paragraph appears in every standard exposition of the notions 'intension' and 'extension.' But it is not at all satisfactory. Why it is not satisfactory is, in a sense, the burden of this entire essay. [...]

[The] traditional doctrine that the notion 'meaning' possesses the extension/intension ambiguity has certain typical consequences. Most traditional philosophers thought of concepts as something mental. Thus the doctrine that the meaning of a term (the meaning 'in the sense of intension,' that is) is a concept carried the implication that meanings are mental entities. Frege and more recently Carnap and his followers, however, rebelled against this 'psychologism,' as they termed it. Feeling that meanings are public property – that the same meaning can be 'grasped' by more than one person and by persons at different times – they identified concepts (and hence 'intensions' or meanings) with abstract entities rather than mental entities. However, 'grasping' these abstract entities was still an individual psychological act. None of these philosophers doubted that understanding a word (knowing its intension) was just a matter of being in a certain psychological state [...].

[...] So theory of meaning came to rest on two unchallenged assumptions:

1. That knowing the meaning of a term [in the sense of 'intension'] is just a matter of being in a certain psychological state (in the sense of 'psychological state' in which states of memory and psychological dispositions are 'psychological states'; no one thought that knowing the meaning of a word was a continuous state of consciousness, of course).

2. That the meaning of a term (in the sense of 'intension') determines its extension (in the sense that sameness of intension entails sameness of extension).

I shall argue that these two assumptions are not jointly satisfied by any notion, let alone any notion of meaning. The traditional concept of meaning is a concept which rests on a false theory.

[...]

[Part II] Are meanings in the head?

That psychological state does not determine extension will now be shown with the aid of a little science fiction. For the purpose of the following science-fiction examples, we shall suppose that somewhere in the galaxy there is a planet we shall call Twin Earth. Twin Earth is very much like Earth; in fact, people on Twin Earth even speak English. In fact, apart from the differences we shall specify in our science-fiction examples, the reader may suppose that Twin Earth is exactly like Earth. He may even suppose that he has a Doppelganger – an identical copy – on Twin Earth, if he wishes, although my stories will not depend on this.

Although some of the people on Twin Earth (say, the ones who call themselves 'Americans' and the ones who call themselves 'Canadians' and the ones who call themselves 'Englishmen,' etc.) speak English, there are, not surprisingly, a few tiny differences which we will now describe between the dialects of English spoken on Twin Earth and Standard English. These differences themselves depend on some of the peculiarities of Twin Earth.

One of the peculiarities of Twin Earth is that the liquid called 'water' is not H_2O but a different liquid whose chemical formula is very long and complicated. I shall abbreviate this chemical formula simply as XYZ. I shall suppose that XYZ is indistinguishable from water at normal temperatures and pressures. In particular, it tastes like water and it quenches thirst like water. Also, I shall suppose that the oceans and lakes and seas of Twin Earth contain XYZ and not water, that it rains XYZ on Twin Earth and not water, etc.

If a spaceship from Earth ever visits Twin Earth, then the supposition at first will be that 'water' has the same meaning on Earth and on Twin Earth. This supposition will be corrected when it is discovered that 'water' on Twin Earth is XYZ, and the Earthian spaceship will report somewhat as follows:

'On Twin Earth the word "water" means XYZ.'

[...]

Note that there is no problem about the extension of the term 'water.' The word simply has two different meanings (as we say): in the sense in which it is used on Twin Earth, the sense of water$_{TE}$, what we call 'water' simply isn't water; while in the sense in which it is used on Earth, the sense of water$_E$, what the Twin Earthians call 'water' simply isn't water. The extension of 'water' in the sense of water$_E$ is the set of all wholes consisting of H_2O molecules, or something like that; the extension of water in the sense of water$_{TE}$ is the set of all wholes consisting of XYZ molecules, or something like that.

Now let us roll the time back to about 1750. At that time chemistry was not developed on either Earth or Twin Earth. The typical Earthian speaker of English did not know water consisted of hydrogen and oxygen, and the typical Twin Earthian speaker of English did not know 'water' consisted of XYZ. Let Oscar$_1$ be such a typical Earthian English speaker, and let Oscar$_2$ be his counterpart on Twin Earth. You may suppose that there is no belief that Oscar$_1$ had about water that Oscar$_2$ did not have about 'water.' If you like, you may even suppose that Oscar$_1$ and Oscar$_2$ were exact duplicates in appearance, feelings, thoughts, interior monologue, etc. Yet the extension of the term 'water' was just as much H_2O on Earth in 1750 as in 1950; and the extension of the term 'water' was just as much XYZ on Twin Earth in 1750 as in 1950. Oscar$_1$ and Oscar$_2$ understood the term 'water' differently in 1750 *although they were in the same psychological state*, and although, given the state of science at the time, it would have taken their scientific communities about fifty years to discover that they understood the term 'water' differently. Thus the extension of the term 'water' (and, in fact, its 'meaning' in the intuitive preanalytical usage of that term) is *not* a function of the psychological state of the speaker by itself.

But, it might be objected, why should we accept it that the term 'water' had the same extension in 1750 and in 1950 (on both Earths)? The logic of natural-kind terms like 'water' is a complicated matter, but the following is a sketch of an answer. Suppose I point to a glass of water and say 'this liquid is called water' (or 'this is called water,' if the marker 'liquid' is clear from the context). My 'ostensive definition' of water [is that] the necessary and sufficient condition for being water is bearing the relation same$_L$ to [i.e. being the same liquid as] the stuff in the glass; but this is the necessary and sufficient condition only if the empirical presupposition is satisfied. If it is not satisfied, then one of a series of, so to speak, 'fallback' conditions becomes activated.

The key point is that the relation same$_L$ is a *theoretical* relation: whether something is or is not the same liquid as *this* may take an indeterminate amount of scientific investigation to determine. Moreover, even if a 'definite' answer has been obtained either through scientific investigation or through the application of some 'common sense' test, the answer is *defeasible:* future investigation might reverse even the most 'certain' example. Thus, the fact that an English speaker in 1750 might have called XYZ 'water,' while he or his successors would not have called XYZ water in 1800 or 1850 does not mean that the 'meaning' of 'water' changed for the average speaker in the interval. [...]

Let us now modify our science-fiction story. I do not know whether one can make pots and pans out of molybdenum; and if one can make them out of molybdenum, I don't know whether they could be distinguished easily from aluminum pots and pans. (I don't know any of this even though I have acquired the word 'molybdenum.') So I shall suppose that molybdenum pots and pans *can't* be distinguished from aluminum pots and pans save by an expert. [...] We will now suppose that molybdenum is as common on Twin Earth as aluminum is on Earth, and that aluminum is as rare on Twin Earth as molybdenum is on Earth. In particular, we shall assume that 'aluminum' pots and pans are made of molybdenum on Twin Earth. Finally, we shall assume that the words 'aluminum' and 'molybdenum' are *switched* on Twin Earth: 'aluminum' is the name of *molybdenum* and 'molybdenum' is the name of *aluminum.*

This example shares some features with the previous one. If a spaceship from Earth visited Twin Earth, the visitors from Earth probably would not suspect that the 'aluminum' pots and pans on Twin Earth were not made of aluminum, especially when the Twin Earthians said they were. But there is one important difference between the two cases. An Earthian metallurgist could tell very easily that 'aluminum' was molybdenum, and a Twin Earthian metallurgist could tell equally easily that aluminum was 'molybdenum.' (The shudder quotes in the preceding sentence indicate Twin Earthian usages.) Whereas in 1750 no one on either Earth or Twin Earth could have distinguished water from 'water,' the confusion of aluminum with 'aluminum' involves only a part of the linguistic communities involved.

The example makes the same point as the preceding one. If Oscar$_1$ and Oscar$_2$ are standard speakers of Earthian English and Twin Earthian English respectively, and neither is chemically or metallurgically sophisticated, then there may be no difference at all in their psychological state when they use the word 'aluminum'; nevertheless we have to say that 'aluminum' has the extension *aluminum* in the idiolect of Oscar$_1$ and the extension *molybdenum* in the idiolect of Oscar$_2$. (Also we have to say that Oscar$_1$ and Oscar$_2$ mean different things by 'aluminum,' that 'aluminum' has a different meaning on Earth than it does on Twin Earth, etc.) Again we see that the psychological state of the speaker does not determine the extension (or the 'meaning,' speaking preanalytically) of the word.

[L]et me introduce a non-science-fiction example. Suppose you are like me and cannot tell an elm from a beech tree. We still say that the extension of 'elm' in my idiolect is the same as the extension of 'elm' in anyone else's, viz., the set of all elm trees, and that the set of all beech trees is the extension of 'beech' in *both* of our idiolects. Thus 'elm' in my idiolect has a different extension from 'beech' in your idiolect (as it should). Is it really credible that this difference in extension is brought about by some difference in our concepts? My concept of an elm tree is exactly the same as my concept of a beech tree (I blush to confess). This shows that the identification of meaning 'in the sense of intension' with concept cannot be correct [...] Cut the pie any way you like, 'meanings' just ain't in the *head*!

[Part III] A socio-linguistic hypothesis

The last two examples depend upon a fact about language that seems, surprisingly, never to have been pointed out: that there is *division of linguistic labor*. We could hardly use such words as 'elm' and 'aluminum' if no one possessed a way of recognizing elm trees and aluminum metal; but not everyone to whom the distinction is important has to be able to make the distinction. Let us shift the example: consider *gold*. Gold is important for many reasons: it is a precious metal, it is a monetary metal, it has symbolic value (it is important to most people that the 'gold' wedding ring they wear *really* consist of gold and not just *look* gold), etc. Consider our community as a 'factory': in this 'factory' some people have the 'job' of *wearing gold wedding rings*, other people have the 'job' of selling gold wedding rings, still other people have the job of *telling whether or not something is really gold*. It is not at all necessary or efficient that everyone who wears a gold ring (or a gold cuff link, etc.), or discusses the 'gold standard,' etc., engage in buying and selling gold. Nor is it necessary or efficient that everyone who buys and sells gold be able to tell whether or not something is really gold in a society where this form of dishonesty is uncommon (selling fake gold) and in which one can easily consult an expert in case of doubt. And it is *certainly* not necessary or efficient that everyone who has occasion to buy or wear gold be able to tell with any reliability whether or not something is really gold.

The foregoing facts are just examples of mundane division of labor (in a wide sense). But they engender a division of linguistic labor: everyone to whom gold is important for any reason has to acquire the word 'gold'; but he does not have to acquire the *method of recognizing* if something is or is not gold. He can rely on a special subclass of speakers. The features that are generally thought to be present in connection with a general name – necessary and sufficient conditions for membership in the extension, ways of recognizing if something is in the extension ('criteria'), etc. – are all present in the linguistic community *considered as a collective body*; but that collective body divides the 'labor' of knowing and employing these various parts of the 'meaning' of 'gold.'

[...]

It seems to me that this phenomenon of division of linguistic labor is one which it will be very important for sociolinguistics to investigate. In connection with it, I should like to propose the following hypothesis:

Hypothesis of the Universality of the Division of Linguistic Labor:

Every linguistic community exemplifies the sort of division of linguistic labor just described, that is, possesses at least some terms whose associated 'criteria' are known only to a subset of the speakers who acquire the terms, and whose use by the other speakers depends upon a structured co-operation between them and the speakers in the relevant subsets.

[O]ne might conjecture that division of labor, including linguistic labor, is a fundamental trait of our species.

It is easy to see how this phenomenon accounts for some of the examples given above of the failure of the assumptions 1 [and] 2. Whenever a term is subject to the division of linguistic labor, the 'average' speaker who acquires it does not acquire anything that fixes its extension. In particular, his individual psychological state *certainly* does not fix its extension; it is only the sociolinguistic state of the collective linguistic body to which the speaker belongs that fixes the extension.

We may summarize this discussion by pointing out that there are two sorts of tools in the world: there are tools like a hammer or a screwdriver which can be used by one person; and there are tools like a steamship which require the cooperative activity of a number of persons to use. Words have been thought of too much on the model of the first sort of tool.

[Part IV] Indexicality and rigidity

The first of our science-fiction examples – 'water' on Earth and on Twin Earth in 1750 – does not involve division of linguistic labor, or at least does not involve it in the same way the examples of 'aluminium' and 'elm' do. There were not (in our story, anyway) any 'experts' on water on Earth in 1750, nor any experts on 'water' on Twin Earth. [...] The example does involve things which are of fundamental importance to the theory of reference [...].

[...]

Suppose I point to a glass of liquid and say 'this is water,' in order to teach someone the word 'water.' [...] Let us now try to clarify further how it is supposed to be taken.

[...]

Let W_1 and W_2 be two possible worlds in which I exist and in which this glass exists and in which I am giving a meaning explanation by pointing to this glass and saying 'this is water.' (We do not assume that the liquid in the glass is the same in both worlds.) Let us suppose that in W_1 the glass is full of H_2O and in W_2 the glass is full of XYZ. We shall also suppose that W_1 is the *actual* world and that XYZ is the stuff typically called 'water' in the world W_2 (so that the relation between English speakers in W_1 and English speakers in W_2 is exactly the same as the relation between English speakers on Earth and English speakers on Twin Earth). Then there are two theories one might have concerning the meaning of 'water.'

1. One might hold that 'water' was world-relative but constant in meaning (i.e., the word has a constant relative meaning). On this theory, 'water' means the same in W_1 and W_2; it's just that water is H_2O in W_1 and water is XYZ in W_2.

2. One might hold that water is H_2O in all worlds (the stuff called 'water' in W_2 isn't water), but 'water' doesn't have the same meaning in W_1 and W_2.

If what was said before about the Twin Earth case was correct, then 2 is clearly the correct theory. When I say 'this (liquid) is water,' [...] the force of my explanation is that 'water' is whatever bears a certain equivalence relation (the relation we called 'same$_L$' [...]) to the piece of liquid referred to as 'this' in the actual world.

[...]

[W]e can understand the relation same$_L$ (same liquid as) as a cross-world relation by understanding it so that a liquid in world W_1 which has the same important physical properties (in W_1) that a liquid in W_2 possesses (in W_2) bears same$_L$ to the latter liquid.

Then the theory we have been presenting may be summarized by saying that an entity x, in an arbitrary possible world, is water if and only if it bears the relation same$_L$ (construed as a cross-world relation) to the stuff we call 'water' in the actual world.

[...]

Words like 'now,' 'this,' 'here,' have long been recognized to be *indexical*, or *token-reflexive* – i.e., to have an extension which varied from context to context or token to token. For these words no one has ever suggested the traditional theory that 'intension determines extension.' To take our Twin Earth example: if I have a *Doppelgänger* on Twin Earth, then when I think 'I have a headache,' *he* thinks 'I have a headache.' But the extension of the particular token of 'I' in his verbalized thought is himself [...], while the extension of the token of 'I' in my verbalized thought is *me* [...]. So the same word, 'I,' has two different extensions in two different idiolects; but it does not follow that the concept I have of myself is in any way different from the concept my *Doppelgänger* has of himself.

Now then, we have maintained that indexicality extends beyond the *obviously* indexical words and morphemes (e.g., the tenses of verbs). Our theory can be summarized as saying that words like 'water' have an unnoticed indexical component: 'water' is stuff that bears a certain similarity relation to the water *around here*. [...]

All the difference in the world

Tim Crane

Source: Crane, T. (1991) 'All the difference in the world', *Philosophical Quarterly*, 41, 162, pp.1–25. Edited as indicated. Numbering of parts, and some subtitles, added.

[Part I] Putnam's thought experiment

Putnam's original aim in 'The Meaning of "Meaning"' (1975 [Reading 3]) was to dispute certain 'grotesquely mistaken' views of language (1975, p. 271) which arise from philosophers' tendency to ignore the contribution made by our natural and social environment to the meanings of our words. Putnam claimed that these views depend on two incompatible assumptions about meaning. The first assumption is that knowing the meaning of a term is a matter of being in a certain psychological state – in general, the meanings of words are fixed by the psychological states of those who use them. I shall call this 'MPS'. The second is that meaning determines reference: a difference in reference is sufficient for a difference in meaning. I shall call this 'MDR'.

Putnam uses the Twin Earth story to show that these two assumptions can be true of no notion – of meaning, Fregean *Sinn,* Carnapian intension or whatever. [He] asks us to suppose that 'somewhere in the galaxy' there is a planet, Twin Earth, as similar as can be to Earth, except that on Twin Earth, the substance people call 'water' is not made up of H_2O, but has a complex chemical constitution whose description we may abbreviate to 'XYZ'. XYZ feels and tastes like H_2O, and the people on Twin Earth do the same things with it. He also supposes that each of us has a duplicate 'twin' or *doppelgänger* on Twin Earth, type-identical to each of us down to the last atom.

Now suppose that on Earth I say 'Water, water everywhere, nor any drop to drink' and my Twin makes the same noises. Do we utter two sentences with the same meaning? Putnam argues that we do not, since the references of our words are different: H_2O and XYZ on Earth and Twin Earth respectively. Since the reference of the two utterances of 'water' is different on each planet, then by MDR, their meanings differ. But what each speaker 'has in mind' (sensations, beliefs about the superficial properties of water, etc.) is the same.

Putnam insists that this difference in meaning between Earth and Twin Earth does not depend on the fact that some scientists on each planet could *tell* that H_2O is not XYZ. To illustrate this he describes Earth and Twin Earth in 1750, before the development of adequate chemistry. In this case no one could tell the difference between the two substances; but the reference of 'water' on each planet differs, according to Putnam. And since the reference differs, so does the meaning, 'in the intuitive, preanalytic use of that term' (1975, p. 224 [Reading 3, p.194]). This is so on the plausible assumption that the meaning of 'water' does not change between 1750 and (say) 1950, simply because scientists found out more about water.

Putnam concludes that MPS is false. The psychological states of twins do not determine the reference of their utterances of 'water'. So if we keep MDR, as he urges we should, then certain meanings aren't determined by psychological states. Meanings aren't 'in the head' (1975, p. 223 [Reading 3, p.196]).

The argument only establishes that MPS is false if my Twin and I are in the same psychological states. So the nature of what is being referred to (H_2O or XYZ) should not affect our psychological states in this sense. These are what Putnam calls psychological states 'in the narrow sense' (1975, p. 221), states which are permitted by 'the assumption of methodological solipsism':

> that no psychological state, properly so called, presupposes the existence of any individual other than the subject to whom these states are ascribed.
>
> (1975, p. 220 [omitted from Reading 3 but discussed later in chapter 3])

Psychological states which do not meet this condition are psychological states in the 'wide' or 'broad' sense: my Twin and I share our narrow psychological states, but differ in our broad psychological states. So what MPS really says is that the *narrow* psychological states of a language-user do not determine meaning.

[...]

[Part II] What is wrong with Putnam's argument?

[...]

Putnam's argument rests on the following three premises:

(1) MDR – meaning determines reference.

(2) My Twin and I are atom-for-atom identical, and so (by definition) share all our narrow [psychological] states.

(3) When I say 'water is wet' and my Twin says the same, our sentences do not have the same truth conditions, since his water is XYZ and mine is H_2O.

From these he concludes that narrow [psychological] states – the states my Twin and I share – do not determine the meanings of our words.

The argument is valid, so we must look at the premises. Premise (1) is just the assumption MDR, which we should accept (*pace*, perhaps, the case of indexicals). Premise (2) is part of the story, and although it is rather irritatingly undermined by the fact that our bodies are composed of water, this is just a feature of the example. There is certainly nothing incoherent in supposing that there can be two people atom-for-atom indistinguishable.

So all the interest rests with (3). Why should we believe it? Why should a difference in the chemical structure of water affect the truth conditions of 'water is wet'? Why should we not say, for instance, that if there were such a substance as XYZ, all this would show is that 'not all water has the same microstructure' (Mellor 1977, p. 303). And indeed, we knew this already, since it would surely be stipulative to deny that heavy water (D_2O) is really *water*. So why does the fact that most of our water is H_2O entail that the truth conditions of 'water is wet' differ across Earth and Twin Earth?

Perhaps a defender of Putnam could respond that 'water' is not really a natural kind term. Perhaps we should accept that there are other kinds of water, because of the different chemical structures that can have similar superficial properties. But when you get to the names of elements you get 'real' natural kind terms – there cannot be different kinds of gold, or lead or helium.

But what about isotopes? Which isotopes of elements are the substances referred to by the 'real' natural kind terms? Which of the two isotopes of chlorine is really chlorine? Maybe they both are – but in that case 'chlorine' like 'water' is not a real natural kind term either, for the same reasons. And this seems to restrict the range of real natural terms to such an extent as to make them a trivial category for metaphysics and the philosophy of science: terms that pick out elements that do not have isotopes. The obvious lesson is that the idea of a natural kind term, as used by essentialists like Putnam, is not very well defined.

It may be responded that when there *is* a clear case of two genuinely different elements – not isotopes of the same element – that are superficially indistinguishable, then Putnam's argument will work. This does somewhat reduce the force of the argument, but it is worth looking at such a case in some detail to see exactly what is wrong with it.

Take aluminium and molybdenum, two practically indistinguishable metals whose names (and relative scarcity) are switched on Earth and Twin Earth. And suppose my Twin and I are atom-for-atom identical. [...] Why not say that we have the same concept (call it '*molyminium*') that applies to aluminium and molybdenum alike? The concept *molyminium* will distinguish less 'finely' between substances than the concepts *aluminium* and *molybdenum*.

[...] Since my Twin and I have an incomplete understanding of the word 'aluminium', our concept *molyminium* does not determine the extension of 'aluminium' as the concept of someone who does have a complete understanding does. Such a person, someone 'in the know', has the more precise concept, and is thus in a position to correct the uses of the word 'aluminium' of those speakers who do not distinguish sufficiently between aluminium and molybdenum. This is just Putnam's division of linguistic labour – but it gives us no reason to think that my Twin and I do not share our concepts.

[...]

[Part III: Putnam's positive theory of reference determination]

What about Putnam's positive proposals? The two major claims made about meaning are that natural kind terms like 'water' are indexical, and that there is a division of linguistic labour (a thesis I mentioned above). These two claims are intended [by Putnam] to compensate for philosophers' lack of concern for the roles of 'the world' and 'other people' respectively in determining meaning. [...] I think that the first claim [...] is [...] inconsistent with other claims of Putnam's [...] .

[T]he Twin Earth cases are meant to demonstrate that the world itself can, as it were, fix the meanings of some of our words. To show how this might work, Putnam introduced the idea that natural kind words have an 'unnoticed indexical component: "water" is stuff that bears a certain similarity relation to the water around here' (1975, p.234 [Reading 3, p.199]). The idea seems to be that once the reference of 'water' has been fixed (perhaps by saying 'This is water'; (Putnam 1975, p.231 [Reading 3, p.198])) then the word can only refer to the substance which is relevantly similar in constitution to the substance referred to. So if meaning still determines reference, then the meaning of a term must be sensitive to the context of the use of that term. [...] [I]t is fairly clear that for Putnam, the relevant features of the context are the microstructure of water, and where the utterance is made.

It is a commonplace that indexical terms fix reference by sensitivity to context. 'I', 'here' and 'now' refer to different speakers, places and times in different contexts of utterance. This is clearly what makes Putnam say that natural kind terms are indexical. [...] So, since the Twin Earth cases are supposed to show that there is no water on Twin Earth, Putnam concludes that 'water' works something like 'I' in picking out different substances in relevantly different contexts.

However, even if we accept that XYZ is not water, this claim is incorrect. For [it implies that] 'water' as used on Twin Earth is a mere homonym of 'water' as used on Earth. But indexicals are not homonyms – indexical type-expressions have a constant meaning. For example, since the work of Kaplan (1977) and Perry (1979), many accept that the constant meaning of (say) the type 'here' is a function which maps contexts (places of utterance) on to a contribution to truth conditions. But Putnam should hold that there is *no* constant meaning in the uses of 'water' across Earth and Twin Earth – since he believes that meaning determines extension. [...]

So if 'water' is genuinely indexical, then all tokens of 'water' must have a constant meaning. But this is inconsistent with the conclusion of the Twin Earth argument. On the other hand, if the Twin Earth argument is sound, then tokens of 'water' spoken on both planets are mere homonyms. But this is inconsistent with the claim that 'water' is an indexical. So if Putnam is to keep the conclusion of the Twin Earth argument, then he ought to abandon the claim that 'water' is indexical.

References

Almog, J., Perry, J. and Wettstein, H. (eds) (1989) *Themes From Kaplan* (Oxford: OUP).

Kaplan, D. (1977) 'Demonstratives', in Almog, Perry and Wettstein (1989).

Mellor, D. H. (1977) 'Natural Kinds', *British Journal for the Philosophy of Science*, 28 pp. 299–312.

Perry, J. (1979) 'The Problem of the Essential Indexical', *Nous*, 13 pp. 3–21.

Putnam, H. (1975) *Mind, Language and Reality* (Cambridge: Cambridge University Press).

Semantic engines: an introduction to mind design

John Haugeland

Source: Haugeland, J. (1981) 'Semantic engines: an introduction to mind design', in J. Haugeland (ed.) *Mind Design: Philosophy, Psychology, Artificial Intelligence*, Montgomery, Vermont, Bradford Books, pp.1–34. Edited as indicated. Subtitles as in the original, with some renumbering.

I. Cognitive science

'Reasoning is but reckoning,' said Hobbes (1651, ch. V), in the earliest expression of the computational view of thought. Three centuries later, with the development of electronic 'computers,' his idea finally began to catch on; and now, in three decades, it has become the single most important theoretical hypothesis in psychology (and several allied disciplines), and also the basis of an exciting new research field, called 'artificial intelligence.' Recently, the expression *cognitive science* has been introduced to cover all these varied enterprises, in recognition of their common conceptual foundation. This term, therefore, does not apply to every scientific theory of cognition, but only to those sharing a certain broad outlook – which is sometimes called the 'information processing' or 'symbol manipulation' approach. Perhaps, at last, Hobbes's philosophical insight has found its home in a proper scientific paradigm.

[...]

A [...] perspective on all the excitement can be gained by asking why it took three hundred years for Hobbes's original proposal to be appreciated. Mainly, three famous philosophical dilemmas stood in the way: (i) the metaphysical problem of mind interacting with matter; (ii) the theoretical problem of explaining the relevance of meanings, without appealing to a question-begging homunculus; and (iii) the methodological issue over the empirical testability (and, hence, respectability) of 'mentalistic' explanations. The computational idea can be seen as slicing through all [three philosophical] dilemmas at a stroke; and this is what gives it, I think, the bulk of its tremendous gut-level appeal.

[(i)] Descartes, a contemporary of Hobbes, gave the mind/matter problem its modern form in his doctrine of metaphysical *dualism*. Mind and body, he said, are two entirely different *kinds* of substance: the one can have (as distinguishing characteristics) various thoughts and feelings, whereas the other can have shapes, motions, and the causal interactions described by physical laws (and not vice versa). Intuitively, this is much more appealing than *materialism* (the main alternative to dualism), according to which everything, including minds, is really just matter, in one form or another. Not only are we reluctant to ascribe thought and feeling to 'mere' matter, but we also find it very hard to ascribe shape and location to minds or ideas. There is, however, one basic problem, which no dualist has ever really solved: how can mind and body *interact*? On the one hand, they certainly *seem* to interact, as when a mental decision leads to a physical action, or when a physical stimulus leads to a mental perception; indeed, it's not clear how perception and action could be possible at all without mind/body interaction. On the other hand, however, physical laws are supposed to describe all motions of all bodies *completely* in terms of their interactions with one another. In other words, physics leaves no room for causal intervention by the mental; hence the price of mind/body interaction is violation of the laws of physics – a price that few philosophers (or scientists) are willing to pay.

[(ii)] Thought itself (quite apart from matter) is not static and not random: it progresses and develops in ways that obey (at least much of the time) various rules of inference and reason. Superficially, this suggests an analogy with material particles obeying the laws of physics. But the analogy breaks down at a crucial point: particles have neither choice nor difficulty in 'obeying' physics – it happens infallibly and automatically. People, on the other hand, often have to work to be reasonable; following the rules of reason is hardly infallible and can be very difficult. But this means there cannot be an explanatory dynamics of thought, which is at all comparable to physical dynamic theories; the respective roles of rules and laws in the two cases are deeply different. In particular, since correct application of the rules of reason to particular thoughts depends on what those thoughts *mean*, it seems that there must be some active rule-applier, which (or: who) *understands* the thoughts (and the rules), and which applies the rules to the thoughts as well as it can. If the activity of this rule-applier, following the rules of reason, is to explain the rationality of our thought processes, then it must be regarded as a complete little person – or *homunculus* (in Latin) – inside the head, directing the thoughts like a traffic cop. The trouble is: a theory that invokes an homunculus to *explain* thinking, has begged its own question, because the homunculus itself has to think, and *that* thinking has *not* been explained.

[(iii)] Finally, there is the question of how the psychology of thought could ever be properly scientific. Thoughts, it seems, cannot be observed; and the difficulty is not that, like electrons or distant galaxies, they are too small or too far away. Rather, they are somehow essentially subjective – we don't even know what it would be like to observe (or measure) them objectively. So all that science has to go on, even in principle, is objective *behavior* (which might include internal 'physiological behavior'); hence, thoughts can enter the picture only as inferred or hypothesized intermediates. Unfortunately, in any given case, invoking beliefs and desires to explain an action is just too easy. Whatever an organism does, one can always trump up a million different ideas and motives that would explain it. If there can be, in principle, no independent, empirical check on which of these hypotheses is the right one, it seems scientifically disreputable to accept any of them, even tentatively. [...]

Cognitive scientists [...] can offer explanations in terms of meaning and rule-following, without presupposing any unexplained homunculus. It all depends on a marvellously rich analogy with computers – the outlines of which we can see with a quick look at everybody's favorite example: a chess-playing machine. [...] [W]e are quite confident [that a chess-playing machine] has no immaterial soul. [Its] decisions clearly cause physical behavior (e.g., in teletypewriters or TV screens), yet no one is worried that the laws of physics are being violated. [...] [W]*hat an inspiration!* If there are no philosophical dilemmas about chess-playing computers, then why should there be any about chess-playing people – or, indeed, about human intelligence in any other form? To put it coldly: why not suppose that people *just are* computers (and send philosophy packing)? Well ... nothing very interesting is ever that simple. Various questions come up, among the first of which is: What exactly is being proposed, anyway?

II. Formal systems

To start at the beginning, we must first say a little bit more carefully what a computer is. It is an automatic formal system. To see what this means, we first consider what a formal system is, and then what it is to automate one.

A *formal system* is like a game in which tokens are manipulated according to rules, in order to see what configurations can be obtained. Basically, to define such a game, three things have to be specified:

(1) what the tokens are;

(2) what the starting position is; and

(3) what moves are allowed in any given position.

Implicit in (2) and (3) is a specification of what positions are possible (for instance, what the board is, if it's a board game). Also, there is sometimes a specified *goal* position, which the player (or each player) is trying to achieve – such as a 'winning position.'

For example, there is a familiar solitaire game in which the tokens are pegs, arranged as follows in the starting position:

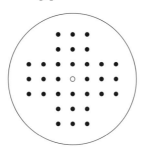

The solid dots are the tokens (pegs), and the circle in the middle is an empty space, into which a token could fit. The only move allowed by the rules is jumping one token over an adjacent one into an empty space, and then removing the token jumped over. This game has a goal; to perform such jumps until only one token remains, and it is in the center space.

[...]

[This definition of formal] systems has the following important consequence: two systems that seem to be quite different may nevertheless be essentially the same. Clearly, the peg-jumping game would be essentially unchanged if the pegs were replaced by marbles, or even by helicopters (given a big enough board) – so long as the same rules were followed. [...] This kind of essential sameness among formal systems is called *formal equivalence*. Two formal systems are formally equivalent if they can be translated back and forth in roughly the following sense:

(1) for each position in one system, there is a unique corresponding position in the other system;

(2) the two starting positions correspond; and

(3) whenever you can get from one position to another in one system, you can get from the corresponding position to the corresponding position in the other system.

[...] [T]his definition [...] leaves room for equivalent systems to be *very* different on the surface, so long as appropriate correspondences can be found.

[...]

III. Automatic formal systems [...]

An *automatic* formal system is a physical device (such as a machine) which automatically manipulates the tokens of some formal system according to the rules of that system. It is like a chess set that sits there and plays chess *by itself*, without any intervention from the players, or an axiomatic system that writes out its own proofs and theorems, without any help from the mathematician. The exciting and astonishing fact is that such systems can be built. Looked at in the right way, this is exactly what computers are. There are two fundamental problems in building an automatic formal system. The first is getting the device to obey the rules (in principle, this problem has already been solved [...]). The second is the 'control' problem – how the device selects which move to make when there are several legal options.

[...]

IV. The control problem

In the last section we considered systems in which each move is completely determined by the rules and the current position. This is essential in the design of an *automatic* system, because each step has to be made 'automatically' – that is, it must be completely fixed by the state of the machine at the time. But in most positions in most formal systems, any one of various moves would be legal; usually, that is what makes them interesting, as games or whatever. Does it follow that such interesting formal systems cannot be automated? No; it only follows that some device for deciding among the several legal options at any point must be automated as well.

The easiest way to think about it is to consider the machine as divided into two parts or 'sub-machines': one to generate a number of legal options, and another to choose from among them. This, of course, is just an extension of the basic point that a given device can be various machines, depending on how you look at it; only now we are looking at it as *two* separate (virtual) machines, interacting with each other on the same level. The advantage is that we can see how the above dilemma is resolved: the move-generating submachine automates an 'interesting' system, in which a variety of moves might be legal at any point; but the combined machine, with both parts together, satisfies the requirement that some *particular* next move be determined by the overall state of the device at each step. Designing the second submachine – the one that makes the choices, given the options – is the *control problem*. In most cases, control design turns out to be the hardest part of automating an interesting formal system.

In an average chess position, for example, [the] hard part – the entire difference between amateurs and world champions – is deciding *which* move to make [...]; and that is the hard part to program as well. At first it might seem that big modern computers, with their tremendous speed and memory, could just look ahead to every possible outcome and see which moves lead to ultimate victory. In principle, this would be possible, since chess is technically finite; and such a machine would be literally invincible. In practical terms, however, such a computation is nowhere near possible. Assuming an average of 31.6 options per play gives a thousand (31.6 x 31.6) possible combinations per full move (each side having a turn). Thus looking ahead five moves would involve a quadrillion (10^{15}) possibilities; forty moves (a typical game) would involve 10^{120} possibilities. (For comparison, there have been fewer than 10^{18} seconds since the beginning of the universe.) These numbers are just preposterously large for any physically conceivable computer. They get that big because the number of choices at each additional step *multiplies* the total number of possible combinations so far. For understandable reasons, this is called the *combinatorial explosion*; it plagues control design for all but the most straightforward problems.

Obviously, human chess-players don't make that many calculations either; in fact, the available evidence indicates that they make rather few. The trick is to consider only the *relevant* possibilities and ignore the rest. [...] So, the approach to the control problem in this case will almost certainly concentrate on determining which possible moves are the relevant ones, deserving further consideration.

Unfortunately, there is no fail-safe way to tell what is and isn't relevant. Everybody knows how a seemingly pointless or terrible move can turn out to be a brilliant stroke (once the opponent takes the bait). Any method that systematically bypasses certain moves as not worth pursuing will inevitably overlook some of these brilliancies. What we want is a method that is efficient at by-passing moves that *really are* worthless, but not easily fooled into ignoring moves that only *seem* worthless.

[...]

V. Semantics

Formal systems (and computers) can be more than mere games, because their tokens can have interpretations that relate them to the outside world. This is the domain of semantics and pragmatics.

Sometimes we say that the tokens in a certain formal system *mean* something – that is, they are 'signs,' or 'symbols,' or 'expressions' which 'stand for,' or 'represent,' or 'say' something. Such relations connect the tokens to the outside world (what they are 'about'), making it possible to use them for purposes like record-keeping, communication, calculation, and so on. A regular systematic specification of what all the tokens of a system mean is called in *interpretation*; and the general theory of interpretations and meanings is called *semantics*. Accordingly, what any token means or says, and hence also whether it is true or false, and so on, are all *semantic properties* of that token.

Semantic properties are not formal properties. A formal system as such is completely self-contained and, viewed in that way, is just a meaningless game. In strictly formal terms, interpretation and meaning are entirely beside the point – they are extraneous 'add ons' that are formally irrelevant. (When discussing a system that is to be interpreted, we call its purely formal characteristics and structure its *syntax*; 'syntactical' is just another word for 'formal,' but it is generally used only when a contrast to 'semantic' is relevant.)

So, formal tokens can lead two lives: *syntactical* (formal) *lives*, in which they are meaningless markers, moved according to the rules of some self-contained game; and (if the system is interpreted) *semantic lives*, in which they have meanings and significant relations to the outside world. The story of how these two lives get together is the foundation of modern mathematics and logic; and it is also the philosophical inspiration of cognitive science. [...] In effect, given an interpreted formal system with true axioms and truth-preserving rules, if you take care of the syntax, *the semantics will take care of itself*.

[...]

An automatic formal system with an interpretation such that the semantics will take care of itself is what Daniel Dennett (1981) calls a *semantic engine*. The discovery that semantic engines are possible – that with the right kind of formal system and interpretation, a machine can handle meanings – is the basic inspiration of cognitive science and artificial intelligence. Needless to say, however, mathematics and logic constitute a very narrow and specialized sample of general intelligence. People are both less and much more than automatic truth-preservers. Consequently, our discussion of interpretation needs to be expanded and generalized considerably; unfortunately, the issues will get messier and murkier as we go.

VI. Interpretation and truth

Interpretation is especially straightforward in the special case of logic and mathematics because in the final analysis, the only semantic property that matters is truth.

[...]

Imagine finding an automatic formal system that uses ordinary numerical tokens, and generates 'theorems' (i.e., outputs) like the following:

$$= 5 = 1 \div \qquad\qquad = \div - 1 - 8 \qquad\qquad + 1 - 5940$$

$$71 \div 92 \text{ x} \qquad\qquad = 61 = 040 \qquad\qquad 84 - 1 \text{ x } 5 =$$

Formally, of course, there is nothing wrong with these tokens; we can imagine any number of (strange and boring) games in which they would be perfectly legal moves. *Semantically*, on the other hand, they look like nonsensical, random gibberish – 'arithmetic salad'. That is, it seems impossible to construe them as expressing claims about the relationships among numbers (e.g., equations). But hold on: this reaction depends on a tacit adoption of the familiar Arabic interpretation of what the numerals and signs mean (the digit '1' stands for the number one, the '+' sign stands for addition, and so on). Formally, however, these numerals and signs are just neutral marks (tokens), and many other (unfamiliar) interpretations are possible (as if the outputs were in a code). Suppose, for instance, we construed the atomic tokens according to the following noncustomary scheme (using '⟹' to abbreviate 'stands for').

'1' ⟹ equals	'6' ⟹ zero	'+' ⟹ five
'2' ⟹ plus	'7' ⟹ one	'–' ⟹ six
'3' ⟹ minus	'8' ⟹ two	'x' ⟹ seven
'4' ⟹ times	'9' ⟹ three	'÷' ⟹ eight
'5' ⟹ div. by	'0' ⟹ four	'=' ⟹ nine

Then, with this table, we could translate the system's outputs back into the familiar notation as:

$$9 \div 9 = 8 \qquad\qquad 98 - 6 = 62 \qquad\qquad 5 = 6 \div 3 \text{ x } 4$$

$$1 = 83 + 7 \qquad\qquad 90 = 94 \text{ x } 40 \qquad\qquad 2 \text{ x } 6 = 7 \div 9$$

Superficially, these look more like equations, and hence, not nearly as random or crazy as the raw (untranslated) outputs. Unfortunately, they're all false – *wildly* false. In fact, on closer inspection, the digits look just as random as before; we still have arithmetic salad, only disguised in regular equation format.

But there are over a trillion possible ways to interpret these fifteen atomic tokens (even sticking to permutations of the ordinary one). Here is just one more possibility, together with the translations it would yield for the original outputs:

'1' $\Rightarrow$ equals	'6' $\Rightarrow$ zero	'+' $\Rightarrow$ five
'2' $\Rightarrow$ div. by	'7' $\Rightarrow$ nine	'−' $\Rightarrow$ four
'3' $\Rightarrow$ times	'8' $\Rightarrow$ eight	'x' $\Rightarrow$ three
'4' $\Rightarrow$ minus	'9' $\Rightarrow$ seven	'÷' $\Rightarrow$ two
'5' $\Rightarrow$ plus	'0' $\Rightarrow$ six	'=' $\Rightarrow$ one

$$1 + 1 = 2 \qquad 12 \times 4 = 48 \qquad 5 = 4 + 7 - 6$$
$$9 = 27 \div 3 \qquad 10 = 16 - 6 \qquad 8 - 4 = 3 + 1$$

What a difference! These not only look like equations, they *are* equations – they are *true*. And, intuitively, that strongly inclines us to prefer this interpretation – to think it 'better' or 'righter' than the ones which yield random nonsense as readings. [...]

[F]ormal tokens in themselves never intrinsically favour one interpretation scheme over any other – from their point of view, all interpretations are equally extraneous and arbitrary. So if some particular interpretation is to be adopted, over all the other possibilities, there must be something distinctive about it, which makes it stand out in the crowd. [...] [I]nterpreting is tantamount to 'making sense of'; hence, if the system doesn't end by making sense (but, rather, makes nonsense), then the interpretation attempt has failed. Arithmetic salad does not make sense (whether clothed in the outer form of equations, or not); and that, primarily, is why random interpretation schemes don't really give *interpretations* at all. In the context of arithmetic, true equations make eminently good sense – hence the preferability of our second scheme.

[...]

VII. Cognitive science (again)

The basic idea of cognitive science is that *intelligent beings are semantic engines* – in other words, automatic formal systems with interpretations under which they consistently make sense. [...] [F]rom this perspective, artificial intelligence can be regarded as psychology in a particularly pure and abstract form. The same fundamental structures are under investigation, but in AI, all the relevant parameters are under direct experimental control (in the programming), without any messy physiology or ethics to get in the way.

References

Dennett, Daniel (1981). 'Three Kinds of Intentional Psychology.' In Healey, 1981.

Healey, R. A. (1981). *Reduction, Time and Reality: Studies in the Philosophy of the Natural Sciences*, Cambridge, England: Cambridge University Press.

Hobbes, Thomas (1651). *The Leviathan*.

Cognitive wheels: the frame problem of AI

Daniel Dennett

Source: Dennett, D.C. (1990) 'Cognitive wheels: the frame problem of AI', in M.A. Boden (ed.) *The Philosophy of Artificial Intelligence*, Oxford, Oxford University Press, pp.147–70. Originally in Hookway, C. (ed.) (1984) *Minds, Machines, and Evolution: Philosophical Studies*, Cambridge, Cambridge University Press, pp.129–51. Edited as indicated. Division into subtitled parts is not in the original.

[Part I: The content and status of the frame problem]

Once upon a time there was a robot, named R_1 by its creators. Its only task was to fend for itself. One day its designers arranged for it to learn that its spare battery, its precious energy supply, was locked in a room with a time bomb set to go off soon. R_1 located the room, and the key to the door, and formulated a plan to rescue its battery. There was a wagon in the room, and the battery was on the wagon, and R_1 hypothesized that a certain action which it called PULLOUT (WAGON,ROOM) would result in the battery being removed from the room. Straightaway it acted, and did succeed in getting the battery out of the room before the bomb went off. Unfortunately, however, the bomb was also on the wagon. R_1 *knew* that the bomb was on the wagon in the room, but didn't realize that pulling the wagon would bring the bomb out along with the battery. Poor R_1 had missed that obvious implication of its planned act.

Back to the drawing board. 'The solution is obvious,' said the designers. 'Our next robot must be made to recognize not just the intended implications of its acts, but also the implications about their side-effects, by deducing these implications from the descriptions it uses in formulating its plans.' They called their next model, the robot-deducer, $R_1 D_1$. They placed $R_1 D_1$ in much the same predicament that R_1 had succumbed to, and as it too hit upon the idea of PULLOUT (WAGON,ROOM) it began, as designed, to consider the implications of such a course of action. It had just finished deducing that pulling the wagon out of the room would not change the colour of the room's walls, and was embarking on a proof of the further implication that pulling the wagon out would cause its wheels to turn more revolutions than there were wheels on the wagon – when the bomb exploded.

Back to the drawing board. 'We must teach it the difference between relevant implications and irrelevant implications,' said the designers, 'and teach it to ignore the irrelevant ones.' So they developed a method of tagging implications as either relevant or irrelevant to the project at hand, and installed the method in their next model, the robot-relevant-deducer, or $R_2 D_1$, for short. When they subjected $R_2 D_1$ to the test that had so unequivocally selected its ancestors for extinction, they were surprised to see it sitting, Hamlet-like, outside the room containing the ticking bomb, the native hue of its resolution sicklied o'er with the pale cast of thought, as Shakespeare (and more recently Fodor) has aptly put it. 'Do something!' they yelled at it. 'I am', it retorted. 'I'm busily ignoring some thousands of implications I have determined to be irrelevant. Just as soon as I find an irrelevant implication, I put it on the list of those I must ignore, and ...' the bomb went off.

All these robots suffer from the *frame problem*. If there is ever to be a robot with the fabled perspicacity and real-time adroitness of R_2D_2, robot-designers must solve the frame problem. It appears at first to be at best an annoying technical embarrassment in robotics, or merely a curious puzzle for the bemusement of people working in Artificial Intelligence (AI). I think, on the contrary, that it is a new, deep epistemological problem – accessible in principle but unnoticed by generations of philosophers – brought to light by the novel methods of AI, and still far from being solved. Many people in AI have come to have a similarly high regard for the seriousness of the frame problem. [...]

I will try here to present an elementary, non-technical, philosophical introduction to the frame problem, and show why it is so interesting. I have no solution to offer, or even any original suggestions for where a solution might lie. It is hard enough, I have discovered, just to say clearly what the frame problem is – and is not. [...]

Since the frame problem, whatever it is, is certainly not solved yet (and may be, in its current guises, insoluble), the ideological foes of AI such as Hubert

Dreyfus [...] are tempted to compose obituaries for the field, citing the frame problem as the cause of death. In *What Computers Can't Do* (Dreyfus 1972), Dreyfus sought to show that AI was a fundamentally mistaken method for studying the mind [...]. Dreyfus never explicitly mentions the frame problem, but is it perhaps the smoking pistol he was looking for but didn't *quite* know how to describe? Yes, I think AI can be seen to be holding a smoking pistol, but [...] it is everyone's problem, not just a problem for AI, which, like the good guy in many a mystery story, should be credited with a discovery, not accused of a crime.

One does not have to hope for a robot-filled future to be worried by the frame problem. [...] How is it that I can get myself a midnight snack? What could be simpler? I suspect there is some leftover sliced turkey and mayonnaise in the fridge, and bread in the breadbox – and a bottle of beer in the fridge as well. I realize I can put these elements together, so I concoct a childishly simple plan: I'll just go and check out the fridge, get out the requisite materials, and make myself a sandwich, to be washed down with a beer. I'll need a knife, a plate, and a glass for the beer. I forthwith put the plan into action and it works! Big deal.

Now of course I couldn't do this without knowing a good deal – about bread, spreading mayonnaise, opening the fridge, the friction and inertia that will keep the turkey between the bread slices and the bread on the plate as I carry the plate over to the table beside my easy chair. I also need to know about how to get the beer out of the bottle into the glass. Thanks to my previous accumulation of experience in the world, fortunately, I am equipped with all this worldly knowledge. [...]

Such utterly banal facts escape our notice as we act and plan, and it is not surprising that philosophers [...] should have overlooked them. [...]

The reason AI forces the banal information to the surface is that the tasks set by AI start at zero: the computer to be programmed to simulate the agent (or the brain of the robot, if we are actually going to operate in the real, non-simulated world), initially knows nothing at all 'about the world.'

[...]

Recall poor R_1D_1, and suppose for the sake of argument that it had perfect empirical knowledge of the probabilities of all the effects of all its actions that would he detectable by it. Thus it believes that with probability 0.7864, executing PULLOUT (WAGON,ROOM) will cause the wagon wheels to make an audible noise; and with probability 0.5, the door to the room will open in rather than out; and with probability 0.999996, there will be no live elephants in the room, and with probability 0.997 the bomb will remain on the wagon when it is moved. How is R_1D_1 to find this last, relevant needle in its haystack of empirical knowledge? A walking encyclopedia will walk over a cliff, for all its knowledge of cliffs and the effects of gravity, unless it is designed in such a fashion that it can find the right bits of knowledge at the right times, so it can plan its engagements with the real world.

[Part II: AI approaches to the frame problem]

The earliest work on planning systems in AI took a deductive approach. [...] [D]esigners hoped to represent all the system's 'world knowledge' explicitly as axioms, and use ordinary logic [...] to deduce the effects of actions. Envisaging a certain situation S was modelled by having the system entertain a set of axioms describing the situation. Added to this were background axioms (the so-called 'frame axioms' that give the frame problem its name) which describe general conditions and the general effects of every action type defined for the system. To this set of axioms the system would apply an action – by postulating the occurrence of some action A in situation S – and then deduce the effect of A in S, producing a description of the outcome situation S'. [...] [T]he deductive approach has not been made to work – the proof of the pudding for any robot – except for deliberately trivialized cases.

Consider some typical frame axioms associated with the action-type: *move x onto y*.

(1) If $z \neq x$ and I move x onto y, then if z was on w before, then z is on w after.

(2) If x is blue before, and I move x onto y, then x is blue after.

Note that (2), about being blue, is just one example of the many boring 'no–change' axioms we have to associate with this action-type. Worse still, note that a cousin of (2), also about being blue, would have to be associated with every other action-type – with *pick up x* and with *give x to y*, for instance. One cannot save this mindless repetition by postulating once and for all something like

(3) If anything is blue, it stays blue,

for that is false, and in particular we will want to leave room for the introduction of such action-types as *paint x red*. Since virtually any aspect of a situation can change under some circumstance, this method requires introducing for each aspect (each predication in the description of S) an axiom to handle whether that aspect changes for each action-type.

This representational profligacy quickly gets out of hand, but for some 'toy' problems in AI, the frame problem can be overpowered to some extent by a mixture of the toyness of the environment and brute force. The early version of SHAKEY, the robot at SRI, operated in such a simplified and sterile world, with so few aspects it could worry about that it could get away with an exhaustive consideration of frame axioms.

Attempts to circumvent this explosion of axioms began with the proposal that the system operate on the tacit assumption that nothing changes in a situation but what is explicitly asserted to change in the definition of the applied action [...]. The problem here is that [...] you don't do just one thing. This was R_1's problem, when it failed to notice that it would pull the bomb out with the wagon. In the explicit representation (a few pages back) of my midnight snack solution, I mentioned carrying the plate over to the table. On this proposal, my model of S' would leave the turkey back in the kitchen, for I didn't explicitly say the turkey would come along with the plate. One can of course patch up the definition of 'bring' or 'plate' to handle this problem, but only at the cost of creating others.

[...]

What is needed is a system that genuinely *ignores* most of what it knows, and operates with a well-chosen portion of its knowledge at any moment. Well-chosen, but not chosen by exhaustive consideration. How, though, can you give a system *rules* for ignoring – or better, since explicit rule-following is not the problem, how can you design a system that reliably ignores what it ought to ignore under a wide variety of different circumstances in a complex action environment?

[...]

[A second] family of approaches, typified by the work of Marvin Minsky and Roger Schank (Minsky 1981; Schank and Abelson 1977), gets its ignoring-power from the attention-focusing power of stereotypes. The inspiring insight here is the idea that all of life's experiences, for all their variety, boil down to variations on a manageable number of stereotypic themes, paradigmatic scenarios – 'frames' in Minsky's terms, 'scripts' in Schank's.

An artificial agent with a well-stocked compendium of frames or scripts, appropriately linked to each other and to the impingements of the world via its perceptual organs, would face the world with an elaborate system of what might be called habits of attention and benign tendencies to leap to particular sorts of conclusions in particular sorts of circumstances. It would 'automatically' pay attention to certain features in certain environments and assume that certain unexamined normal features of those environments were present. Concomitantly, it would be differentially alert to relevant divergences from the stereotypes it would always begin by 'expecting'.

Simulations of fragments of such an agent's encounters with its world reveal that in many situations it behaves quite felicitously and apparently naturally, and it is hard to say, of course, what the limits of this approach are. But there are strong grounds for skepticism. Most obviously, while such systems perform creditably when the world co-operates with their stereotypes, and even with *anticipated* variations on them, when their worlds turn perverse, such systems typically cannot recover gracefully from the misanalyses they are led into. In fact, their behaviour *in extremis* looks for all the world like the preposterously counter-productive activities of insects betrayed by their rigid tropisms and other genetically hard-wired behavioural routines.

[...]

In effect, [this] approach is an attempt to *pre-solve* the frame problems the particular agent is likely to encounter. While insects do seem saddled with such control systems, people, even when they do appear to he relying on stereotypes, have back-up systems of thought that can deal more powerfully with problems that arise. Moreover, when people do avail themselves of stereotypes, they are at least relying on stereotypes of their own devising, and to date no one has been able to present any workable ideas about how a person's frame-making or script-writing machinery might he guided by its previous experience.

[...]

References

Dreyfus, H. L. (1972). *What Computers Can't Do*. New York: Harper & Row.

Minksy, M. (1981). 'A Framework for Representing Knowledge.' Originally published as MIT AI Lab. Memo 3306. Quotation drawn from excerpts repr. in J. Haugeland (ed.), *Mind Design*, pp. 95–128. Cambridge, Mass.: MIT Press/Bradford Books.

Schank, R. C., and Abelson, R. P. (1977). *Scripts, Plans, Goals, and Understanding: An Inquiry into Human Knowledge*. Hillsdale, NJ: Erlbaum.

Meaning and the world order

Jerry A. Fodor

Source: Fodor, J.A. (1987) 'Meaning and the world order', in *Psychosemantics: The Problem of Meaning in the Philosophy of Mind*, Cambridge, Mass., MIT Press, pp.97–111. Numbering of parts added but subtitles as in original. The use of apostrophes to pluralize 'A' and 'B' in the original has been suppressed here.

[Part I] Introduction

I suppose that sooner or later the physicists will complete the catalogue they've been compiling of the ultimate and irreducible properties of things. When they do, the likes of *spin, charm,* and *charge* will perhaps appear upon their list. But *aboutness* surely won't; intentionality simply doesn't go that deep. It's hard to see, in face of this consideration, how one can be a Realist about intentionality without also being, to some extent or other, a Reductionist. If the semantic and the intentional are real properties of things, it must be in virtue of their identity with (or maybe of their supervenience on?) properties that are themselves *neither* intentional *nor* semantic. If aboutness is real, it must be really something else.

[...]

[W]e would have largely solved the naturalization problem for a propositional-attitude psychology if we were able to say, in nonintentional and nonsemantic idiom, what it is for a primitive symbol of Mentalese to have a certain interpretation in a certain context.

Alas, I don't know how to carry out this program. But I see no principled reason why it can't be carried out; I even imagine that we might make a little progress within the foreseeable future. In particular, I think it's plausible that the interpretation of [...] Mentalese symbols is determined by certain of their causal relations. For example, what makes it the case that (the Mentalese symbol) 'water' expresses the property H_2O is that tokens of that symbol stand in certain causal relations to water samples. Presumably if tokens of 'water' have a different interpretation on Twin-Earth [...], that is all because it's XYZ that bears to [these] tokens the sort of causal relations that H_2O bears to tokens of 'water.'

So the causal story goes. I think it points a promising route to the naturalization of such semantics as RTM [i.e. the Representational Theory of Mind, Fodor's label for CTM] requires. At a minimum, I think that some of the standard objections to that sort of story can be met; that's what I propose to argue in the following.

Here, then, are the ground rules. I want a *naturalized* theory meaning; a theory that articulates, in nonsemantic and nonintentional terms, sufficient conditions for one bit of the world to *be about* (to express, represent, or be true of) another bit. [...] I'm prepared that it should turn out that smoke and tree rings represent only relative to our interests in predicting fires and ascertaining the ages of trees, that thermostats represent only relative to our interest in keeping the room warm, and that English words represent only relative to our intention to use them to communicate our thoughts. I'm prepared, that is, that only mental states (hence, according to RTM, only mental representations) should turn out to have semantic properties *in the first instance;* hence, that a naturalized semantics should apply, strictu dictu, to mental representations only.

But it had better apply to them.

[Part II] The Crude Causal Theory

Let's start with the most rudimentary sort of example: the case where a predicative expression ([the Mentalese symbol] 'horse', as it might be) is said of, or thought of, an object of predication (a horse, as it might be). Let the Crude Causal Theory of Content be the following: In such cases the symbol tokenings denote their causes, and the symbol types express the property whose instantiations reliably cause their tokenings. So, in the paradigm case, my utterance of 'horse' says *of* a horse that it *is* one.

'Reliable causation' requires that the causal dependence of the tokening of the symbol upon the instancing of the corresponding property be counterfactual supporting: either instances of the property actually do cause tokenings of the symbol, or instances of the property *would* cause tokenings of the symbol *were they to occur,* or both. I suppose that it is necessary and sufficient for such reliable causation that there be a nomological – lawful – relation between certain (higher-order) properties of events; in the present case, between the property of being an instance of the property *horse* and the property of being a tokening of the symbol 'horse.' The intuition that underlies the Crude Causal Theory is that the semantic interpretations of mental symbols are determined by, and only by, such nomological relations.

You can see straight off why the Crude Causal Theory has a much better chance of working for mental representations than it does for (e.g.) English words. CCT wants the tokening of a symbol to depend upon the instantiation of the property it expresses. But whether an English word gets tokened (e.g., uttered) depends not just on what it means but also upon the motivations, linguistic competences, and communicative intentions of English speakers. Giving voice to an utterance, unlike entertaining a thought, is typically a voluntary act.

[...]

In short, the causal dependence of tokenings of mental representations upon semantically relevant situations in the world is typically more reliable than the causal dependence of tokenings of English expressions upon semantically relevant situations in the world. That's because the chains that connect tokenings of mental representations to their semantically relevant causes are typically *shorter than* (indeed, are typically links in) the chains that connect tokenings of English sentences to their semantically relevant causes. This is the principal reason why it is mental representations, and not the formulas of any natural language, that are the natural candidates for being the primitive bearers of semantic properties. If, however, mental representations are the bearers of semantic properties in the first instance, then it is the semantic properties of mental representations that are, in the first instance, apt for naturalization. CCT and RTM are made for one another.

Which is not, of course, to say that the Crude Causal Theory will work for mental representations; only that it's unlikely to work for anything else. CCT has – I admit it – lots of problems. I want to argue, however that some of what look to be its worst problems have natural and appealing solutions. This makes me hopeful that maybe, someday, some refinement of the Crude Causal Theory might actually be made to work. Maybe.

The Crude Causal Theory says, in effect, that a symbol expresses a property if it's nomologically necessary that *all* and *only* instances of the property cause tokenings of the symbol. There are problems with the 'all' part (since not all horses actually do cause 'horse' tokenings) and there are problems with the 'only' part (cows sometimes cause 'horse' tokenings; e.g., when they are mistaken for horses). The main business of this [extract] will be the consideration of [the second problem].

[...]

[Part III] Error in the Crude Causal Theory

An embarrassment: It seems that, according to CCT, there can be no such thing as *misrepresentation*. Suppose, for example, that tokenings of the symbol 'A' are nomologically dependent upon instantiations of the property *A*; viz., upon As. Then, according to the theory, the tokens of the symbol denote As (since tokens denote their causes) and they represent them *as* As (since symbols express the property whose instantiations cause them to be tokened). But symbol tokenings that represent As as As are ipso facto veridical. So it seems that the condition for an 'A'-token meaning *A* is identical to the condition for such a token being true. How, then, do you get *un*veridical 'A' tokens into the causal picture?

This may not look awfully worrying so far, since it invites the following obvious reply: "*Sometimes* 'A' tokens are caused by As (and thus represent their causes as As, and are thus veridical); but other times 'A' tokens are caused by Bs where, as we may suppose, whatever is B is *not* A. Well, since 'A' tokens express the property of being A, 'A' tokens that are caused by Bs represent Bs as As and are ipso facto not veridical. 'A' tokens that are caused by Bs are ipso facto *mis*representations of their causes. *That's* how misrepresentation gets into the causal picture."

But though that answer sounds all right, CCT can't make it stick. Since there are B-caused tokenings of 'A,' it follows that the causal dependence of 'A's upon As is imperfect; As are sufficient for the causation of 'A's, *but so too are Bs*. If, however, symbols express the properties whose instantiations reliably cause them, it looks as though what 'A' must express is not the property of *being A* (or the property of *being B*) but rather the *disjunctive property of being*

(A ∨ B). [Note: ' ∨ ' abbreviates 'or' (disjunction), just as '&' abbreviates 'and' (conjunction).]

But if 'A' expresses the property *(A ∨ B)*, then B-caused 'A' tokenings are veridical after all. They're not misrepresentations since, of course, *Bs are A ∨ B*. But if B-caused 'A' tokenings are true of their causes, then we don't yet have a theory of misrepresentation.

That's what I'll call the 'disjunction problem.' We can put it that a viable causal theory of content has to acknowledge *two* kinds of cases where there are disjoint causally sufficient conditions for the tokenings of a symbol: the case where the content of the symbol is disjunctive ('A' expresses the property of *being (A ∨ B)*) and the case where the content of the symbol is *not* disjunctive and some of the tokenings are false ('A' expresses the property of *being A*, and B-caused 'A' tokenings misrepresent). The present problem with the Crude Causal Theory is that it's unable to distinguish between these cases; it always assigns disjunctive content to symbols whose causally sufficient conditions are themselves disjoint.

The disjunction problem is extremely robust; so far as I know, it arises in one or another guise for every causal theory of content that has thus far been proposed. Accordingly, there are various ideas for circumventing it in the literature in which such theories are espoused. None of these proposals has been very satisfactory, however; and the rumor has gotten around that the problem that causal theories have with misrepresentation is perhaps intrinsic and ineliminable. [...] I'm about to try and scotch that rumor. First, however, let's look at [one of] the remedies currently on offer.

[Part IV] Dretske's solution

Fred Dretske's important book *Knowledge and the Flow of Information* was largely responsible for the present widespread enthusiasm for causal theories of content, so his treatment of misrepresentation bears careful consideration. For Dretske, the cardinal semantic relation is the one that holds between two events when one of them (the tokening of a symbol, as it might be) *transmits information about* the other. Here is how he proposes to construe misrepresentation in that theoretical context:

In the learning situation special care is taken to see that incoming signals have an intensity, a strength, sufficient unto delivering the required piece of information *to* the learning subject.... Such precautions are taken in the learning situation ... in order to ensure that an internal structure is developed with ... the information that s is *F*.... But once we have meaning, once the subject has articulated a structure that is selectively sensitive to information about the *F*-ness of things, instances of this structure, tokens of this type, can be triggered by signals that *lack* the appropriate piece of information.... We [thus] have a case of misrepresentation – a token of a structure with a false content. We have, in a word, meaning without truth.

(KFI, 194–195; emphases Dretske's)

All you need to know to understand this well enough for present purposes is that Dretske's notion of information is fundamentally that of counterfactual-supporting correlation: events of type 'A' carry information about events of type A to the extent that the latter sort of events are reliably causally responsible for events of the former sort. (There is, in fact, rather more than this to Dretske's official account of information; but none of the rest is essential to his treatment of the problem of false content.)

So information reduces to a certain sort of correlation. And the problem is this: Correlations can be better or worse – more or less reliable – but there is no sense to the notion of a *mis*correlation, so there appears to be nothing for Dretske to make a theory of misinformation out of. His solution is to enforce a strict distinction between what happens in the learning period and what happens thereafter. The correlation that the learning period establishes determines what 'A' events represent, and it's the teacher's function to ensure that this correlation reliably connects 'A' tokens to As. It may be, however, that *after* the learning period 'A' tokens are brought about by something *other than* As (by Bs, for example); if so, then these are, as I'll sometimes say, 'wild' tokenings, and their content is false.

I think this move is ingenious but hopeless. Just for starters, the distinction between what happens in the learning period and what happens thereafter surely isn't principled; there is no time after which one's use of a symbol stops being merely shaped and starts to be, as it were, in earnest. [...] Moreover, if Dretske insists upon the learning-period gambit, he thereby limits the applicability of his notion of misrepresentation to *learned* symbols. This [...] leaves no way for innate information to be false [...].

But the real problem about Dretske's gambit is internal. Consider a trainee who comes to produce 'A' tokens in A circumstances during the learning period. And suppose that the teacher does his job and ensures that *only* As elicit 'A' tokenings in the course of training. Well, time passes, a whistle blows (or whatever), and the learning period comes to an end. At some time later still, the erstwhile trainee encounters an instance of B and produces an 'A' in causal consequence thereof. The idea is, of course, that this B-elicited tokening of 'A' is ipso facto wild and, since it happened after the training ended, it has the (false) content *that A.*

But this won't work; it ignores counterfactuals that are clearly relevant to determining *which* symbol-to-world correlation the training has brought about. Imagine, in particular, what *would have* happened if an instance of B *had* occurred during the training period. Presumably what would have happened is this: it would have caused a tokening of 'A.' After all, Bs are supposed to be sufficient to cause 'A' tokenings *after* training; that's the very supposition upon which Dretske's treatment of wild 'A' tokenings rests. So we can also assume – indeed, we can stipulate – that if a B had occurred *during* training, it too would have brought about an 'A.' But that means, of course, that if you take account of the relevant counterfactuals, then the correlation that training established is (not between instances of A and tokenings of 'A' but) between instances of $A \vee B$ and tokenings of 'A.' [...] So we have the old problem back again. If 'A's are correlated with $(A \vee B)$s, then the content of a tokening of 'A' is *that $A \vee B$.* So a B-caused 'A' tokening isn't false. So we're still in want of a way out of the disjunction problem.

[...]

[Part V] How to solve the disjunction problem

We need a way to break the symmetry between A-caused 'A' tokenings (which are, by hypothesis, true) and B-caused 'A' tokenings (which are, by hypothesis, false). In particular, we need a difference between A-caused 'A' tokenings and B-caused 'A' tokenings that can be expressed in terms of nonintentional and nonsemantic properties of causal relations; for nonintentional and nonsemantic properties of causal relations are all that the Crude Causal Theory of Content has to play with. My suggestion is that [we need to appeal] to the *counterfactual* properties of the causal relations between As and 'A's, on the one hand, and Bs and 'A's, on the other. [...]

It's an old observation – as old as Plato, I suppose – that falsehoods are *ontologically dependent* on truths in a way that truths are not ontologically dependent on falsehoods. The mechanisms that deliver falsehoods are somehow *parasitic on* the ones that deliver truths. In consequence, you can only have false beliefs about what you can have true beliefs about (whereas you can have true beliefs about anything that you can have beliefs about at all). So the intuition goes, and I think that there is something to it. What's more, I think that it points the way out of the disjunction problem.

Consider the following situation: I see a cow which, stupidly, I misidentify. I take it, say, to be a horse. So taking it causes me to effect the tokening of a symbol; viz., I say 'horse.' Here we have all the ingredients of the disjunction problem (set up, as it happens, for a token of English rather than a token of Mentalese; but none of the following turns on that). So, on the one hand, we want it to be that my utterance of 'horse' means *horse* in virtue of the causal relation between (some) 'horse' tokenings and horses; and, on the other hand, we *don't* want it to be that my utterance of 'horse' means *cow* in virtue of the causal relation between (some) 'horse' tokenings and cows. But if the causal relations are the same, and if causation makes representation, how can the semantic connections not be the same too? What we want is the situation in [the diagram] (where the dashed line stands for the representation relation and the other lines stand for causal relations); but how are we to get what we want?

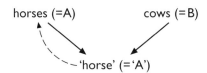

horses (=A)   cows (=B)

'horse' (='A')

Answer: As previously remarked, the causal relations aren't identical in their counterfactual properties. In particular, misidentifying a cow as a horse wouldn't have led me to say 'horse' *except that there was independently a semantic relation between 'horse' tokenings and horses*. But for the fact that the word 'horse' expresses the property of *being* a *horse* (i.e., but for the fact that one calls *horses* 'horses', it would not have been *that* word that taking a cow to be a horse would have caused me to utter. Whereas, by contrast, since 'horse' does mean *horse*, the fact that horses cause me to say 'horse' does not depend upon there being a semantic – or, indeed, any – connection between 'horse' tokenings and cows.

From a semantic point of view, mistakes have to be *accidents:* if cows aren't in the extension of 'horse,' then cows being called horses can't be *required* for 'horse' to mean what it does. By contrast, however, if 'horse' didn't mean what it does, being mistaken for a horse wouldn't ever get a cow called 'horse.' Put the two together and we have it that the possibility of saying 'that's a horse' falsely presupposes the existence of a *semantic setup* for saying it truly, but not vice versa. Put it in terms of CCT, and we have it that the fact that cows cause one to say 'horse' depends on the fact that horses do; but the fact that horses cause one to say 'horse' does *not* depend on the fact that cows do.

So, the causal connection between cows and 'horse' tokenings is, as I shall say, *asymmetrically dependent* upon the causal connection between horses and 'horse' tokenings. So now we have a necessary condition for a B-caused 'A' token to be wild: B-caused 'A' tokenings are wild only if they are asymmetrically dependent upon non-B-caused 'A' tokenings.

What we've got [...] is, in effect, a theory that understands wildness in terms of an empirical dependence among causal relations. [...] [A]ll the notions employed are naturalistic, as per prior specifications.

References

Dretske, F. *(KFI). Knowledge and the Flow of Information.* Cambridge, Mass., MIT Press, 1981.

Representational systems

Fred Dretske

Source: Dretske, F. (1988) 'Representational systems', in *Explaining Behavior: Reasons in a World of Causes*, Cambridge, Mass., MIT Press, pp.51–69. Edited as indicated. Numbering of parts added.

[Part I] Conventional systems of representation: Type I

By a representational system (RS) I shall mean any system whose function it is to indicate how things stand with respect to some other object, condition, or magnitude. If RS's function is to indicate whether O is in condition A or B, for instance, and the way RS performs this function *(when* it performs it) is by occupying one of two possible states, a (indicating that O is A) and b (indicating that O is $B)$, then a and b are the expressive elements of RS and *what they represent* (about O) is *that* it is A (in the case of a) and *that* it is B (in the case of b).

Depending on the kind of function involved, and on the way a system manages to carry out this function (the way it manages to *indicate)*, representational systems can be variously classified. What follows is one possible classification. My chief interest is in *natural* representations (systems of Type III), but the special properties of such systems are best understood by comparing and contrasting them with their conventional (to varying degrees) cousins. So I begin with conventional systems of representation [Types I and II].

Let this dime on the table be Oscar Robertson, let this nickel (heads uppermost) be Kareem Abdul-Jabbar, and let this nickel (tail uppermost) be the opposing center. These pieces of popcorn are the other [basketball] players, and this glass is the basket. With this bit of stage setting I can now, by moving coins and popcorn around on the table, represent the positions and movements of these players. I can use these objects to describe a basketball play I once witnessed.

[...]

The coins and the popcorn do their job [...] only insofar as some *other* indicator system is functioning satisfactorily, only insofar as there is something in the manipulator of these symbols (in this case, something *in me*) that indicates how things stood on the basketball court at the time in question. If I am ignorant of what Oscar and Kareem did with the ball, the coins and the popcorn are unable to perform the function they have been assigned – unable to indicate, by their various positions and movements, what took place on the court that day. This is merely to acknowledge that these objects are, considered by themselves, representationally lifeless. They are merely my representational instruments.

The elements of Type I systems have no *intrinsic* powers of representation – no power that is not derived from us, their creators and users. Both their function (what they, when suitably deployed, are *supposed* to indicate) and their power to perform that function (their success in indicating what it is their function to indicate) are derived from another source: human agents with communicative purposes. Many familiar RSs are like this: maps, diagrams, certain road signs (of the informational variety), prearranged signals, musical notation, gestures, codes, and (to some degree, at least) natural language. I call the representational elements of such systems *symbols*. Symbols are, either explicitly or implicitly, *assigned* indicator functions, functions that they have no intrinsic power to perform. *We* give them their functions, and *we* (when it suits our purposes) see to it that they are *used* in accordance with this function. Such representational systems are, in this sense, *doubly* conventional: *we* give them a job to do, and then *we* do it for them.

[Part II] Natural signs and information

In contrast with the relationship between popcorn and professional basketball players, we don't have to *let* tracks in the snow, bird songs, fingerprints, and cloud formations stand for the things we take them to indicate. There is a sense in which, whether we like it or not, these tracks, prints, songs, and formations indicate what they do quite independent of us, of how we exploit them for investigative purposes, and of whether we even recognize their significance at all. These are what are sometimes called *natural* signs: events and conditions that derive their indicative powers, not (as in the case of symbols) from us, from our *use* of them to indicate, but from the way they are objectively related to the conditions they signify.

To understand conventional systems of representation of Type II and the way they differ from RSs of Type I, it is important to understand the difference between symbols and signs. In systems of Type II, natural signs are *used* in a way that exploits their *natural* meaning, their *unconventional* powers of indication, for representational, and partly conventional, purposes. This makes systems of Type II a curious blend of the conventional and the natural.

[...]

I have occasionally used the verb "mean" as a synonym for "indicate." Let me explain. Paul Grice (1957) distinguished what he called a natural sense from a non-natural sense of the word "meaning." The natural sense of "meaning" is virtually identical to that of "indicate," and that is how I shall normally use the word. The 24 rings in a tree stump, the so-called growth rings, mean (indicate) that the tree is 24 years old. A ringing bell – a ringing *door*bell – means (indicates) that someone is at the door. A scar on a twig, easily identified as a leaf scar, means, in this natural sense, that a leaf grew there. As Grice observes, nothing can mean that *P* in the *natural* sense of "meaning" if *P* is not the case. This distinguishes it from non-natural meaning, where something (e.g., a statement) can mean that *P* without *P*'s being the case. A person can *say*, and *mean*, that a quail was here without a quail's having been here. But the tracks in the snow cannot mean (in this natural sense of "meaning") that a quail was here unless, in fact, a quail *was* here. If the tracks were left by a pheasant, then the tracks might, depending on how distinctive they are, mean that a pheasant was here. But they certainly do not mean that a quail was here, and the fact that a Boy Scout *takes* them to mean that cannot *make* them mean that.

[...]

When there is any chance of confusing this use of the word "meaning" with what Grice calls non-natural meaning – the kind of meaning associated with language, the kind of meaning that is [...] closer to what it is the *function* of something to mean (naturally) or indicate – I shall either combine the word "meaning" with the word "natural" or use it together with its synonym "indicate." The word "represent" is sometimes used in a way that I am using "indicate" and "mean" (naturally). Since I wish to reserve the idea of representation for something that is closer to genuine meaning, the kind of meaning (Grice's non-natural meaning) in which something can mean that *P without P*'s being the case, I will *never* use the words "represent" and "indicate" interchangeably. As I am using these words, there can be no *mis*indication, only misrepresentation.

[...]

[Part III] Conventional systems of representations: Type II

In systems of Type II, natural signs take the place of symbols as the representational elements. A sign is given the job of doing what it (suitably deployed) can already do.

It should be remembered that what a system *represents* is *not* what its (expressive) elements indicate or mean. It is what these elements have the *function* of indicating or meaning. It is important to keep this point in mind, since the natural signs used in systems of Type II typically indicate a great many things. Normally, though, they are used to represent only *one* of these conditions – a condition which we, for whatever reason, take a special interest in [...]. If a full tank of gas means (because of the weight of the gas) that there is a large downward force on the bolts holding the tank to the car's frame, then the fuel gauge indicates a large downward force on these bolts whenever it indicates a full tank of gas. [...] Given the way these gauges operate, they cannot indicate (i.e., have their behavior depend on) the amount of fuel in the tank without indicating (exhibiting at least the same degree of dependency on) [this] related condition.

Nevertheless, we take one of these indicated conditions to be what the gauge *represents,* one of these correlated conditions to define what *kind* of gauge it is. It is, or so we say, a *fuel* gauge [...] Since we are interested in the amount of gasoline in the tank, not (except derivatively) in these correlated conditions, we *assign* the gauge the function of indicating the amount of gasoline in the tank. We *give* it the job of delivering *this* piece of information, calibrate and label it accordingly, and ignore the collateral pieces of information it necessarily supplies in the process. Since what an instrument or gauge represents is what it is *supposed* to indicate, what it has the *function* of indicating, and since *we* determine these functions, *we* determine what the gauge represents. If, by jacking up the fuel tank, I remove the force on the bolts securing the tank to the car frame, the fuel gauge, though still indicating the amount of fuel in the tank, no longer indicates the amount of force on these bolts. But, under these unusual conditions, the gauge does not *misrepresent* the force on these bolts the way it could, and the way gauges sometimes *do*, misrepresent the amount of fuel in the tank. The reason it doesn't is because the gauge, even when things are operating normally, does not *represent* (though it does *indicate*) the magnitude of this force. Its *representational* efforts – and therefore its representational failures, its *mis*representations – are limited to what it has the *function* of indicating. [...]

You can't assign a rectal thermometer the job of indicating the Dow-Jones Industrial Average. The height of the mercury doesn't depend on these economic conditions. The mercury and the market fluctuate independently. Trying to use a thermometer in this way is like assigning a rock the job of washing dishes. My son can be given this job (even if he never does it) because he, unlike the rock, *can* wash dishes. The functions we assign to instruments are similarly restricted to what the instruments *can* do, or, [...] what [...] we *think* they can do. This makes the functions of systems of Type II restricted in a way that those of Type I systems are not restricted. It is this fact, together with the fact that once a device has been given such a function it performs without any help from us, that makes such systems only *partly* conventional.

[...]

[Part IV] Natural systems of representation [(Type III)]

A natural system of representation is not only one in which the elements, like the elements of Type II systems, have a power to indicate that is independent of the interests, purposes, and capacities of any other system, but also one in which, in contrast with systems of Type II, the functions determining what these signs *represent* are also independent of such extrinsic factors. Natural systems of representation, systems of Type III, are ones which have *their own* intrinsic indicator functions, functions that derive from the way the indicators are developed and used *by the system of which they are a part*. In contrast with systems of Type I and II, these functions are not assigned. They do not depend on the way *others* may use or regard the indicator elements.

Whatever one might think about the possibility of intrinsic functions, the type of functions that define Type III systems (a contentious point to which I will return in a moment), it is clear that what I have been calling natural signs – events, conditions, and structures that somehow indicate how things stand elsewhere in the world – are essential to every animal's biological heritage. Without such internal indicators, an organism has no way to negotiate its way through its environment, no way to avoid predators, find food, locate mates, and do the things it has to do to survive and propagate. This, indeed, is what sense perception is all about. An animal's senses [...] are merely the diverse ways nature has devised for making what happens inside an animal depend, in some indicator-relevant way, on what happens outside. If the firing of a particular neuron in a female cricket's brain did not indicate the distinctive chirp of a conspecific male, there would be nothing to guide the female in its efforts to find a mate (Huber and Thorson 1985). The *place, misplace,* and *displace* neural units in the rat's brain (O'Keefe 1976), units that guide the animal in its movements through its environment, are merely internal indicators of place, of alterations in place, and of movement through a place. [...]

We are accustomed to hearing about biological functions for various bodily organs. The heart, the kidneys, and the pituitary gland, we are told, have functions – things they are, in this sense, *supposed to do.* The fact that these organs are supposed to do these things, the fact that they have these functions, is quite independent of what *we* think they are supposed to do. Biologists *discovered* these functions, they didn't invent or assign them. We cannot, by agreeing among ourselves, *change* the functions of these organs in the way that I can change, merely by making an appropriate announcement, what the coins and the popcorn in my basketball game stand for. The same seems true for sensory systems, those organs by means of which highly sensitive and continuous dependencies are maintained between external, public events and internal, neural processes. Can there be a serious question about whether, in the same sense in which it is the heart's function to pump the blood, it is, say, the task or function of the noctuid moth's auditory system to detect the whereabouts and movements of its arch-enemy, the bat?

Some marine bacteria have internal magnets, magnetosomes, that function like compass needles, aligning themselves (and, as a result, the bacterium) parallel to the Earth's magnetic field (Blakemore and Frankel 1981). Since the magnetic lines incline downward (toward geomagnetic north) in the northern hemisphere, bacteria in the northern hemisphere, oriented by their internal magnetosomes, propel themselves toward geomagnetic north. Since these organisms are capable of living only in the absence of oxygen, and since movement toward geomagnetic north will take northern bacteria away from the oxygen-rich and therefore toxic surface water and toward the comparatively oxygen-free sediment at the bottom, it is not unreasonable to speculate, as Blakemore and Frankel do, that *the function* of this primitive sensory system is to indicate the whereabouts of benign (i.e., anaerobic) environments.

Philosophers may disagree about how best to analyze the attribution of function to the organs, processes, and behaviors of animals and plants [...], but that some of these things *have* functions – functions, like those of the bacterium's magnetic sense or the moth's auditory sense, to be *discovered* (not invented or assigned) – seems evident not only from a common-sense standpoint but also from the practice, if not the explicit avowals, of biologists and botanists.

This is, nevertheless, a controversial topic, at least among philosophers [...]. [F]or the moment I take the biological examples as more or less (depending on your point of view) plausible illustrations of intrinsic functions – plausible examples, therefore, of sensory systems that, by having such functions, qualify as *natural* systems of representation.

[...]

[Part V] Intentionality: misrepresentation

Philosophers have long regarded intentionality as a mark of the mental. One important dimension of intentionality is the capacity to misrepresent, the power (in the case of the so-called propositional attitudes) to *say* or *mean* that *P* when *P* is not the case. The purpose of this section is to describe how systems of representation, as these have now been characterized, possess this capacity and, hence, exhibit some marks of the mental. [...]

Before we begin, it is perhaps worth noting that, since systems of Types I and II derive their representational powers, including their power to misrepresent, from systems (typically humans) that already have the full range of intentional states and attitudes (knowledge, purpose, desire, etc.), *their* display of intentional characteristics is not surprising. As we shall see, the traces of intentionality exhibited by such systems are merely *reflections* of the minds, *our* minds, that assign them the properties, in particular the functions, from which they derive their status as representations. This is not so, however, for systems of Type III. If there are such systems, *their* intentionality will not be a thing of *our* making. They will have what Haugeland (1981b) calls *original* intentionality and Searle (1980) calls *intrinsic* intentionality.

[...]

The capacity for misrepresentation is easy enough to understand in systems of Type I. For here the power of the elements to misrepresent depends on *our* willingness and skill in manipulating them in accordance with the (indicator) functions we have assigned them. Since I am responsible for what the coins and the popcorn in my basketball game stand for, since I assigned them their indicator function, and since I am responsible for manipulating them in accordance with this function, the arrangement of coins and popcorn can be made to misrepresent whatever *I*, deliberately or out of ignorance, make them misrepresent. Their misrepresentations are really *my* misrepresentations.

Misrepresentation in systems of Type II is not quite so simple an affair, but, once again, its occurrence ultimately traces to whoever or whatever assigns the functions that determine the system's representational efforts. Since there is no such thing as a *mis*indication, no such thing as a natural sign's meaning that something is so when it is not so, the only way a system of natural signs can misrepresent anything is if the signs that serve as its representational elements fail to indicate something they are *supposed* to indicate. [...] Putting chilled alcohol in a glass cylinder doesn't generate a misrepresentation unless somebody calibrates the glass, hangs it on the wall, and calls it a thermometer.

Only when we reach RSs of Type III – only when the functions defining what a system is supposed to indicate are intrinsic functions – do we find a *source*, not merely a reflection, of intentionality. Only here do we have systems sufficiently self-contained in their representational efforts to serve, in this one respect at least, as models of thought, belief, and judgment.

A system could have acquired the *function* of indicating that something was *F* without, in the present circumstances, or any longer, or perhaps *ever*, being able to indicate that something is *F*. This is obvious in the case of a Type II RS, where, by careless assembly, a device can fail to do what it was designed to do. As we all know, some shiny new appliances don't work the way they are supposed to work. They *never* do what it is their function to do. When what they are supposed to do is indicate, such devices are doomed to a life of misrepresentation. Others leave the factory in good condition but later wear out and no longer retain the power to indicate what it is their function to indicate. Still others, though they don't wear out, are used in circumstances that curtail their ability to indicate what they were designed to indicate. A compass is no good in a mineshaft, and a thermometer isn't much good in the sun. In order to do what they are supposed to do, care has to be taken that such instruments are used when and where they can do their job.

The same is true of RSs of Type III. Suppose a primitive sensory ability evolves in a species because of what it is capable of telling its possessors about some critical environmental condition F. Let us assume, for the sake of the example, that the manner in which this indicator developed, the way it was (because of its critical role in delivering needed information) favored by the forces of selection, allows us to say that this indicator has the function of indicating F. Through some reproductive accident, an individual member of this species (call him Inverto) inherits his F-detector in defective (let us suppose inverted) condition. Poor Inverto has an RS that always misrepresents his surroundings: it represents things as being F when they are not, and vice versa.[1] Unless he is fortunate enough to be preserved in some artificial way – unless, that is, he is removed from a habitat in which the detection of Fs is critical – Inverto will not long survive. He emerged defective from the factory and will soon be discarded. On the other hand, his cousins, though emerging from the factory in good condition, may simply wear out. As old age approaches, their RSs deteriorate, progressively losing their ability to indicate when and where there is an F. They retain their function, of course, but they lose the capacity to perform that function. Misrepresentation becomes more and more frequent until, inevitably, they share Inverto's fate.

And, finally, we have the analogue, in a Type III system, of an instrument used in disabling circumstances – the compass in a mineshaft, for instance. Consider a sensitive biological detector that, upon removal from the habitat in which it developed, flourished, and faithfully serviced its possessor's biological needs, is put into circumstances in which it is no longer capable of indicating what it is supposed to indicate. We earlier considered bacteria that relied on internal detectors (magnetosomes) of magnetic north in order to reach oxygen-free environments. Put a northern bacterium into the southern hemisphere and it will quickly destroy itself by swimming in the wrong direction. If we suppose [...] that it is the function of these internal detectors to indicate the whereabouts of anaerobic conditions, then misrepresentation occurs – in this case with fatal consequences.

Put a frog in a laboratory where carefully produced shadows simulate edible bugs. In these unnatural circumstances the frog's neural detectors – those that have, for good reason, been called "bug detectors" – will no longer indicate the presence or the location of bugs. They will no longer indicate this (even when they are, by chance, caused to fire by real edible bugs) because their activity no longer *depends* in the requisite way on the presence of edible bugs. Taking a frog into the laboratory is like taking a compass down a mineshaft: things no longer work the way they are supposed to work. Indicators stop indicating. If we suppose, then, that it is the function of the frog's neural detectors to indicate the presence of edible bugs, then, in the laboratory, shadows are misrepresented *as* edible bugs. The frog has an analogue of a false belief. Occasionally, when an edible bug flies by, the frog will correctly represent it as an edible bug, but this is dumb luck. The frog has the analogue of a true belief, a *correct* representation, but no *knowledge,* no *reliable* representation. Taking a compass down a mineshaft will not change what it "says" (namely, that whichever way the needle points is geomagnetic north), but it will change the reliability, and (often enough) the truth, of what it says. Likewise, taking a frog into the laboratory will not change what it "thinks," but it will change the number of times it *truly* thinks what it thinks.

Notes

[1] An artificial approximation of this situation occurred when R. W. Sperry (1956) and his associates rotated, by surgical means, the eyeball of a newt by 180°. The vision of the animal was permanently reversed. As Sperry describes it: "When a piece of bait was held above the newt's head it would begin digging into the pebbles and sand on the bottom of the aquarium. When the lure was presented in front of its head, it would turn around and start searching in the rear."

References

Blakemore, R. P., and R. B. Frankel. 1981 Magnetic navigation in bacteria. *Scientific American* 245: 6.

Grice, P. 1957. Meaning. *Philosophical Review* 66: 377–388.

Haugeland, J. (ed.) 1981a. *Mind Design*. Cambridge, Mass. : MIT Press. A Bradford Book.

Haugeland, J. 1981b. Semantic engines: An introduction to mind design. In Haugeland 1981a.

Huber, F., and J. Thorson. 1985. Cricket auditory communication. *Scientific American* 253, no. 6: 60–68.

O'Keefe, J. 1976. Place units in the hippocampus of freely moving rat. *Experimental Neurology* 51: 78–109.

Searle, J. 1980. Minds, brains and programs. *Behavioral and Brain Sciences* 3, no. 3: 417–457.

Sperry, R. W. 1956. The eye and the brain. Reprinted (from *Scientific American*) in *Perception: Mechanisms and Models* (San Francisco: Freeman).

Advertisement for a semantics for psychology

Ned Block

Source: Block, N. (1994) 'Advertisement for a semantics for psychology', in S. Stich and T.A. Warfield (eds) *Mental Representation: A Reader*, Oxford, Basil Blackwell, pp.81–135. Heavily edited with some silent restructuring of paragraphs. Neither numbering of parts nor subtitles in original. The use of apostrophes to pluralize 'S' and 'T' in the original has been suppressed here.

[Part I: Conceptual role semantics]

Meaning is notoriously vague. So, it should not be surprising that semanticists (those who study meaning) have had somewhat different purposes in mind, and thus have sharpened the ordinary concept of meaning in somewhat different ways. It is a curious and unfortunate fact that semanticists typically tell us little about what aspects of meaning they are and are not attempting to deal with. One is given little guidance as to what extent "rival" research programs actually disagree. My purpose here is to advocate an approach to semantics relevant to the foundations of psychology, or, rather, one approach to one branch of psychology, namely cognitive science. I shall be talking in terms of some of the leading ideas of cognitive science, most importantly the representational theory of mind [i.e. CTM] [...]. The representationalist doctrine that my argument depends on is that thoughts are structured entities. [...]

The view that I am advertising is a variant on the functionalism familiar in the philosophy of mind. However, I will not be attempting to counter the objections that have been raised to that view (except briefly, and in passing). My bet is that looking at functionalism from the point of view of meaning (rather than mentality) and with an eye to its fertility and power rather than its weaknesses will provide a rationale for working on its problems. [...]

Conceptual role semantics (CRS) [...] has been suggested, independently, by both philosophers and cognitive scientists. [...] CRS says meaning is conceptual role. If someone uses a word (or a word functions in her brain) that has the conceptual role of "dog," then the word in question means the same as "dog." If a person's brain changes so as to cause a word to be used (by her or her brain) so as to have the conceptual role in question, then she has acquired the concept of a dog [...].

[W]hat makes an expression meaningful is that it has a conceptual role of a certain type, one that we may call "appropriate." The difference between "cat" and "glurg" is that "cat" has an appropriate conceptual role, whereas "glurg" does not. What gives "cat" the particular meaning that it has is its particular conceptual role. The difference between meaningful expressions with different meanings ("cat" and "dog") is a conceptual role difference *within* the category of appropriate conceptual roles. [...]

The internal factor, conceptual role, is a matter of the causal role of the expression in reasoning and deliberation and, in general, in the way the expression combines and interacts with other expressions so as to mediate between sensory inputs and behavioral outputs. A crucial component of a sentence's conceptual role is a matter of how it participates in inductive and deductive inferences. A word's conceptual role is a matter of its contribution to the role of sentences.

For example, consider what would be involved for a symbol in the internal representational system, "→," to express the material conditional. The "→" in "FELIX IS A CAT → FELIX IS AN ANIMAL" expresses the material conditional if, for example, when the just quoted sentence interacts appropriately with:

> "FELIX IS A CAT," the result is a tendency to inscribe "FELIX IS AN ANIMAL" (other things equal, of course).
>
> [With] "FELIX IS NOT AN ANIMAL," the result is a tendency to prevent the inscription of "FELIX IS A CAT," and a tendency to inscribe "FELIX IS NOT A CAT."
>
> [With] "IS FELIX AN ANIMAL?," the result is a tendency to initiate a search for "FELIX IS A CAT."

Conceptual role is *total causal role*, abstractly described. Consider, by way of analogy, the causal role of herring. They affect what they eat, what eats them, what sees them and runs away, and, of course, they causally interact with one another. Now abstract away from the total causal role of herring to their culinary role, by which I mean the causal relations involving them that have an effect on or are affected by human dining. Presumably, some of what affects herring and what they affect will not be part of their culinary role: for example, perhaps herring occasionally amuse penguins, and this activity has no culinary causes or effects. Similarly, elements of language have a total causal role, including, say, the effect of newsprint on whatever people wrap in it. Conceptual role abstracts away from all causal relations except the ones that mediate inferences, inductive or deductive, decision-making and the like. [...] (Calling the causal roles CRS appeals to "conceptual" or "inferential" shouldn't mislead anyone into supposing that the theory's description of them can appeal to their meanings – that would defeat the point of reductionist theories.) [...]

A crucial question for CRS (*the* crucial question) is what counts as identity and difference of conceptual role. Clearly, there are many differences in reasoning that we do not want to count as relevant to meaning. For example, if you take longer than I do in reasoning from x to y, we do not necessarily want to see this as revealing a difference between your meanings of x and/or y and mine. Our reasoning processes may be the same in all inferentially important respects.

Further, CRS must fact the familiar "collateral information" problem. Suppose you are prepared to infer from "TIGER" to "DANGEROUS," whereas I am not. Do our "TIGER"s have the same conceptual role or not? More significantly, what if we differ in inferring from "TIGER" to "ANIMAL"? Does the first difference differ in kind from the second? [...]

If CRS is to be developed to the point where it can be evaluated seriously, definite proposals for individuating conceptual roles must be framed and investigated. One of the purposes of this paper is to try to make it plausible that CRS is worth pursuing. [...]

CRS aims for a reductionist account, indeed, a naturalistic-reductionist account, in proposing to explain a semantic property in terms of a naturalistic, non-semantic property: causation. CRS's reductionism and naturalism allow it to promise an answer to "What makes a meaningful expression meaningful?" [...]

[Part II: The reductionist alternatives]

There are two competing families of approaches to semantics that [are also] reductionist [...] One of them is the approach of reducing meaning to *mental content*. Call this type of approach "Gricean." The Gricean approach [...] reduces speaker meaning to the content of speaker's intentions. [...] Although I do not want to belittle the Gricean accomplishment, without a naturalistic account of the mental, the Gricean approach has little to contribute to the project I am discussing. [...] Is there some way in which the Gricean account could be extended to internal language? Computation in internal symbol systems appears to be of a rather "automatic" sort which gains efficiency through inflexibility. For example, if one memorizes a list of six letters, say "UEKNMG," and one is asked whether "E" is on the list, one does an "exhaustive" serial search, looking at all six letters, one by one, even if "E" is the first letter in the list. (This is one of the better tested results in all of cognitive psychology.) Is it at all plausible that one forms an *intention* to look at all the items, or to do an exhaustive serial search? Further, even if the uses of the internal system are intentional in some sense, surely the intentions are not intentions to *communicate*, as in the standard Gricean theories. [...]

There is a second family of reductionist approaches to semantics that could be claimed to satisfy my desiderata: what I called "indicator semantics." Dretske (1981) and Stampe (1977) have similar versions, which I believe have been refuted by Fodor [this volume, pp.227–30]. [...] Dretske and Stampe say what it is for a sentence S to have the content that T in terms of tokens of S carrying information about T; carrying information, in turn, is cashed in terms of a nomological relation between Ss and Ts (roughly, an S nomologically requires a T). Fodor objects that, if error is possible, then a non-T can cause a tokening of S; but then why should we regard T as the state of affairs with which S is nomologically correlated when S has a *better* correlation with the disjunctive state of affairs whose disjuncts are T and the non-T state that causes S? So it seems that, on the Dretske/Stampe view, error is not possible. [...]

[Many reductionist semantic theories appeal to] the idea that the cognitive system is *supposed* to function in a certain way. How is this teleological talk supposed to be understood? [...] Some [...] talk in terms of a notion of teleology provided by evolutionary theory. The cognitive system is supposed to function a certain way in that [that] is what evolution designed it to do. [... But ...] one cannot rely on evolution in such a simple way, since one can imagine a molecule-for-molecule duplicate of a baby who comes into being by chance and grows up in the normal way. Such a person would have language with the normal semantic properties, but no evolutionary "design."

[Part III: Psychological explanation and narrow meaning]

It would be surprising if the nature of meaning (what meaning *is*) were utterly irrelevant to explaining [...] how it is that the brain's grasp of meanings has effects on the world[.] Meanings are (at least apparently) non-physical abstract objects. And the relation between a brain and the meanings it grasps does not seem to be like the relation between a metal bar and the number of degrees Celsius that is its temperature – a case in which there are proposals about how a change in the value of the temperature can cause, say, expansion of the bar [...]. Yet the difference between a brain that grasps a certain meaning and a brain that does not makes for a difference in the causal properties of that brain. A brain that grasps the meaning of "transmogrify" can win a quiz show for its owner, transporting the two of them to a hotel in [Hawaii]. We need an account of how such a [...] relation between a brain and a meaning can make a causal difference.

How does the brain confer meaning on its representations? [My answer]: by conferring the right causal roles on the representations. What is it for a person to grasp the meaning of a word? [My answer]: for a person to grasp the meaning of a word is for the word (or its standard Mentalese associate) to have a certain causal role in his or her brain. How can it be that a person grasping an abstract object can propel the person (and his or her brain) to Hawaii? [My answer]: the difference between grasping a meaning and not grasping it is a difference in the causal role of entities in the person's brain, and differences in such causal roles can make for differences in behavior and the rewards that are contingent on behavior. [...]

The version of conceptual role semantics that I [am] defending characterizes *narrow* meaning in terms of conceptual role. [...] Consider the difference between the beliefs I would express by uttering (1), as compared with (2):

(1) I am in danger of being run over.

(2) Ned Block is in danger of being run over.

Believing (2) cannot be guaranteed to have the same life-saving effect on my behavior as believing (1), since I may not know I am Ned Block (I may think I am Napoleon). So there is an important difference between (1) and (2) with respect to causation (and therefore causal explanation) of behavior. This observation is one motivation for a familiar way of thinking about meaning and belief content in which, when you and I have beliefs expressed by our (respective) utterances of (1), we have beliefs with the same content. This is the way of individuating in which two lunatics who say "I am Napoleon" have the *same delusion*. [...]

Nonetheless, (1), said by me, and (2) express the same proposition, according to a familiar [but different] way of individuating propositions. In a familiar sense of "meaning" in which two sentence-tokens have the same meaning just in case they express the same proposition, (1), said by me, and (2) have the same meaning. If we individuate contents of beliefs as we individuate the propositions believed, the belief I express by (1) would have the same content as the belief I express by (2). Further, the belief I express by (1) would have different content from the belief you express by (1); similarly, the meaning of my utterance of (1) would be different from your utterance of (1).

Call the former scheme of individuation *narrow* individuation and the latter *wide* individuation [...]. Wide individuation groups token sentences together if they attribute the same properties to the same individuals [...]. [N]arrow individuation abstracts from the question of (i.e., ignores) whether the same individuals are involved and depends instead on how the individuals are referred to. [...] One can think of narrow and wide individuation as specifying different aspects of meaning, narrow and wide meaning. [...] Narrow meaning is "in the head," in the sense of this phrase in which it indicates supervenience [roughly: dependence] on physical constitution, and narrow meaning captures the semantic aspect of what is in common to utterances of (e.g.) (1) by different people. Wide meaning, by contrast, depends on what individuals outside the head are referred to, so wide meaning is not "in the head." The type of individuation that gives rise to the concept of narrow meaning also gives rise to a corresponding concept of narrow belief content. Two utterances have the same narrow meaning just in case the beliefs they express have the same narrow content. [...]

Narrow meaning/content and wide meaning/content are relevant to psychological explanation in quite different ways. For one thing, the narrow meaning of a sentence believed is more informative about the mental state of the believer. Thus narrow meaning (and narrow content) is better suited to predicting and explaining what someone decides or does, so long as information about the external world is ignored. Thus, if you and I both have a belief we would express with (1), one can explain and predict our sudden glances at nearby vehicles and our (respective) decisions to leap to the side. Wide meanings are less suited to this type of prediction and explanation, because they "leave out" information about the way one refers to oneself. Since the wide meaning of (1) said by me and (2) are the same, if you are told I believe a sentence with this wide meaning (i.e., the wide meaning common to my [1] and [2]), you know that I believe something – me, as it happens, but you aren't told that I know it's me – is in danger of being run over. Thus, information is omitted, since you aren't told how I conceive of the thing in danger. [...]

I have been talking so far about the meaning of sentences with indexicals, but the points I have been making can be extended to names and, more controversially, to natural kind terms. [...] [The case of names] is illustrated by "Cicero orates" and "Tully orates." [...] [H]ow you represent something that you refer to can affect your psychological states and behavior. So if you know that Cicero orates and you don't know that Cicero = Tully, you are not in a position to make use of the fact that Tully orates. [...]

[For natural kind terms, consider] Putnam's original Twin Earth story. My doppelgänger (again, a physical duplicate) uses "water" to refer to XYZ. Suppose, along with Putnam, that XYZ is *not* a type of water. Further, we may add into the story ideas developed by Burge (Burge, 1979) that show the differences in how our different language communities use words can determine differences in the meanings of our words, even when they do not result in differences in stimuli impinging on our surfaces. Suppose my twin and I both say to ourselves:

> My pants are on fire. But luckily I am standing in front of a swimming pool filled with water. Water, thank God, puts out fires.

If Burge and Putnam are right (and I am inclined to agree with them), there are substantial differences between my twin's and my meanings and thought contents because of the differences in physical and social environment. Nonetheless – and here, again, is the crucial idea behind my advocacy of narrow meaning and content – *there is some aspect of meaning in common to what he says and what I say (or at least a common partial determinant of meaning), and this common semantic aspect of what we say provides part of a common explanation of why we both jump into our respective pools.* And if current ideas about the representational theory of mind are right, narrow meaning and content will be usable to state nomological generalizations relating thought, decision, and action. [...]

Why is narrow meaning relevant to the explanation of behavior, and why is it relevant in the same way for me and my twin? Taking the second question first: since my twin and I are physically identical, all of our representations have exactly the same internal causal roles, and hence the same narrow meanings. But why is narrow meaning relevant to the explanation of behavior in the first place? To have an internal representation with a certain narrow meaning is to have a representation with certain likely inferential antecedents and consequents. Hence, to ascribe a narrow meaning is to ascribe a syndrome of causes and effects, including, in some cases, behavioral effects (or at least impulses in motor-output neurons). The reason my twin and I both jump is that we have representations with conceptual roles that have, as part of their syndrome of effects, jumping behavior. The reason that wide meaning is not as relevant to the explanation of behavior as is narrow meaning is that differences in wide meaning that do not involve differences in narrow meaning (e.g., the difference between me and my twin) do not cause behavioral differences. [...] "I am in the path of danger" and "Ned Block is in the path of danger" can have systematically different conceptual roles, depending on whether I know I am Ned Block (rather than, say, Napoleon). "I," used by a speaker, differs systematically from the speaker's own name in its conceptual role, even though they refer to the same thing. Hence CRS assigns them different narrow meanings. Thus the thought I express with "I" (or its internal associate) is different in narrow content from the thought I would have expressed were my name to have replaced "I."

Thus, narrow meaning, as articulated by CRS, can [...] serve the purpose[s of psychological explanation]. Similar points apply to the examples using names [...]. "Cicero [orates]" and "Tully [orates]" have different conceptual roles; so despite the fact that they have identical wide meanings, we can see why believing these different sentences could have different effects on other mental states and behavior.

[Part IV: Individuation of conceptual roles]

Let us say that a propositional attitude or meaning ascription is individualistic if it is supervenient on the physical state of the individual's body, where physical state is specified non-intentionally and independently of physical and social conditions obtaining outside the body. I believe that there is an important individualistic scheme of individuation of beliefs, belief contents, and the meanings of the sentences believed. There is a strong element of individualistic individuation in ordinary thought, but its main home lies in scientific thinking about the mind, especially in contemporary cognitive science. I also agree with [...] Putnam that there is an important non-individualistic scheme of individuation in ordinary thought. No incompatibility yet.

But Putnam [...] and others have also argued against individualistic individuation. Putnam's conclusion (1983) is based on an argument that it is impossible to come up with identity conditions on content or meaning, individualistically considered. I don't have identity conditions to offer, but I am inclined to regard this not as an insurmountable obstacle but as an issue to be dissolved by theory construction. My guess is that a scientific conception of meaning should do away with the crude dichotomy of same/different meaning in favour of a multidimensional gradient of similarity of meaning [...] – by moving from the crude pigeonholes of *believes/doesn't believe* to degrees of belief. [...]

[I]n this paper, I have not attempted to elaborate CRS [...]. Rather, I have tried to provide reason for suppressing the "put up or shut up" reflex that dogs talk of conceptual roles in the absence of identity conditions for them. My hope is that this theory will get more attention and that more detailed versions of it will allow us to evaluate its prospects better.

References

Block, N. (1983). "Mental pictures and cognitive science," *Philosophical Review*, 92, pp. 499–541.

Burge, T. (1979). "Individualism and the mental," *Midwest Studies in Philosophy*, 4, pp. 73–121.

Dretske, F. (1981). *Knowledge and the Flow of Information*. Cambridge, MA: MIT Press.

Putnam, H. (1983). "Computational psychology and interpretation theory," in *Philosophical Papers*, vol. 3: *Realism and Reason* (Cambridge: Cambridge University Press).

Stampe, D. (1977). "Towards a causal theory of linguistic representation," *Midwest Studies in Philosophy*, 2, pp. 42–63.

Holism, content similarity, and content identity

Jerry Fodor and Ernest Lepore

Source: Fodor, J.A. and Lepore, E. (1992) 'Introduction: a geography of the issues', in *Holism: A Shopper's Guide*, Cambridge, Mass. and Oxford, Blackwell. Subtitles and numbering of parts added.

[Part I: Generalizations in scientific psychology]

Lots of people, including most cognitive scientists and many riders on the Clapham omnibus, hold the following view of behavior: that higher animals act out of their beliefs and desires. According to this view, there are counterfactual-supporting generalizations that connect the mental states of higher animals with their behaviors (and with one another) *and which subsume mental states in virtue of their intentional contents.* Consider such shopworn examples as "If you see the moon *as being on the horizon,* then you will see it *as oversized"* or "If someone asks you what's the first thing salt makes you think of, you'll think of pepper" or "If someone asks you what's the first color you think of, you'll think of red."

And so forth.

We emphasize that it's in virtue of *what they are thoughts about* that thoughts fall under a generalization like "If you think of a color, the first color you think of is red" – that is, it's in virtue of their being thoughts about color and thoughts about red (reading "thoughts about" de dicto). A fortiori, the generalization subsumes you and me (as it might be) only if we both *have* thoughts about color and about red.

But now suppose that holism is true about thought content. Then, since you and I surely have widely different belief systems (think of all the things you know that I don't) and since, by definition, a property is holistic only if nothing has it unless many other things do, it may well turn out that none of your thoughts [are the same in content as] any of mine. It would follow that not more than one of us ever has thoughts about color or thoughts about red. So, at most one of us is subsumed by the generalization that if you think of a color, then the first color you think about is red. In fact, it might well turn out that, at most, one *time slice* of one of us is subsumed by this generalization since, after all, vastly many of one's beliefs change from moment to moment, and, on the present assumptions, belief individuation is holistic.

These sorts of considerations suggest that it might turn out that if [the individuation of thought content] is holistic, there are no *robust*, counterfactual-supporting intentional generalizations, none that is ever satisfied by more than an individual at an instant. Many philosophers have indeed drawn this sort of inference. Since, they argue, mental properties are holistic, there couldn't really be intentional laws; and since there can't really be intentional laws, intentional explanations can't be fully factual. [...] Presumably, if there aren't fully factual intentional generalizations, then there can't be an intentional science of human nature (or a scientific epistemology or a scientific moral psychology) in anything like the sense of "science" that the physical and biological sciences have in mind. "Behavioral science," "social science," "cognitive science," and the like are therefore, strictly speaking, oxymorons if semantic holism is true.

[...]

[Part II: Why content similarity presupposes content identity]

Why, then, aren't many people outside philosophy (many cognitive/ behavioral/social scientists, for example) worried about the holism issues? One reason is that they may not have noticed the undesirable consequences of holism [...]. Another reason is that it's widely supposed that even if holism precludes a robust notion of content *identity*, still it permits a robust notion of content *similarity*. [...] Taking this for granted seems like just common sense. After all, there does *seem* to be a colloquial notion of belief similarity. We do say things like "What I believe is a lot like what the President believes" or "Her world view is sort of similar to Dracula's" [...] and so on. So maybe this colloquial sense of "similar belief" can be co-opted to provide for a robust formulation of intentional generalizations. Maybe the right generalization is: If somebody asks you something *sort of like* what is the first color you think of, then you will think of something *sort of like* red.

The trouble is that we really have no idea what it would be like for this new generalization to be true (or false) and, barring some illumination in this quarter, the suggestion that appealing to content similarity may mitigate the severer consequences of semantic holism is simply *empty*. This point is so important, and so widely goes unrecognized, that we propose to spend a little time rubbing it in.

No doubt, one does know (sort of) what it is like to more or less believe the same things as the President does; it's to share *many of the President's beliefs*. For example, the President believes P, Q, R, and S, and I believe P, Q, and R; so my beliefs are similar to his. An alternative, compatible reading is: the President believes P and *Q very strongly* and I believe them equally strongly or almost as strongly, so again my beliefs are similar to his. But neither of these ways of construing belief similarity helps with the present problem. The present problem is not to make sense of believing-most-of-P, -Q, -R, -and-S or of more-or-less-strongly-believing-P; it's to make sense of believing *something-similar-to-P* – that is, believing *more-or-less-P*.

The colloquial senses of "similar belief" *presuppose* some way of *counting* beliefs, so they presuppose some notion of belief *identity*. If you have most of the beliefs that I have, then, a fortiori, there are (one or more) beliefs that we both have. And if there is a proposition that you sort of believe and that I believe strongly, then, a fortiori, there is a proposition that is the object of both of our beliefs. But precisely because these colloquial senses of belief similarity *presuppose* a notion of belief identity, they don't allow us to *dispense with* a notion of belief identity *in favor of* a notion of belief similarity. In consequence, if you're a holist and your notion of belief identity is very unrobust, so that, de facto, people can hardly ever have the same belief, then it will also turn out that, in either of the colloquial senses just discussed, people can hardly ever have *similar* beliefs. [...]

It's not, of course, incoherent to imagine a notion of "similar belief" which, unlike these colloquial ones, is compatible both with meaning holism and with there being robust intentional generalizations. The trouble is, as we remarked above, that nobody seems to have any idea what this useful new sense of "similar belief" might be.

References

Putnam, H., "Philosophers and human understanding," in *Realism and Reason*, pp. 184–204.

Putnam, H., *Realism and Reason. Philosophical Papers*, vol. 3, Cambridge University Press, Cambridge, 1983.

True believers: the intentional strategy and why it works

Daniel Dennett

Source: Dennett, D.C. (1990) 'True believers: the intentional strategy and why it works', in W.G. Lycan (ed.) *Mind and Cognition: A Reader*, Cambridge, Mass. and Oxford, Basil Blackwell, pp.15–165. Edited as indicated. Numbering and some subtitling of parts added.

[Part I: Is belief inside the head or all just a matter of interpretation?]

Sometimes belief attribution appears to be a dark, risky, and imponderable business – especially when exotic, and more particularly religious or superstitious, beliefs are in the limelight. These are not the only troublesome cases; we also court argument and scepticism when we attribute beliefs to non-human animals, or to infants, or to computers or robots. Or when the beliefs we feel constrained to attribute to an apparently healthy, adult member of our own society are contradictory, or even just wildly false. [...]

On [...] normal occasions, when familiar beliefs are the topic, belief attribution looks as easy as speaking prose, and as objective and reliable as counting beans in a dish. Particularly when these straightforward cases are before us, it is quite plausible to suppose that in principle (if not yet in practice) it would be possible to confirm these simple, objective belief attributions by *finding something inside the believer's head* – by finding the beliefs themselves, in effect. "Look," someone might say, "You either believe there's milk in the fridge or you don't believe there's milk in the fridge" (you might have no opinion, in the latter case). But if you do believe this, that's a perfectly objective fact about you, and it must come down in the end to your brain's being in some particular physical state. If we knew more about physiological psychology we could in principle determine the facts about your brain state, and thereby determine whether or not you believe there is milk in the fridge, even if you were determined to be silent, or disingenuous on the topic. In principle, on this view physiological psychology could trump the results – or non-results – of any "black box" method in the social sciences that divines beliefs (and other mental features) by behavioral, cultural, social, historical, *external* criteria.

[...]

I think this is a mistake. My thesis will be that while belief is a perfectly objective phenomenon (that apparently makes me a realist), it can be discerned only from the point of view of one who adopts a certain *predictive strategy*, and its existence can be confirmed only by an assessment of the success of that strategy (that apparently makes me an interpretationist).

First I will describe the strategy, which I call the intentional strategy, or adopting the intentional stance. To a first approximation, the intentional strategy consists of treating the object whose behavior you want to predict as a rational agent with beliefs and desires and other mental states exhibiting what Brentano and others call *intentionality*. The strategy has often been described before, but I shall try to put this very familiar material in a new light, by showing *how* it works, and by showing *how well* it works.

Then I will argue that any object – or as I shall say, any *system* – whose behavior is well predicted by this strategy is in the fullest sense of the word a believer. *What it is* to be a true believer is to be an *intentional system*, a system whose behavior is reliably and voluminously predictable via the intentional strategy. I have argued for this position before, and my arguments have so far garnered few converts and many presumed counterexamples. I shall try again here, harder, and shall also deal with several compelling objections.

[Part II] The intentional strategy and how it works

There are many strategies, some good, some bad. Here is a strategy, for instance, for predicting the future behavior of a person: determine the date and hour of the person's birth, and then feed this modest datum into one or another astrological algorithm for generating predictions of the person's prospects. This strategy is deplorably popular. Its popularity is deplorable only because we have such good reasons for believing that *it does not work*.

When astrological predictions come true this is sheer luck, or the result of such vagueness or ambiguity in the prophecy that almost any eventuality can be construed to confirm it. But suppose the astrological strategy did in fact work well on some people. We could call those people *astrological systems* – systems whose behavior was, as a matter of fact, predictable by the astrological strategy. [...]

So far as we know, however, the class of astrological systems is empty, so the astrological strategy is of interest only as a social curiosity. Other strategies have better credentials. Consider the physical strategy, or physical stance: if you want to predict the behavior of a system, determine its physical constitution (perhaps all the way down to the micro-physical level) and the physical nature of the impingements upon it, and use your knowledge of the laws of physics to predict the outcome for any input. This is the grand and impractical strategy of Laplace for predicting the entire future of everything in the universe, but it has more modest, local, actually usable versions. The chemist or physicist in the laboratory can use this strategy to predict the behavior of exotic materials, but equally the cook in the kitchen can predict the effect of leaving the pot on the burner too long. [...]

Sometimes, in any event, it is more effective to switch from the physical stance to what I call the design stance, where one ignores the actual (possibly messy) details of the physical constitution of an object, and, on the assumption that it has a certain design, predicts that it will behave *as it is designed to behave* under various circumstances. [...] [A]lmost anyone can predict when an alarm clock will sound on the basis of the most casual inspection of its exterior. One does not know or care to know whether it is spring wound, battery driven, sunlight powered, made of brass wheels and jewel bearings or silicon chips – one just assumes that it is designed so that the alarm will sound when it is set to sound, and it is set to sound where it appears to be set to sound, and the clock will keep on running until that time and beyond, and is designed to run more or less accurately, and so forth. For more accurate and detailed design stance predictions of the alarm clock, one must descend to a less abstract level of description of its design; for instance, to the level at which gears are described, but their material is not specified.

Only the designed behavior of a system is predictable from the design stance, of course. If you want to predict the behavior of an alarm clock when it is pumped full of liquid helium, revert to the physical stance. Not just artifacts, but also many biological objects (plants and animals, kidneys and hearts, stamens and pistils) behave in ways that can be predicted from the design stance. They are not just physical systems but designed systems.

Sometimes even the design stance is practically inaccessible, and then there is yet another stance or strategy one can adopt: the intentional stance. Here is how it works: first you decide to treat the object whose behavior is to be predicted as a rational agent; then you figure out what beliefs that agent ought to have, given its place in the world and its purpose. Then you figure out what desires it ought to have, on the same considerations, and finally you predict that this rational agent will act to further its goals in the light of its beliefs. A little practical reasoning from the chosen set of beliefs and desires will in many – but not all – instances yield a decision about what the agent ought to do; that is what you predict the agent *will* do.

The strategy becomes clearer with a little elaboration. Consider first how we go about populating each other's heads with beliefs. A few truisms: sheltered people tend to be ignorant; if you expose someone to something he comes to know all about it. In general, it seems, we come to believe all the truths about the parts of the world around us we are put in a position to learn about. *Exposure* to x, that is, sensory confrontation with x over some suitable period of time, is the *normally sufficient* condition for knowing (or having true beliefs) about x.

[...]

Of course we do not come to learn or remember all the truths our sensory histories avail us. In spite of the phrase 'know all about', what we come to know, normally, are only all the *relevant* truths our sensory histories avail us. I do not typically come to know the ratio of spectacle-wearing people to trousered people in a room I inhabit, though if this interested me, it would be readily learnable. [...] So one rule for attributing beliefs in the intentional strategy is this: attribute as beliefs all the truths relevant to the system's interests (or desires) that the system's experience to date has made available. This rule leads to attributing somewhat too much – since we all are somewhat forgetful, even of important things. It also fails to capture the false beliefs we are all known to have. But the attribution of false belief, *any* false belief, requires a special genealogy⁻, which will be seen to consist in the main in true beliefs.

[...]

An implication of the intentional strategy, then, is that true believers mainly believe truths.

[...]

How do we attribute the desires (preferences, goals, interests) on whose basis we will shape the list of beliefs? We attribute the desires the system *ought to have*. That is the fundamental rule. It dictates, on a first pass, that we attribute the familiar list of highest, or most basic, desires to people: survival, absence of pain, food, comfort, procreation, entertainment. Citing any one of these desires typically terminates the "Why?" game of reason giving. One is not supposed to need an ulterior motive for desiring comfort or pleasure or the prolongation of one's existence. Derived rules of desire attribution interact with belief attributions. Trivially, we have the rule: attribute desires for those things a system believes to be good for it. Somewhat more informatively, attribute desires for those things a system believes to be best means to other ends it desires. The attribution of bizarre and detrimental desire thus requires, like the attribution of false beliefs, special stories.

[...]

That is enough, on this occasion, about the principles of belief and desire attribution to be found in the intentional strategy. What about the rationality one attributes to an intentional system? One starts with the ideal of perfect rationality and revises downwards as circumstances dictate. That is, one starts with the assumption that people believe all the implications of their beliefs, and believe no contradictory pairs of beliefs. This does not create a practical problem of clutter (infinitely many implications, for instance), for one is interested only in ensuring that the system one is predicting is rational enough to get to the particular implications that are relevant to its behavioral predicament of the moment. [...]

For I want to turn from the description of the strategy to the question of its use. Do people actually use this strategy? Yes, all the time. There may someday be other strategies for attributing belief and desire and for predicting behavior, but this is the only one we all know now. And when does it work? It works with people almost all the time. [...]

The strategy works on birds, and on fish, and on reptiles, and on insects and spiders, and even on such lowly and unenterprising creatures as clams (once a clam believes there is danger about, it will not relax its grip on its closed shell until it is convinced that the danger has passed). It also works on some artifacts: the chess-playing computer will not take your knight because it knows that there is a line of ensuing play that would lead to losing its rook, and it does not want that to happen. More modestly, the thermostat will turn off the boiler as soon as it comes to believe the room has reached the desired temperature.

The strategy even works for plants. In a locale with late spring storms you should plant apple varieties that are particularly *cautious* about *concluding* that it is spring – which is when they *want* to blossom, of course. [...]

[Part III] True believers as intentional systems

Now clearly this is a motley assortment of "serious" belief attributions, dubious belief attributions, pedagogically useful metaphors, *façons de parler*, and perhaps worse: outright frauds. [...] Does our definition of an intentional system exclude any objects at all? For instance, it seems the lectern in this lecture room can be construed as an intentional system, fully rational, and believing that it is currently located at the centre of the civilized world (as some of you may also think); and desiring above all else to remain at that centre. What should such a rational agent so equipped with belief and desire do? Stay put, clearly, which is just what the lectern does. I predict the lectern's behavior, accurately, from the intentional stance, so is it an intentional system? If it is, anything at all is.

What should disqualify the lectern? For one thing, the strategy does not recommend itself in this case, for we get no predictive power from it that we did not antecedently have. We already knew what the lectern was going to do – namely nothing – and tailored the beliefs and desires to fit in a quite unprincipled way. In the case of people, or animals, or computers, however, the situation is different. In these cases often the only strategy that is at all practical is the intentional strategy; it gives us predictive power we can get by no other method. [...] The decision to adopt the intentional stance is free, but the facts about the success or failure of the stance, were one to adopt it, are perfectly objective.

Once the intentional strategy is in place, it is an extraordinarily powerful tool in prediction. [...]

The power of the intentional strategy can be seen [...] with the aid of an objection first raised by Robert Nozick some years ago. Suppose, he suggested, some beings of vastly superior intelligence – from Mars, let us say – were to descend upon us, and suppose that we were to them as simple thermostats are to clever engineers. Suppose, that is that they did not *need* the intentional stance – or even the design stance – to predict our behavior in all its detail. They can be supposed to be Laplacean super-physicists, capable of comprehending the activity on Wall Street, for instance, at the micro-physical level. Where we see brokers and buildings and sell orders and bids, they see vast congeries of subatomic particles milling about – and they are such good physicists that they can predict days in advance what ink marks will appear each day on the paper tape labelled 'Closing Dow Jones Industrial Average'. They can predict the individual behaviors of all the various moving bodies they observe without ever treating any of them as intentional systems. Would we be right then to say that from *their* point of view we really were not believers at all (any more than a simple thermostat is)? If so, then our status as believers is nothing objective, but rather something in the eye of the beholder – provided the beholder shares our intellectual limitations.

Our imagined Martians might be able to predict the future of the human race by Laplacean methods, but if they did not also see us as intentional systems, they would be *missing something* perfectly objective: the *patterns* in human behavior that are describable from the intentional stance, and only from that stance, and which support generalizations and predictions. Take a particular instance in which the Martians observe a stock broker deciding to place an order for 500 shares of General Motors. They predict the exact motions of his fingers as he dials the phone, and the exact vibrations of his vocal cords as he intones his order. But if the Martians do not see that indefinitely many *different* patterns of finger motions and vocal cord vibrations – even the motions of indefinitely many different individuals – could have been substituted for the actual particulars without perturbing the subsequent operation of the market, then they have failed to see a real pattern in the world they are observing. Just as there are indefinitely many ways of *being a spark plug*[,] so there are indefinitely many ways of *ordering 500 shares of General Motors* [...].

Suppose, pursuing our Martian fantasy a little further, that one of the Martians were to engage in a predicting contest with an Earthling. [...] The Earthling's performance would look like magic! How did the Earthling know that the human being who got out of the car and got the bottle in the shop would get back in? [...] There *are* patterns in human affairs that impose themselves, not quite inexorably but with great vigor, absorbing physical perturbations and variations that might as well be considered random; these are the patterns that we characterize in terms of the beliefs, desires, and intentions of rational agents.

[...]

It is important to recognize the objective reality of the intentional patterns discernible in the activities of intelligent creatures, but also important to recognize the incompleteness and imperfections in the patterns. The objective fact is that the intentional strategy *works as well as it does,* which is not perfectly. No one is perfectly rational, perfectly unforgetful, all-observant, or invulnerable to fatigue, malfunction, or design imperfection. This leads inevitably to circumstances beyond the power of the intentional strategy to describe, in much the same way that physical damage to an artifact, such as a telephone or an automobile, may render it indescribable by the normal design terminology for that artifact. How do you draw the schematic wiring diagram of an audio amplifier that has been partially melted, or how do you characterize the program state of a malfunctioning computer?

[...]

Now the reason for stressing our kinship with the thermostat should be clear. There is no magic moment in the transition from a single thermostat to a system that *really* has an internal representation of the world around it. The thermostat has a minimally demanding representation of the world, fancier thermostats have more demanding representations of the world, fancier robots for helping around the house would have still more demanding representations of the world. Finally you reach us. [...]

The principles, and problems, of interpretations that we discover when we attribute beliefs to people are the *same* principles and problems we discover when we look at the ludicrous, but blessedly simple, problem of attributing beliefs to a thermostat. The differences are of degree, but nevertheless of such great degree that understanding the internal organization of a simple intentional system gives one very little basis for understanding the internal organization of a complex intentional system, such as a human being.

[Part IV] Why does the intentional strategy work?

If the intentional system in question is a person, there is [...] an ambiguity in our question. The first answer to the question of why the intentional strategy works is that evolution has designed human beings to be rational, to believe what they ought to believe and want what they ought to want. [...] The more difficult version of the question asks, in effect, how the machinery which Nature has provided us works. And we cannot yet give a good answer to that question. We just do not know. We do know how the *strategy* works, and we know the easy answer to the question of why it works, but knowing these does not help us much with the hard answer.

[...]

A currently [...] popular explanation is that the account of how the strategy works and the account of how the mechanism works will (roughly) *coincide*: for each predictively attributable belief, there will be a functionally salient internal state of the machinery, decomposable into functional parts in just about the same way the sentence expressing the belief is decomposable into parts – that is, words or terms. The inferences we attribute to rational creatures will be mirrored by physical, causal processes in the hardware; the *logical* form of the propositions believed will be copied in the *structural* form of the states in correspondence with them. This is the hypothesis that there is *a language of thought* coded in our brains, and our brains will eventually be understood as symbol manipulating systems in at least rough analogy with computers. Many different versions of this view are currently being explored, in the new research program called cognitive science, and provided one allows great latitude for attenuation of the basic, bold claim, I think some version of it will prove correct.

But I do not believe that this is *obvious*. Those who think that it is obvious, or inevitable, that such a theory will prove true (and there are many who do), are confusing two different empirical claims. The first is that intentional stance description yields an objective, real pattern in the world – the pattern our imaginary Martians missed. This is an empirical claim, but one that is confirmed beyond skepticism. The second is that this real pattern is *produced* by another real pattern roughly isomorphic to it within the brains of intelligent creatures. Doubting the existence of the second real pattern is not doubting the existence of the first. There *are* reasons for believing in the second pattern, but they are not overwhelming. The best simple account I can give of the reasons is as follows. As we ascend the scale of complexity from simple thermostat, through sophisticated robot, to human being, we discover that our efforts to design systems with the requisite behavior increasingly run foul of the problem of *combinatorial explosion*. [...] Now somehow the brain has solved the problem of combinatorial explosion. It is a gigantic network of billions of cells, but still finite, compact, reliable, and swift, and capable of learning new behaviors, vocabularies, theories, almost without limit. Some elegant, *generative*, indefinitely extendable principles of representation must be responsible. We have only one model of such a representation system: a human language. So the argument for a language of thought comes down to this: what else could it be? We have so far been unable to imagine any plausible alternative in any detail. That is a good enough reason, I think, for recommending as a matter of scientific tactics that we pursue the hypothesis in its various forms as far as we can. But we will engage in that exploration more circumspectly, and fruitfully, if we bear in mind that its inevitable rightness is far from assured. One does not well understand even a true empirical hypothesis so long as one is under the misapprehension that it is necessarily true.

Acknowledgements

Grateful acknowledgement is made to the following sources for permission to reproduce material within this book:

Readings

Grice, H. P. (1957) 'Meaning', *The Philosophical Review*, Vol. 66, Issue 3, July 1957, The Philosophical Review;

Searle, J. R. 'What is a speech act?', in Black, M. (ed.) (1965) *Philosophy in America*. Allen and Unwin and Cornell University Press;

Putnam, H. 'The Meaning of "Meaning"', in Harnish, R. M. (1994) *Basic Topics in the Philosophy of Language*, Harvester Wheatsheaf. Pearson Education;

Crane, T. (1991) 'All the Difference in the World', *The Philosophical Quarterly*, Vol. 41, No. 162, January 1991, Blackwell Publishing Ltd;

Haugeland, J. (1981) 'Semantic engines: an introduction to mind design', *Mind Design*, MIT Press;

Dennett, D. 'Cognitive Wheels: The Frame Problem of AI', in Hookway, C. (ed.) (1990) *Minds, Machines & Evolution: Philosophical Studies*. © Cambridge University Press, reproduced with permission of the publisher and author;

Fodor, J. A. (1987) *Psychosemantics – The problem of meaning in the philosophy of mind*, MIT Press;

Dretske, F. (1991) *Explaining Behaviour: Reasons in a World of Causes*. MIT Press, © 1988 Massachusetts Institute of Technology;

Block, N. (1994) 'Advertisement for a Semantics for Psychology', in Stich, S. and Warfield, T. A. (eds) *Mental Representation: A Reader*. Blackwell Publishers Limited;

Fodor, J. and Lepore, E. (1992) *Holism: A Shopper's Guide*. Blackwell Publishers Limited;

Lycan, W. G. (1990) *Mind and Cognition: A reader*. Blackwell Publishers Limited.